JUDGMENT DAY

The struggle for life on earth

PAUL COLLINS

'God's anger has come, and the day for judging . . .
and for destroying those who destroy the earth'
–The Book of Revelation

Maryknoll, New York 10545

Founded in 1970, Orbis Books endeavors to publish works that enlighten the mind, nourish the spirit, and challenge the conscience. The publishing arm of the Maryknoll Fathers and Brothers, Orbis seeks to explore the global dimensions of the Christian faith and mission, to invite dialogue with diverse cultures and religious traditions, and to serve the cause of reconciliation and peace. The books published reflect the views of their authors and do not represent the official position of the Maryknoll Society. To learn more about Maryknoll and Orbis Books, please visit our website at www.maryknollsociety.org.

Published in 2011 in the United States by Orbis Books, Maryknoll, NY 10545-0302.

First published in 2010 by
University of New South Wales Press Ltd.
University of New South Wales
Sydney NSW 2052
Australia
www.unswpresscom.au

Queries regarding rights and permissions should be addressed to: Orbis Books, P.O. Box 302, Maryknoll, NY 10545-0302.

Typeset in Australia. Printed in the United States of America
Cover Design by Committee, photo by Gettey images

Library of Congress Cataloging-in-Publication Data

Collins, Paul, 1940-
Judgment day : the struggle for life on earth / Paul Collins.
p. cm.
Includes bibliographical references and index.
ISBN 978-1-57075-920-8 (pbk.)
1. Human ecology—Religious aspects—Christianity. I. Title.
BT695.5.C652 2011
261.8'8—dc22

2010040482

In loving memory of Pam Garrett,
who died on 5 September 2009.

A woman who 'girded herself with strength' (Proverbs 31:17)
and stood for goodness, justice, integrity and hope.

Contents

Introduction

A question: can you name the first entirely carbon neutral state on earth? I have heard many answers to this, but the correct one is the Vatican City State. Sure, it is the smallest state in the world and it is hardly suffering from a population explosion, given that the majority of its 824 inhabitants are celibate. Natural increase is exceptionally low! Most people are surprised to hear about the Vatican's carbon neutrality, but it is a sign that the church is beginning to take the world environmental crisis seriously. Without doubt Catholicism specifically, and Christianity generally, have a long way to go in the process of coming to grips with what is happening to the natural world, but at least a beginning has been made. There is a clear recognition that we face a crisis.

The purpose of this book is to push that recognition further. While my background and inspiration are specifically Catholic, what I argue applies equally to all those who call themselves Christian, to believers of any of the great religious traditions, and to people of goodwill. It also has relevance to people who see the ecological crisis as a profound spiritual and moral issue. For that is precisely what it is.

Fifteen years ago I published a book entitled *God's Earth: Religion as if matter really mattered* (1995), in which I made my first foray into what can be loosely called 'environmental theology'. This book takes the application of theological and moral categories to ecology a lot further. A lot has happened environmentally since then. Although it was hardly mentioned in public discussion in those days, global warming is now a reality that looms over us all, and ecological devastation continues apace. Governments continue to wring their hands, but they have done little to care for the natural world. More and more species are becoming extinct. The world's population continues to increase. Industrialisation, based on non-renewable pollutants such as coal and petroleum, continues to fuel the old industrial world as well as the new, expanding economies such as those of India, China and Brazil. Pollution levels continue to increase. And some people imagine that despite the world financial meltdown of 2008–09, unfettered capitalism can still reign supreme and we can continue the developmental binge that the Western world began at the start of the industrial revolution in the late 18th century.

But the picture is not all bad: there is increasing public awareness of environmental concerns, focused by the threat of global warming, throughout communities in the Western world. Environmental issues have reached the mainstream, although it is still very difficult to get politicians to take them seriously. While they indulge in ecological rhetoric and there is a lot of environmental window-dressing, governments still have a long way to go before one could claim that they are taking this issue seriously. In the European Union some good work has been done in developing ecological awareness and a legislative framework, but the United States, at least under former President George W. Bush, was actively opposed to any form of environmental legislation and saw global warming as a myth. What the world needs from President Barack Obama is genuine leadership on this issue.

The Christian churches, including many evangelicals and even some fundamentalists, have also realised that environmentalism is an important issue facing us all. The Patriarch of the Eastern Orthodox Churches,

Bartholomew I, is often called the 'green patriarch', and he has certainly influenced Pope Benedict XVI, who speaks increasingly often about the environmental challenge we face. Many Catholic bishops' conferences and the mainstream Protestant churches have also taken up the challenge. The other great world religious traditions have joined in the struggle to increase the importance of environmentalism in their ethical and belief agendas.

But we humans are strangely illogical creatures. Despite our extraordinary reflective powers, we still find it hard to get things into perspective. So often the immediate overwhelms us and we become blinded to the real, but not immediate, threats and issues that face us. Take, for instance, the global financial crisis of 2008–09. Perhaps our loss of perspective is the fault of the media, which for months was besotted with this situation. The rhetoric was strident. We were told that we faced an 'unprecedented catastrophe', that it would be much worse than the Depression of the 1930s, that it was a crisis in capitalism with billions of dollars being wiped off the value of shares. Many businesses and people were 'going to the wall', while executive salaries remained obscene. All of this panic combined to push everything else off the front pages and out of the headlines. The far more important issue of global warming was literally relegated to at most a single column somewhere between pages six and ten in the newspapers and right off the radio and TV news. For the media the immediate is always more important than the significant.

It has been almost miraculous to see tight-fisted governments which previously said that running a deficit was something like baby-killing suddenly being able to find hundreds of billions of dollars to bail out failed banks, insurance companies and financial institutions. Apparently now government debt is not such a bad thing after all.

But while governments work themselves into a lather trying to save the financial system, global warming, population increase and environmental destruction move on inexorably. More species slide into extinction. Even countries like those in the European Union that had made commitments at Bali in early 2008 to reducing greenhouse gas emissions by between 25 and 40 per cent by 2020 are now backing down. There is hope, of course, that President Obama will bring the United States on board to tackle climate change and that this will influence reluctant Western governments, but there is also a danger that he will be swamped by financial, employment and environmental crises in the United States and be unable to tackle the main game. All of this means that we could drift on for several more years with nothing serious being done about global warming. This would lead to an unprecedented crisis, as the number of extreme weather events such as hurricanes increase, bush and forest fires grow in intensity and velocity, ice sheets melt, sea levels continue to rise and deserts creep across more and more of the landscape.

Part of the problem is that many people have still not really been grabbed at the gut level by the dire threat that global warming poses, and many are still hoodwinked by the kind of propaganda put out by well-funded climate change deniers. The polluting industries still have a massive amount of clout with governments, media and opinion makers as they ruthlessly threaten the loss of jobs through taking their operations overseas, or attempt to persuade governments to wait for action by other countries before acting.

Another part of the problem of understanding global warming and environmental devastation is that quite a few people are untrained in thinking comprehensively. In order to grasp what global warming is about you need to be able to comprehend a very big picture. It is universal in size and you need to know a fair amount of weather history to see it in perspective. But many people are the products of an education system that offered them few critical tools, little in terms of powers of discrimination between the significant and the trivial, and a distrust of what might be called over-arching narratives or big picture issues such as global warming. They also tend to think that every opinion is equally important and that no one has the professional authority to speak without being challenged, even by those who know little or nothing about the issue. They almost delight in maverick opinions. So they all too readily listen to climate change deniers who present themselves as a persecuted minority overwhelmed by a gullible majority of scientists who, they argue, only support the global warming push because they want funding for their research, or are too afraid to oppose the dominant opinion. The deniers snipe from the sidelines, attempting to pick minor holes in the evidence presented by mainstream scientists. The tragedy is that uncritical people tend to take them far more seriously than they deserve.

So the challenges are great. However, there is an increasing determination among many religious people, and many others of goodwill, to do something about the situation we confront. This book is meant as a small contribution to those discussions and challenges.

None of us, of course, is completely original. We owe debts, both intellectual and personal, to many people. My debt to the late Thomas Berry (1914–2009) is both profound and obvious. As this book makes clear, Tom was one of the rare, truly creative thinkers. Such people are few and far between in the church, and in a world full of hackneyed half-truths, superficial media commentary, spin and politically correct slogans. It was through reading Berry over a number of years and then later talking to him, in personal conversations and in interviews for radio and television, that I first came to articulate what I felt and thought about ecology and theology. His influence continues to grow, and in many quarters has become pervasive. I was also helped a lot by interviews I did and conversations I had with two other leading theologians in the Christian world: Jürgen Moltmann and Hans Küng.

I also owe much to my friend, Australian Anglican theologian Graeme Garrett. He never lets me forget that my context and roots are explicitly and deeply Christian and that it was only within that context that I would make sense to myself, let alone to others. This book owes much to him. It is dedicated to his dear wife and my friend Pam, who died just before the text was completed.

Many others have contributed. Historian of environmentalism William J. Lines has contributed much to my thinking about ecology and population over the last five years, as have members of Sustainable Population Australia, particularly Jenny Goldie. I am also very much in the debt of Dr Andrew Glikson, earth and paleo-climate scientist from the Australian National University (ANU), who has helped me understand the implications of global warming. Emeritus Professor John Mulvaney of the ANU, one of Australia's truly distinguished historians and archaeologists, has always been generous with advice and help, as has ecologist Professor Brendan Mackey, also of the ANU. Rev Dr Charles Rue has also helped me on many occasions with his comments on environmental issues and with material he has sent me. Rev Dr Normal Habel, editor of *The Earth Bible*, read the manuscript and made several very helpful suggestions.

Thanks also to my agent Mary Cunnane, to Phillipa McGuinness and Heather Cam at UNSW Press and to Sarah Shrubb, who edited the book. And, as always, thanks to Marilyn Hatton for her constant support, advice and love.

PART I

SEEING OURSELVES IN PERSPECTIVE

1 Cursed

For even the most clear-minded people, it is very hard to see ourselves as others see us. It is even more difficult to imagine how people in the future will think of us. Usually our main concern is what our family, friends, work mates and neighbours think about us. And that's the problem when we consider our impact on the natural world: we usually don't experience the real effects of our environmental actions and decisions. Their impact will only be seen three or four decades down the track, so it's hard to see the long-term effects of our behaviour. However, we may not evade responsibility completely: already the drying out of the climate is resulting in increasingly intense and fast-moving wildfires in eastern and southwestern Australia, California and the western United States, western Canada, especially British Columbia, Greece, Portugal, Spain and southern France.[1]

Despite our inability to foresee the future in detail, it is my view that:

> those of us whose lives have spanned the seven decades since the beginning of the Second World War will be among the most despised and cursed generations in the whole history of humankind. The reason why we will be hated by our own grandchildren and by those who come

> after them is simple: never before have human beings so exploited, damaged, and degraded the earth to the extent that we have.[2]

We still refuse to confront our impact on the natural world, and we continue to be enormously destructive and insatiably voracious.

It is no use kidding ourselves that it is just bad luck for people in the future or that they will somehow find a technological fix for the damage we have wrought. Our exploitation of the natural world is inescapably a moral and ethical issue. By destroying the earth, consuming resources and wiping out thousands of species we involve ourselves in a profoundly sinful situation. In a sense we are committing the primal sin: we are pretending that we are 'like God' (Genesis 3:5) and that we control the earth and all that is on and in it. We simply assume that we have to answer to no one, least of all to God the Creator. But as the Genesis story of Adam and Eve points out, a day of reckoning always comes. The good thing is that increasing numbers of people are starting to wake up to this. Global warming has been a key issue in focusing this growing realisation. The election of President Barack Obama seems to signal that the most powerful nation in the world will at least recognise the reality of global warming. He has promised a green, renewable economy; time will tell whether or not he can deliver. The United Kingdom has also shown some leadership in the area of renewables, as have most EU countries. There is a new openness in many people and a feeling that something might be done, but the power of vested interests is still enormous.

The origins of this change of social attitude go back to late 2006 or early 2007. It is hard to pin down exactly what happened, but suddenly there was a sense that many people had re-engaged with broader community issues. The language of change and hope articulated in the 2008 presidential campaign by Obama resonated particularly with young people. At the same time there was a dawning realisation that global warming and the environmental challenges confronting us could no longer be swept aside by pretending that they didn't exist, or that if they did they should be solved by someone else, preferably the government, without cost to individuals. People started to realise that the capitalist and neo-rationalist economic clichés proposed over the last two decades by the political, media, business and opinion-forming élites were wrong and that the solutions they had offered were either superficial or mere spin. For a moment there was a feeling that for once we might just get it right on the environment.

Then, just as optimism was growing in mid 2008 and people were beginning to take global warming seriously, the global financial crisis lurched onto the scene. It has distracted governments and let them off the hook, and again there is a danger that the ecological crisis will be swept aside as the most important issue facing us. But it is unlikely to be pushed aside completely.

As this book goes to press Barack Obama is facing the greatest environmental crisis of his presidency so far, and the tragedy is that he seems to have little to offer. The Gulf of Mexico oil spill is fast becoming the worst oil spill not just in US history, but in world history. It may well challenge Saddam Hussein's deliberate oil spill at the end of the first Gulf War in early 1991, when around 10 million barrels (about 1.17 billion litres) of crude oil were released into Kuwait's land and coastal environment and the Persian Gulf. Everyone remembers the *Exxon Valdez* disaster in King William Sound in Alaska in March 1989, but many of us forget another disaster: in the Gulf of Mexico in 1978 a large volume of crude oil, possibly as much as 10 million barrels, escaped a broken well. We also now know that the chemical dispersants used to try to clean up spills often have worse environmental consequences than the actual oil spill itself. So this is not the first time that humankind has faced such a disaster, but our culture appears to be still so besotted with cheap oil that we will pay any environmental price for it.

The result is that as the US government and the owners of the well try one thing after another, a whole regional ecosystem is being destroyed: birds, fish and animals are being killed, and the natural world is being devastated. This is not the US President's fault; nor is it a failure of policy. It is the fault of a culture that thinks its technology can do anything, that there is a 'fix' for everything, that human ingenuity is so great that it can plug a gaping hole in the seabed 1.5 kilometres below the surface. Perhaps it can, but at the time of writing, about 9 million litres per day of crude oil have spilled into the sea.

Why do companies drill for oil in such risky environments? The usual answer is money. That's true, but the deeper, cultural reason is the kind of irresponsible technological mania mentioned above. The extractive industries particularly are dominated by this attitude. We seem unable to control our mania to interfere; the sole guideline seems to be that if something can be done, then it should be done. And when anything goes wrong – as it has on a massive scale in the Gulf of Mexico – the techno-freaks rush to tell us that there will be a fix of some sort, even though it was technological interference that created the problem. No one had worked out what to do if something went wrong. The presumption seems to have been that if difficulties arose they could somehow be fixed technologically, but the problem is that before we can work out what to do an enormous amount of damage has already been done to the natural world.

You might expect that in this context there would be a moratorium on the approval of further off-shore drilling, or drilling in ecologically sensitive environments such as the Arctic, until what happened to cause the Gulf disaster was established. At least President Obama had the decency to put a temporary kybosh on any further off-shore drilling, but other countries showed no such hesitation. The Australian government, for instance, approved 31 new off-shore oil exploration leases on 17 May 2010 during the escalation of the Gulf of Mexico disaster. Again the assumption is that technology will solve any problems. But what we don't talk about is the fact that the technocratic mindset is so built into the way we think and has so penetrated our intellectual horizons and the way we perceive reality that we can't think outside this context. Our unquestioned, instinctual reaction to nature is now that it must be used, whatever the cost. If the oil is there, we have an unrestricted moral right to take it. No one asks about the ethics of tearing the world apart, polluting it, destroying it.

This is a theme to which we will return often in this book.

Global warming has focused many people's minds and shocked them out of their apathy regarding the environment. They know the world is warming up. Weather patterns are changing: there are more hurricanes, droughts, floods, wildfires and other disasters. There is an awareness that the Arctic and Antarctic ice is melting and sea levels are rising. This means that low-level coastlines right across the world will be threatened and literally hundreds of millions of people will be displaced. If this process is already further advanced than we think and still speeding up, if the methane trapped in the Siberian tundra is released (methane has a much higher global warming potential than carbon dioxide), and if the Greenland ice sheet melts (this process has already begun), the future looks bleak indeed. There is a broad consensus in the community that we have to do something, and quickly. Many people seem to understand these issues better than governments do, and their thinking is well ahead of that of some politicians.

We non-scientists tend to use 'global warming' as a code term, and hope that as long as we deal with this we will have somehow dealt with all our ecological problems and saved the environment. The term 'global warming' now represents a whole series of intersecting issues which all have to be addressed if we are to begin to deal with the environmental crises we face. In other words, climate change is not a single issue, but an interconnected series of human impacts on nature that are having serious, even disastrous consequences. We also need to remember that population is a central driver of global warming and that these two issues are intimately connected: the more people there are, the more energy will be used, and the more greenhouse gases will be released. At a deeper level the climate change process has become a symbol for the clash between modern culture, with its individualism, consumerism and capitalist economics, and the natural processes of the planet. In the end the two are not compatible, no matter how much we try to persuade ourselves that they are.

The major religious traditions are also beginning to understand the way global warming has focused public concern about environmental issues. Until the end of the 20th century the churches and the major religions had been, at best, less than half-hearted in their response to the contemporary ecological crisis. However, recently there has been an important shift. A true pioneer in this has been Bartholomew I, the Ecumenical Patriarch of the Orthodox churches, who has been correctly dubbed the 'green patriarch'. He has bluntly said that those who commit 'crimes against the natural world' are sinners who need to confess, repent and make restitution. From his home in Istanbul he has worked hard to highlight the pollution and threatened destruction of the Black Sea, the Aegean Sea and the Danube River. He has also influenced the Vatican to become much more environmentally aware and has found an ally in Pope Benedict XVI, who has spoken increasingly of the need to protect the environment. Pollution is now on a Vatican list of 'deadly sins'! Benedict has linked the attainment of peace with the protection of creation, especially in his Message for the World Day of Peace of January 2010. He says: 'The environment must be seen as God's gift to all people, and the use we make of it entails a shared responsibility for all humanity, especially the poor and future generations.'

A number of Catholic bishops' conferences have begun to show some leadership. The Philippine bishops have been speaking out for several decades about environmental destruction in their country: they have denounced the clear-felling of tropical forests with the resultant loss of topsoil, as well as the destruction of coral reefs. However, they have still failed to confront the problem of over-population in the Philippines, and this weakens the strength of their other stances. Recently the Brazilian Catholic bishops have become strong, outspoken defenders of the Amazonian rainforests, and some of the Australian bishops are starting to show concern for the environment, as witnessed by their establishment of Catholic Earthcare Australia. At the grassroots level in Catholicism we are also beginning to see a real commitment to environmental sustainability in many Catholic religious orders, parishes and lay people. Little or nothing of significance has been heard from the US bishops on environmental issues.

A minority of mainstream Protestants has been aware of the ecological crisis for decades and, as we will see, the Process Theology movement, which explores a fascinating theoretical basis for ecological concerns, had its roots in the Protestant theological tradition. There is also growing evidence that large communities at the more evangelical end of the Protestant spectrum are also beginning to 'go green'. Fundamentalists such as Rev Jerry Falwell were always deeply suspicious of environmentalism as a kind of 'liberal plot', and just before his death in 2007 Falwell criticised 'naïve Christian leaders' for being 'duped' by environmentalism, which he said 'was Satan's attempt to redirect the church's primary focus' away from evangelism.[3] The evangelical emphasis has traditionally been on the Bible, worship and the use of the world for the betterment of humankind. Fundamentalists saw environmental degradation as a symptom of the coming 'end times', when those who were saved and those who were damned would be spectacularly sorted out following a cosmic cataclysm. However, there are increasing numbers of 'green evangelicals' who, while suspicious of environmentalists who may be trying to create a new 'ecological religion', understand the challenge and the threat that global warming poses for our society and are determined to do something practical about it.

But the 'greening' of Christianity should not be exaggerated. It remains a deeply anthropocentric faith in all its forms and it still has a long way to go before a thoroughgoing ecological approach is integrated into theology and belief. In Australia, for instance, it is clear that the mainstream churches – Catholic, Anglican and Uniting – have paid lip service to greening the church, but as Steven Douglas has pointed out:

> Creation-care remains an optional extra for [church] organizations, and economic and institutional gains still take precedence over ecological protection in the vast majority of situations … the almighty dollar and the interests of the Church still take absolute priority … even in the face of parishioners' opposition.[4]

Environmental awareness is not confined to Christianity. The other major religious traditions show some acquaintance with our impact on the world. The most ancient of these traditions is, of course, Hinduism. It is impossible to define Hinduism, and it ranges from an elitist, caste-bound, stratified religion to, at its best, a sublime form of mysticism and an insight into unifying truth.[5] The result is that it is impossible to generalise about environmentalism and Hinduism. The best in traditional Hindu spirituality is profoundly unworldly, so environmentalism is a very modern concern among Hindus. But India faces difficult environmental conundrums and choices. The enormous and growing urban middle class is putting extraordinary pressure on the ecology of the subcontinent and contributing much to greenhouse gases; the rural masses want more arable land; and caught between the two are the dispossessed, the former rural poor, who live on the fringes of the big cities. Within this context it is difficult to focus on environmental concerns. We will return to these issues in the chapter on population.

Buddhism has always been more in harmony with the natural world than other religious systems and traditionally it has placed far less emphasis on the dichotomy between humans and the non-human world. The notion of the interrelatedness of all beings seems to promote an egalitarianism that is non-anthropocentric, but that doesn't mean that Buddhism is inherently friendly to the natural world. Scholars point out that there are several Buddhist traditions and that not all of them accept the emerging strain of 'green Buddhism'. Nevertheless, many Buddhists, including the Dalai Lama, have integrated ecological principles into their spirituality. It has been Western Buddhists, particularly American Buddhists, who have taken the lead in the greening of Buddhism.

As Judaism will be largely dealt with in the chapter on the Bible, I will only touch on the modern Jewish faith's relationship to ecology here. The first issue for most Jews in a post-Holocaust world has been the physical survival of the Jewish people. As a result there has been an especially strong emphasis among the traditionalist groups on high rates of fertility to replace the millions who were killed. The other major issue facing Jews is the question of their place in the world, and especially the place of Israel in its prolonged struggle for survival. Among secular Zionists the ideal was to create a new kind of Jew, one wedded to the land of Israel rather than to the Jewish faith and tradition. A kind of secular religion of agricultural labour developed in Israel, especially on the kibbutzim, but this does not mean that the country has been particularly careful about its physical environment. The desert is a relatively hostile and difficult environment, so secular Israelis – mainly those who came to Israel from America, England, Canada and Australia – are usually more likely to espouse Western environmentalism than to draw on the Hebrew Scriptures as an inspiration. Jews from post-Holocaust Europe and those from Arabic countries tend to be more religious in the narrow sense and less concerned about the protection of the land and environment.

Traditional Islamic writers often refer to Muhammad's concern for the equitable distribution of the goods of the earth and to the Qur'an's many references to land, air and water, as well as to the creativity of God, some of which are remarkably like verses in the Hebrew Bible. For instance 'Praise be to Allah who created the heavens and the earth and made the darkness and the light' (Q. 6:1) expresses the same sentiment as Genesis 1:1–5 and 'The seven heavens and the earth, and all beings therein, declare His glory; there is not a thing but celebrates His praise' (Q. 17:44) has much in common with Psalm 19. However, ecological awareness is not well developed in Islamic societies. The focus is on technological development, and as members of post-colonialist societies many modern Muslims feel that Western environmentalism is a form of neo-imperialism designed to keep them in subservience. This means that Muslim countries like Iran are more likely to focus on social justice than on the environment. While self-criticism and knowledge of other religions is generally lacking in these societies, there are individual Muslims who stand out.

One such is the Iranian-born Islamic writer Seyyed Hossein Nasr, born in 1933 in Tehran. He argues that the separation of modern Western science from the idea of nature as sacred and revelatory, a movement which began in Renaissance Humanism, 'gave rise to a world centered on man instead of God. Human reason was no longer bounded by allegiance to anything beyond itself.' He believes that this destructive separation is:

> rooted in modern Western science and its domination of our view of nature, a view that separates nature from the sacred ... I'm not hostile to Western science, but [to] its claim to be the only valid science of the natural world. There are other ways of 'knowing' ... We can't save the natural world except by rediscovering the sacred in nature.[6]

He believes that this alienation from nature has been deepened by the theory of evolution – 'Darwinism has eradicated the sense of the sacred' in the natural world – and argues that harmony and co-operation, rather than the survival of the fittest, are 'basic'. He sees the West as attempting to set the agenda for Islamic societies, but argues that in a true Islamic country political leaders would be guided:

> by the shari'ah as set out by the doctors of the law. If they pronounced polluting industries and certain kinds of development in violation of Islamic principles, political leaders would have to take strong action against transgressors.

While to the democratic mind this seems rather theocratic, at least something would be done. The problem is finding a true Islamic society.

In a way this book takes up Seyyed Hossein Nasr's challenge: it is fundamentally about the recovery of a notion of the sacredness and revelatory nature of the cosmos. It focuses on the natural world, God, environment, theology, spirituality and us, and the profound interconnections between all these realities. It examines a series of pivotal human and spiritual questions that arise from the new vision of the natural world that has developed since the 1950s. The book grew out of my conviction that environmentalism is the most significant human, moral and theological problem confronting the contemporary world, and that if we don't face up to the issues embedded in the ecological crisis we will have no future as sane, ethical and spiritual beings. We really will be cursed by the people who come after us, because we will have denied them their birthright by destroying so much of the beauty and resources of the natural world in our selfish and self-engrossed attempt to seize everything for ourselves. Until now, extinctions were the result of natural or cosmic processes, such as the large-scale destruction of the sea reptiles and dinosaurs at the end of the Cretaceous, some 67 million years ago. What is happening now is different: we are presiding over an unnatural apocalyptic extinction that results directly from our activities and decisions.

Certainly we are the first generations of humans who have been able to exploit the natural world to such a destructive extent. We have the technology that people in the past lacked. Previous generations, armed with comparable technology, probably would have acted in a similarly destructive manner, although the extent of their depredation would have depended on their cultural, religious and ethical context and attitudes. However, there is no doubt that our individualistic, Western, consumer-based, capitalist culture has encouraged a range of attitudes that have led to our present impasse.

The capitalist system is based on two myths: first, that economic growth (that is, a constant increase in the value and amounts of goods and services) is essentially infinite and that no limits should ever be imposed on it; and second, that affluence and individualism lead to happiness. Both of these are patently wrong. The dawning realisation that we are running out of resources such as oil and water in many places shows that there is a real limit to growth. And neither has affluence led to happiness. Rather, we seem to have an epidemic of depression and suicide, especially among the young. While the capitalist system is decreasingly able to meet our needs, most people still expect that we can solve environmental problems while maintaining business as usual. They are unaware of how subversive genuine environmental commitment is to prevailing economic models. However, apologists for capitalism have glimpsed this and use it as an argument against those they cast as 'extreme environmentalists' or, in an even more derogatory tone as 'fairies at the bottom of the garden'. Personally, I think environmentalists ought to be proud of the fact that what we are proposing directly challenges much of our economic system and many of the cultural and religious underpinnings of our society. Commitment to the environment provides us with a real opportunity to break out of our destructive living patterns, and to work to recover those aspects of the natural world that are now under threat. Sadly, we cannot bring back what has already been lost to extinction.

In essence, what I want to ask is: what is the role of religion, and specifically Christianity and Catholicism, in all this? While modern environmental consciousness arises from the interconnection of a number of scientific disciplines and it is obvious that these will continue to influence it deeply, it is also true that belief, spirituality and ethics will have to become an essential part of our rethinking. For our self-definition as human brings is derived from two primal sets of relationships. The first is our relationship to ourselves, to each other and to the natural world and all that is in it; this is what we call morals or ethics. The second is our mysterious and intangible relationship with the transcendent; it is in this context that we sort out the ultimate meaning of our existence. This is what we call spirituality and religion; theology provides a kind of clarification and commentary on this. Although their origins are very different, modern environmentalism is absolutely central to the future of religion and vice versa. I contend that religion generally, and Christianity specifically, will gradually cease to exist if the natural world continues to be devastated at the present rate. There is a deep and dependent relationship between the development of religious attitudes and the sustaining of the natural world. Thus religion and theology can play important roles in deepening both ethical and spiritual approaches to environmentalism. One of the primary aims of this book is to develop a theology of the natural world.

We are also confronted with another problem that even committed environmentalists try to avoid: the fact that the world is grossly overpopulated. It is obvious that it is human beings and our insatiable desire for ever-higher living standards which destroy the natural infrastructure of the earth and that this destruction will escalate if the increase in the human population is not slowed. This increase has placed extraordinary strains on all other natural systems, and our very existence has for some time threatened many species of animals and plants with extinction. Since human action is responsible for virtually all environmental destruction, does this not imply that some ethical limits have to be placed on human reproduction? This key moral question confronts all the religious traditions, particularly Catholicism. It is still the major test of the credibility of the church's most senior leadership.

The problem is that if the present levels of population growth and environmental destruction continue, they will eventually lead to the earth becoming nothing more than the foundation for a food supply for human beings. Everything will have to be subsumed to this. But humans living in a feed-lot world where all wildernesses have been destroyed, most species driven to extinction and nature driven out, would lose touch with the possibility of the development of culture, art, religion and spirituality. Deprived of the natural world, with its beauty, multiplicity, mystery, complexity and otherness, our imaginations would shrivel up and we would lose our ability to perceive and experience the deeper feelings that give meaning to our lives. For nature is the source of our human origin and the context of our continuing evolution and spiritual development. If we were to lose this, we would cease to have a sense of ourselves as human beings at all.

The result: the poetic, mystical core of our spirituality, art and culture would dry up, for there would be nothing to renew and nurture it. Our imaginations need the inspiration of natural beauty and ecological diversity; without it we would lose the ability to conjure up the new possibilities that actually drive us creatively forward as a species. We would gradually lose the essence of our humanity and descend into a hopeless, mad, paranoid world in which we would destroy ourselves. It is our imagination that saves us from the delusional monism that is the essential core of insanity. Thomas Berry illustrates this through a comparison: 'If we lived on the moon our knowledge of God would reflect the lunar landscape, our imaginations would be as empty as the moon, and our intellect would be completely thwarted.'[7] While this seems an apocalyptic scenario it remains a real threat because so much of our contemporary religious, political, and economic thinking is so short-sighted.

As we move further into the new millennium, we will have to make decisions about the environmental issues that confront us. As the December 2009 Copenhagen Climate Summit made clear, we have very little time left, for much of the beauty and complexity of the natural world has already been permanently lost. Many scientists believe that we are already trapped in an irreversible process of global warming. Even if we're not, surely prudence demands that we don't rush headlong along the path to global warming, like the herd of Gadarene swine in St Matthew's Gospel who, possessed by demons, 'rushed down the steep bank into the sea and perished in the waters' (Matthew 8:32).

Part of the reason for our situation is that many of the sources that in the past have provided constructive approaches to our problems have failed us. Democratically elected governments seem unwilling and unable to tackle the hard issues. Governments seem dominated by the kind of compromise constantly pushed in the media and in public policy debates by industry, neo-liberal economists and technocratic planners who lack the vision to grasp the real issues of our world. While the influence of the neo-conservatives was weakened by the disastrous Bush-Cheney presidency in the United States and the global financial crisis, they should not be underestimated. Another element making it hard to grasp the big picture is the fact that our ability to analyse what is happening to us culturally and socially has been to some extent crippled by modern educational theories that deny the possibility of constructing any coherent 'meta-narrative', or overarching understanding of what is happening in society and culture, and instead maintain that all we can grasp are the kind of temporary, subjective and limited visions characteristic of particular groups and individuals.

There is also still a lot of environmental window-dressing among Christians. The reason is that the bottom line for the tradition of

Christian theology inherited by the churches is the emphasis on the absolute priority of humanity over the rest of creation. In this tradition, everything in the world plays a secondary role to humankind and its needs. No matter what their rhetoric about environmentalism, the mainstream Christian churches are still crippled by an anthropocentrism that dominates their unconscious reactions and guides their value judgments. Since I am going to use this ugly word 'anthropocentrism' often in this book, I will explain its meaning. It comes from the Greek word *anthropos*, meaning man in the generic sense of humankind. To be anthropocentric is to be focused on humankind and its needs and aspirations to the exclusion of all other species and priorities. It is the unconscious assumption that the earth exists for us and that its total meaning is derived from us. Thomas Berry says that anthropocentrism is rooted in 'our failure to think of ourselves as a species like other species, interconnected with and biologically interdependent on the rest of reality'.[8] Instead, we think of ourselves in ethnic, cultural, linguistic or economic terms and see all other species as existing simply to satisfy us and fulfil our needs. Putting it another way, we take ourselves and our needs as the focus, norm, and final arbiter of all that exists.

I personally find it sad that many hierarchs of my own Catholic tradition, rather than being out there with the 'green' Patriarch Bartholomew, are still largely preoccupied with the minutiae of sexual behaviour and reproduction, or with the church's struggle to free itself from the self-engrossed and defensive hangovers of the 16th century Counter-Reformation. The saddest aspect of contemporary Catholicism is the widespread retreat by the institutional church into a new conservatism and a narrow orthodoxy that is as contemptuous of the true Catholic tradition as it is of those Catholics who have tried to live their lives in critical harmony with contemporary society. Even the Catholic Church's significant and important stand on social justice is still focused on the needs of humankind, although there is an increasing acknowledgment that there can be no genuine justice for people when the natural world, the source of life for all, is exploited and destroyed.

While near the end of his life Pope John Paul II expressed some concern about environmental destruction, he is a commonplace example of Christian anthropocentrism. He argues that human beings differ radically from animals and the rest of reality because they have an interior life:

> A person differs from a thing in structure and degree of perfection. To the structure of the person belongs an 'interior', in which we find the elements of spiritual life, and it is this that compels us to acknowledge the spiritual nature of the human soul, and the peculiar perfectibility of the human person. A person must not be put on the same level as a thing ... Between the psyche of an animal and the spirituality of a man there is an enormous distance, an un-crossable gulf.[9]

One of my main purposes in this book is to show just how wrong it is to say that there is an 'un-crossable gulf' between human personhood and the other beings of the natural world, especially sentient, conscious animals. Modern science rejects this dichotomy, as must we, for genetically and biologically we are profoundly interconnected with the rest of the living world. And why argue for such a radical disjunction? An animal is not just a thing like a machine. It is a living being with its own independent existence. Its life has intrinsic value and purpose and its own specific interiority.

John Paul's comments are symptomatic of a Christian anthropocentrism that has no base in the genuine Catholic tradition, or in modern scientific knowledge. Is it true that human beings have an interiority that sets them apart from the rest of nature? Is the value of the human person to be exalted at the expense of every other living thing on earth? A prayer of St Basil the Great (330–79) certainly seems to contradict

John Paul's comments: 'May we realize that they [animals] live not for us alone, but for themselves and for You [God], and that they love the sweetness of life as we do, and serve You better in their place than we in ours.' St Thomas Aquinas (1225–74) says unequivocally that animals have souls. Admittedly, he says they are non-rational, sensitive souls and that they 'perish along with the body', in contrast to the human soul, which is immortal.[10] This is not to claim that Aquinas is somehow sentimental about animals; it is merely that he recognises that they have something spiritual about them. What his discussion makes clear is that animals are not mere complex machines, as the philosopher René Descartes (1596–1650) maintained. They have real individuality and independence (as anyone who has dealt with a cat knows), feel affection and attachment, have real social lives (especially herd animals), can feel pain and sorrow and have highly developed perceptivity. Rather than speaking of uncrossable gulfs, Aquinas seems to indicate that there is a real relationship between the feeling soul of animals and more rational human souls. In this he has more in common with Princeton University ethicist Peter Singer than with John Paul II. Singer has argued that animal rights are based not so much on their intelligence as on their ability to feel pain, which indicates a level of consciousness that, while perhaps not the same as that of humankind, is certainly real. In fact animal intelligence is remarkable, and in many areas it exceeds that of humans.

So if all our usual religious, social, philosophical and cultural sources have let us down, and I believe they have, we have to turn elsewhere. We need to turn back to the natural world from which we came, and begin to reinterpret our religious, spiritual and cultural experience in the light of our interaction with that natural world. So at heart this book is about the deep theological, human and cultural shift that contemporary environmentalism implies.

This shift will involve, first, the way in which we perceive God and

God's relationship to us. There are strong traditions running through all religions and theologies, including Christian theology, that posit the natural world as the primary symbol that reveals the presence of the transcendent in earthly existence. What is needed is a shift in the way theology views revelation – here the word 'revelation' refers to the way in which the divine is manifested to us. Actually, in this ordinary people are already way ahead of theologians. Many today are finding traces of the transcendent in the world around them: in nature, beauty and the wilderness. Urbanised people, as they escape from the city and abandon the superficial scientism that underpins much of contemporary culture, are starting to rediscover what the mystics have always known: that the natural world palpitates with a sense of an unseen presence that points beyond itself to spirituality, to a transcendence that transforms our whole view of existence. Talk to bushwalkers or environmentalists, many of them non-believers, about what has happened to them in the wilderness, and they will report spiritual experiences very similar to those of the mystics. As Berry says, our primary relationship with the world is 'ecstatic', from the Greek *ekstatikos*, meaning to stand outside oneself.[11] It is precisely this kind of experience that many people have in the wilderness.

This book also argues that none of our modern religious traditions can turn away from the consequences of environmentalism without rendering themselves irrelevant to the major issue of our time. As one of the largest world religions, Christianity will have to face up to some radical shifts of emphasis in its theology in order to remain in touch with the environmental age. The consequences for Christianity will include refocusing on our notion of God and deepening our understanding of the meaning of transcendence. Environmentalism will also have consequences for the theology of revelation: it will mean that we will slowly come to recognise that we are just as likely to encounter the transcendent presence of God in the natural world as in the Bible or the church. In fact, the natural world is the revelatory starting point for the discovery of the divine.

For Christians, Christ is central. He is seen in theology as the focal point of history. But much of the evidence of modern science implicitly questions this. It posits the long history and gargantuan size of the cosmos as the primary given, with some scientists arguing that the cosmos is infinite. So while maintaining the centrality of Christ, contemporary theology has to try to confront this challenge. In contrast to the history of the universe (15 billion years), salvation history (the story of Judaism, Christ and Christianity) is extraordinarily brief, a mere 3500 years. Also, if you posit the natural world as a kind of primal revelation, it throws up questions about the Bible, Christ and the church as revelatory sources. In the final chapter, on Christ, I will tackle these questions and try to articulate a response.

It is at this point that some of the most difficult and contentious questions will have to be faced. Despite the fact that Christ himself always pointed outward to the mysterious God who sent him and whose kingdom he proclaimed, many believers will find it hard to cope with a theology that places Christ in this much wider cosmic context. In practice, many enthusiastic and fundamentalist Christians today are caught up in a focus on Jesus that is essentially idolatrous. The Trinitarian nature of God becomes obscured. In a theology influenced by environmentalism, the focus will shift more to God, the mysterious transcendent presence that underpins all reality that is manifest in the natural world. Nature points us outwards towards the mystery of the divine reality that stands beyond our limited perceptions.

Environmentalism and science inevitably raise questions that are by their very nature theological. It was in this sense that the Roman thinker Cicero (106–43BC) and the early Christian theologians Sts Basil and Augustine (354–430) saw the beauty of the world as a pointer to God. Augustine speaks of 'traces' of God in the world, and the poetry of the 16th century Spanish mystic St John of the Cross (1542–91) also illustrates the notion that mysticism begins with the contemplation of nature and the discovery of the intangible presence that stands behind and beyond the world. It was this perennially attractive mystery that 'lit and led' John through to the profound 'presence' that stands at the core of everything.[12] So, in a way, this book is an attempt to restate a kind of natural theology in a new context. It moves well beyond the argument from design formulated in the late 18th century by the Anglican divine William Paley (1743–1805), which resulted in a natural theology that eventually either drove God totally from the world or devolved into pantheism. My aim is to take the natural world seriously as the primal revelation of God and, working from that, try to find what we can discover of the transcendent from this world.

In all of this we have one thing going for us. As human beings we have a unique ability: we have a self-awareness that allows us to see ourselves in perspective. Alone of all creatures we can comprehend our context, reflect upon ourselves within the parameters of history and culture and sketch the borders that create our world and environment. This possibility has greatly expanded recently as our knowledge of history (cosmic, biological and human), science, psychology and culture have increased. Though most of us judge reality from the narrow, parochial experience of our individual lives and cultures, the stark environmental choices that confront us now are beginning to force us to look at ourselves in a wider context than ever before.

We are facing a series of decisions, both locally and on a worldwide scale, that will require that rare ability to see ourselves within a broad historical and scientific context. We are experiencing profound shifts as the political, cultural and economic hegemony of Western Europe retreats. Within the broad sweep of decolonisation and an emerging world culture, we see the development of new constellations of power and influence based on either geography (as in Asia, Africa and Latin America), or religious ideology (as in the revival of Islam and the emergence of fundamentalism in all the great faiths). The emergence of fundamentalism across the whole religious spectrum is one of the most frightening aspects of the contemporary world. This primitive, anti-spiritual religiosity is the antithesis of everything that I will argue for in this book. Religious fundamentalism of any kind is very destructive.

But it is not with the geopolitical issues, or even with cultural issues, that I am primarily concerned. My interest is explicitly environmental, and ultimately spiritual and theological. Issues associated with environmentalism and spirituality have become pivotal factors in the new world that is emerging. But given the increased rate of destruction of the natural world and the increase in world population, one thing is clear: unless human attitudes and ethical values change, and change quickly in all societies, the 'new world' will be very bleak indeed. It is an illusion to hope that people will eventually just change. Human beings need intellectual convictions, ethical structures and a spiritual motivation if lasting and far-reaching adjustment is to occur. Contemporary environmentalism is not just about tinkering at the edges; it demands a deep-seated shift of attitude, akin to a conversion. This is where faith and belief have a pivotal role to play.

I should declare my hand right from the start. It is my view that the underlying theological substratum of Catholic Christianity is probably one of the best religious systems in the contemporary world from within which to develop a coherent environmental theology and ethic. Its strength lies, paradoxically, in its notion of tradition. The English word 'tradition' is misleading. We usually take the word to mean looking backwards, living in the past. But the word is actually derived from the Classical Latin verb *trado*, which means to hand over, deliver, transmit. This implies an active process, which suggests the possibility of development: in the very process of handing on a belief it is actually subtly changed and amplified. So tradition in Catholic theology refers to the idea that belief develops and evolves within a broad interpretation of the parameters of biblical revelation and the church's ongoing articulation of its experience of itself and its beliefs in interaction with the world around it. The Latin word *traditor* (traitor or betrayer) is closely related. In this sense a traitor is primarily one who fails to hand on the tradition.

Certainly Catholicism has a very dubious track record in terms of dealing with the natural world. But inherent in Catholic theology is the idea of the evolution and development of doctrine, and among Catholics in touch with the genuine tradition there is a unique openness to cultural and historical experience. It is in the interaction between this sense of continuity and contemporary culture that Catholic Christianity can be most creative. It is less rigidly tied to an unchanging biblical word than are the more evangelical elements of Protestant Christianity. I will develop these arguments in more detail in later chapters. What I aim to do is provide a context within which we can begin to look at environmental and religious questions more creatively. I also want to try to articulate some theological principles upon which a practical set of environmental ethics can be based. At the deepest level, we need to undergo a form of conversion so that attitudes can be changed and outdated ideologies jettisoned.

Many people feel that the odds against this happening are high and that it will be impossible to achieve the necessary changes in time to reverse global warming and save the many species that are now in danger. There is much to support this pessimistic view. Often despair seems justified as the facts about environmental destruction are spelled out and politically and economically powerful forces remain arrayed against change. Even so, we should remember that despair is not coterminous with surrender. Already an enormous amount has been achieved. Even the most reactionary and pro-development governments and polluting industries have at least felt the need to dress up their policies in pseudo-environmental rhetoric. This is also where theology and spirituality step in: Christianity sees hope as a pivotal virtue. Hope is the ability to imagine something different, to be creative enough for change to be achieved. Hope is the passionate determination to achieve change despite governments and vested interests. So if this book is about anything, it is about hope. If we have this, there is a possibility that we will be able to save something of the natural world for the future. Without it, descent into the madness of a human monoculture is inevitable.

I have adopted here a basic and firm moral conviction: that the good of the planet must come before everything else. The absolute, non-negotiable moral basis of human behaviour is that the natural world is the creation of God and that, as Berry has said:

> If we lose the splendour of the natural world, we lose our true sense of the divine ... All human institutions, professions, programs and activities must now be judged primarily by the extent to which they inhibit, ignore or foster a mutually enhancing human–earth relationship.[13]

We must take the world seriously, and in order to do that we need to learn the humility of seeing ourselves in perspective. First, human beings have been on the earth for a very short time – the cosmos has been in the process of evolution for 15 billion years and the earth for 4 billion years. At most, *Homo sapiens* has been here for 130,000 to 140,000 years, perhaps a little longer. Second, we are totally dependent on this world, the world which we are tearing apart with reckless and contemptuous disregard for the future. Again, as Berry says, 'We now experience ourselves as the latest arrivals after some 15 billion years of universe history, and after some 4.5 billion years of earth history. Here we are, born yesterday.'[14]

Our most deadly sin is not lust, or greed, or pride, or envy, or sloth, or any of the other deadly sins. There is a sense in which they are all summed up in the sin of anthropocentrism, the conviction that somehow we are the centre of everything, that the world was made for us alone and that we are the sum total of its meaning. It is this that is at the core of our existential resentment at the sheer vulnerability of our existence and at our complete dependence on the world around us. It also explains our environmental destructiveness and it makes plain why we are willing to sacrifice everything in the natural world to satisfy ourselves.

My hope is that this attitude is beginning to change and that increasing numbers of people of goodwill are determined to get humankind back into perspective, back to the sense that this is our only home, the one place where we 'belong', and that without it we will be truly homeless and adrift.

PART II

THE FACTS

2 Warming

I have visited Kiribati, the former British colony in the mid-Pacific which will be the first country in the world to be drowned by global warming. Kiribati is a collection of 33 coral atolls made up of the Gilbert, Phoenix and Line Islands, and Banaba (Ocean) and Christmas Islands. With a total land area of 811 square kilometres, it sits astride the equator, and is spread out over 3.5 million square kilometres of ocean. With the exception of Banaba, a formally phosphate-rich island, the highest point on the atolls is less than 2 metres above sea level. The population at the end of 2009 was about 110,850. Kiribati President Anote Tong admitted that he 'doesn't know how long we've got' – depending on the speed of global warming, the atolls will all be submerged sometime between 2025 and 2040. The country is already subject to king tides and flooding by the sea.

Tuvalu, another former British colony in the central Pacific, faces the same fate. Its highest point is 4.5 metres above sea level and it has a population of about 12,400. It was Tuvalu that created a storm at the December 2009 UN Copenhagen Climate Change Conference, when it demanded a legally binding agreement to limit temperature rises to 1.5°C, rather than the 2°C degrees favoured by industrialised nations. According to the country's Prime Minister, Apisai Ielemia, 'To go over that limit … will be a graveyard for all the living things in Tuvalu … 1.5°C is our bottom line.' Other Pacific countries facing a similar immediate fate are the Maldives and the Marshall Islands. The 2°C limit agreed to at the last minute seems to spell the end for these low-lying islands, which have little influence in world affairs. But at least for a couple of days at Copenhagen they succeeded in getting some attention from the rest of the world.

On 7 February 2009, 10 months before the Copenhagen conference, Australians also got a glimpse into the near future. And what they saw was terrifying. On that day parts of the state of Victoria were hit by the most disastrous bushfires experienced in Australia since European settlement. One-hundred and seventy-three people were killed, more than double the number of deaths in any previous bushfire. As a result of this extraordinary fire a new category was introduced into fire assessment: 'catastrophic'.[1]

Southeastern Australia is the world's most fire-prone landscape, even compared with California and western North America. The dominance of eucalypts and combustible scrub, plus very hot summers, recurrent long-term drought and extreme hot northerly and northwesterly winds, can turn the southeast corner of the continent into a tinderbox. The whole region faces the danger of destructive bushfires every summer. Nevertheless, that first Saturday of February 2009 was different from anything experienced before. People accustomed to bushfires had never seen anything like the velocity and intensity of the fire.

Two other bushfire days are seared into the cultural memory of Australians: Black Friday (13 January 1939) and Ash Wednesday (16 February 1983).[2] Seventy-one people died in Victoria on Black Friday and 47 on Ash Wednesday. These figures show that the impact of these fires was considerably less than that of 7 February 2009, now known as 'Black Saturday'. The actual trajectories of the Black Friday 1939 and Black

Saturday 2009 fires were almost exactly the same, but the area burnt out on Black Friday was double that burnt on Black Saturday. So what explains the fact that just over twice as many people were killed in 2009? It is not that more people lived in the bush in 2009 than in 1939. While exact statistics are hard to compile, there were probably almost as many people living in the path of the fire in 1939 as there were in 2009.

So what was the new element on Black Saturday? The answer is: southeastern Australia is drying out, and the most plausible cause is global warming. Victoria has had a 20 per cent drop in rainfall over the last 12 years. Recent summers have been the hottest and driest on record, way outside the normal range. The weather systems that used to bring rain to southeastern Australia are shifting further south, so that much of the rain now falls either over the ocean or on southwestern Tasmania. It is misleading to talk about a 'drought', because the word implies that things will eventually return to 'normal'. In fact, the present weather conditions are the new 'normal'. This will lead to bushfires that are more frequent, more intense and more widespread. No longer are Black Friday and Ash Wednesday the norms by which fires are judged; the new measure is Black Saturday. Psychologically, this has left many people, especially in Victoria, numb. They are unable to comprehend what has happened, let alone believe that Black Saturday is the norm for future bushfires. It is too much to take in and is too threatening.

Just take the issue of temperature. On 7 February 2009:

> An all-time record was set at Hopetoun, in [Victoria's] north-west, where the temperature reached 48.8°C, exceeding the old record of 47.2°C, set at Mildura in January 1939 ... Seven other sites, in the Wimmera and in the area immediately west of Melbourne, also exceeded the old record ... The Hopetoun temperature is also believed to be the highest ever recorded in the world so far south ... [In] Melbourne (with 154 years of record) ... the temperature reached

> 46.4°C, far exceeding its previous all-time record of 45.6°C set on Black Friday 1939 … Record high temperatures for February were set over 87 per cent of Victoria.[3]

But Black Saturday wasn't just the culmination of a 10-day, record-setting heatwave. Humidity and wind speed are also key factors in bushfires. Climatologist David Karoly says that the wind pattern and velocity 'were similar to those on Ash Wednesday and Black Friday and … do not appear to be exceptional nor related to climate change'. However, he says unequivocally that the heatwave and the record high temperatures were the result of climate change:

> A recent analysis of observed and modelled extremes in Australia finds a trend to warming of temperature extremes and a significant increase in the duration of heat waves from 1957 to 1999. Hence, anthropogenic climate change is likely an important contributing factor in the unprecedented maximum temperatures on 7 February 2009.[4]

Karoly admits that there are no specific studies that relate the very low humidity of late January and early February 2009 'to anthropogenic climate change, but it is consistent with increased temperatures and reduced rainfall … due to climate change in southern Australia'.[5]

Another clear example of the effects of climate change can be found at the other end of the earth, in the Arctic. Here previous weather systems are changing rapidly. Researcher David Spratt, one of the authors of *Climate Code Red*, says that 'Eight million kilometres of sea-ice – an area the size of Australia – is melting … The complete loss of sea-ice in summer is now irreversible.'[6] It will most likely happen within the next decade. 'The Arctic is often cited as the canary in the coal mine for climate warming … and now as a sign of climate warming, the canary has died.'[7] The Arctic is even more important than Antarctica, because it is the key driver of global climate systems. What happens there influences the whole world. Writer George Monbiot explains:

> As the ice disappears the region becomes darker, which means that it absorbs more heat ... The extra warming caused by disappearing sea ice penetrates 1500 km inland, covering almost the entire region of continuous permafrost. Arctic permafrost contains twice as much carbon as the entire global atmosphere.[8]

The reason for this is that the permafrost contains methane. This most dangerous of gases, with a very high global warming potential, continually develops from vast quantities of rotting vegetable matter of all sorts, most of which is trapped in silt in river deltas, in seabed deposits in the oceans and under permafrost layers in northern latitudes (places such as Siberia, Scandinavia and Canada). The methane remains naturally stable as long as the temperatures and conditions in which the gas is stored remain stable. However, if sea temperatures rise or the Arctic permafrost melts, the release of methane will be catastrophic. Already there has been considerable warming of the Arctic Sea: it has become warmer by up to 4°C in the years 2005–08 relative to averages from 1951 to 1980. In 2008 methane was reported to be bubbling up from the Arctic Ocean seabed off the eastern Siberian coast and off Svalbard in Norway.[9] Also, nitrous oxide emissions – and nitrous oxide is an even more dangerous greenhouse gas than methane – are already starting to occur in the Western Siberian peat bogs. It is difficult to say what the time frame for the release of these gases is, because they have not been studied closely.[10] However, once methane gets into the atmosphere in large amounts the whole process of global warming will escalate rapidly. Methane remains in the atmosphere for 40 or more years before it breaks down. So we are in a situation which could be quite catastrophic. Spratt says we need to get summer ice back into the Arctic, or it 'will kick the climate system into run-on warming and create a new climate state many, many degrees hotter'.[11]

The Arctic Sea ice melt is also intimately linked with the collapse of the Greenland ice sheet. The island is 85 per cent ice covered, holding 10 per cent of the world's fresh water. If it melts, sea levels will rise by up to 7 metres. While no one knows exactly how long this will take, all the evidence indicates that it is happening already and that it is happening fast. Some think that it has already passed its tipping point. Even a partial melt will have disastrous effects on coastal cities across the world and low-lying countries such as Kiribati, the Maldives and Bangladesh. In the Antarctic, ice shelves such as the Wilkins ice shelf are also disintegrating, due to warming seas. Another symptom is the melting of glaciers. Peru, Ecuador and Bolivia, for instance, are dominated by the Andes Mountains and much of their water supply comes from glaciers. It is often forgotten that Peru and Ecuador are in the tropics – Quito is virtually on the equator and Lima is only 1300 kilometres south. These countries have already lost 12 per cent of their fresh water. If this loss continues – and it is predicted that the northern Andes will lose most of its glaciers in the next 15 to 20 years – the coastal plain will be turned into desert.

An element that may be slowing down the process of global warming slightly is called 'global dimming'. Essentially this is a kind of photochemical smog or smokescreen around the globe, and it is particularly prevalent in areas of high industrialisation such as China; it results from burning fossil fuels. Dimming reflects the sun's rays and prevents incoming sunlight getting through to the earth's surface. While some think that this has been masking the true impact of global warming, most scientists are more cautious – they are uncertain of the consequences of the process. Over the last decade its effects seem to be diminishing. It is certainly no panacea for global warming.

I often talk to scientists, and the utter frustration and despair I increasingly see in climatologists and earth scientists, despite the fact that they are highly rational people, is striking. Try as they might, they cannot get their message through to enough of our politicians and policy makers. They often blame themselves, because they feel the message is too complicated. While the details require concentration, any intelligent person who applies their mind to it will get the message. Even after Copenhagen 2009 many policy makers are still resistant. They seem to be influenced by the lobbyists employed by the polluting industries, and for them the short political cycle is always a pressing factor.[12] Politicians love 'problems' they can be seen to 'solve', such as the global financial crisis. They bear a terrible moral burden for their inactivity and lack of leadership on global warming.

The danger we face has been reinforced recently by a group of leading atmospheric scientists from the United States, the United Kingdom and France, led by the prestigious climatologist Professor James E. Hanson of NASA and Columbia University in New York. They have already shown that the earth's climate system is far more sensitive to CO_2 than the Intergovernmental Panel on Climate Change (IPCC) and others had at first thought. The Hanson group's work is based on better data on climate history and further evidence from the polar regions. In their view, an optimum level of CO_2 in the atmosphere should be less than 350 parts per million (ppm). Most predictions used by politicians and policy makers have set 450 ppm, or even higher, as the real danger level. If Hanson and his colleagues are correct, with a November 2009 level of 385.99 ppm and an annual increase of just of over 2 ppm, we are actually moving further *into* the danger zone, rather than just moving towards it.[13] The evidence that coal is the major source of atmospheric pollution is overwhelming, and the authors say that 'the only realistic way to sharply curtail CO_2 emissions is to phase out coal use except where CO_2 is captured and sequestered'. They argue that if coal emissions were phased out by 2030, CO_2 in the atmosphere would peak at 400 to 425 ppm and then slowly decline. Reforestation and improved agricultural practices could be used as forms of remediation; they seriously question the use of technological or geo-engineering solutions to remove CO_2 from the atmosphere. Geo-engineering 'is defined as "the deliberate large-scale manipulation of the planetry environment to counteract anthropogenic climate change". Methods fall into two types: carbon dioxide removal from the atmosphere and solar radiation management aimed at reducing heat coming or reflecting more of it out.'[14] In other words, the use of more technological fixes for problems that we are causing by our behaviour.

Dr Andrew Glikson, of the Australian National University (ANU), points out that 'life on earth depends on a delicate balance between the atmosphere, the oceans and the biosphere'. The atmosphere acts as 'the lungs of the biosphere', and the ocean currents as the vein system, 'modulating temperatures around the globe'.[15] He argues that present carbon dioxide levels 'are already leading earth toward conditions similar to about 3 million years ago, when CO_2 levels reached 400 ppm, global temperature rose by 2–3°C and sea level rose 25 ± 12 metres', and claims that the IPCC and government plans for emission caps and reduction targets 'such as 15 per cent by 2020 or 60 per cent by 2060' completely underestimate the sensitivity of the atmosphere.[16] We already know, he says, that warming and cooling events can happen within 'time scales of a few years to decades'. He concludes that 'plans for climate stabilization at 450 ppm may not be able to prevent melting of the polar ice sheets. Plans for stabilization at 650 ppm may not be able to stop runaway greenhouse effects and associated extinctions.'[17] And high temperatures resulting from runaway greenhouse effects will be a long-term problem, because CO_2 remains in the atmosphere for 100 years.

It is useful to place this whole scenario in a historical perspective.[18] Humans first made their presence decisively felt on earth during the great megafaunal extinctions that came in the late Pleistocene, between

10,000 and 20,000 years ago. This saw the end of the woolly mammoth in northern Eurasia, the *diprotodon* (a giant marsupial browser) and many other large marsupials in Australia, and a later wave of extinctions in the Americas. The domestication of animals (dogs, cattle, sheep and horses), the use of fire for forest clearing, irrigation, and the beginning of agriculture were further steps in the process of taming, manipulating and exploiting the environment. Then, in the late 10th century AD, coal began to be used in China both for the production of iron and for heating. This came slightly later in England and Europe. The result was that 'Preindustrial societies could and did modify coastal and terrestrial ecosystems, but they did not have the numbers, social and economic organization, or technologies needed to equal or dominate the great forces of Nature in magnitude or rate.'[19] That came with industrialisation, which began in about 1800. This is increasingly being called the first stage of the 'Anthropocene' – the age when industry, technology and human population began to rival nature for control of the world. The second stage of this is the industrial acceleration that occurred immediately after the end of World War II in 1945. The impact of this on the atmosphere has been enormous. As climatologist Will Steffen points out, 'Nearly three-quarters of the anthropogenically driven rise in CO_2 concentration has occurred since 1950, from about 310 to 380 ppm, and about half of the total rise (48 ppm) has occurred in just the last 30 years.'[20]

This brief overview nicely illustrates the problem we face. Coal and oil are such convenient fuels. They are easy to use and perfectly adapted to the lifestyle we've come to expect. Coal provides cheap electricity, fuel-driven cars and aircraft have given us extraordinary mobility, and small petrol-driven machines, from lawnmowers to chainsaws, have made life easier and cheaper. No longer do we need working animals and our own muscle power to survive, as did all generations prior to the industrial revolution. Coal and oil have provided us with a powerful source of energy that is, above all, cheap. That is why persuading people to surrender this source of power is difficult; these industries, and these goods, are deeply embedded in the capitalist-industrialist system. Perhaps all of us unconsciously perceive just how radical the change that we need to bring about to live more sustainably will be, and are unwilling to abandon our comfort zone.

It was this refusal to face the facts of climate change that frustrated climatologist James Hanson. In a 23 June 2008 briefing for the US House of Representatives Select Committee on Energy Independence and Global Warming, he bluntly told members of Congress that 'we have used up all the slack' and that we are on the edge of climate catastrophe. He pointed out that politicians and business leaders have had 20 years to come to grips with this problem, but have at best dithered and at worst lied and prevaricated, and still need to be shaken out of their complacency. Hanson argued that something must be done *now*: 'Otherwise it will become impractical to constrain atmospheric carbon dioxide, the greenhouse gas produced in burning fossil fuels, to a level that prevents the climate system from passing tipping points that lead to disastrous climate changes that spiral dynamically out of humanity's control.' Hanson believes that the wealthy, powerful, industrial special interests that prevent political action have to be neutralised and their influence eliminated. If they are uncooperative, they need to be forced to conform.

He sees the coal industry as the worst of these: 'CEOs of fossil energy companies know what they are doing and are aware of the long-term consequences of continued business-as-usual. In my opinion these CEOs should be tried for high crimes against humanity and nature.' Yet these people still put enormous pressure on governments. That is why I said at the beginning of this book that we will be cursed by our children and grandchildren and those who follow them because we have surrendered so easily to grossly selfish and fundamentally evil people. To deal with these corporations Hanson called for a carbon tax – on coal, oil and gas – which would be returned in its entirety to the public to be 'deposited monthly in an individual's bank account'. In this way people would be funded to pay for rising prices for energy. He pointed out that 'low and middle income people will find ways to limit their carbon tax and come out ahead … [and] profligate energy users will have to pay for their excesses'.[21] Another element preventing many business leaders from confronting global warming is that they have done nothing about risk management. Many businesses have simply failed to factor global warming into their business plans. Hanson is confident that we can bring atmospheric carbon dioxide back to 350 ppm 'if we phase out global coal emissions within 20 years and prohibit emissions from unconventional fossil fuels such as tar sands and oil shale … [and] if policies make it uneconomic to go after every last drop of oil', and if we improve forestry and agricultural practices. Otherwise 'it is a dead certainty that continued high emissions will create a chaotic dynamic situation … with deteriorating climate conditions out of … [people's] control'.[22]

Yet countries such as the United States, Australia and the Czech Republic continue to mine coal on a massive scale. While Saudi Arabia is still the world's largest producer of oil, Canada is now developing the world's second-largest oil reserves – in the Athabasca region in northeastern Alberta. Oil is extracted from tar sands in the world's largest open cut mines, in a process that uses enormous amounts of energy and produces toxic waste on a vast scale. The strip mines are about 60 metres deep and the oil is extracted from bitumen via a process using scalding water that is heated by natural gas. The leftover material (made up of water, sand, oil and toxic materials such as naphthenic acid) is dumped in tailings ponds, some close to the Athabasca River. The region is currently producing 1.3 million barrels of oil per day. The present Conservative Party government of Stephen Harper protects this highly polluting industry and has repudiated the greenhouse gas targets Canada set for itself under the Kyoto Protocol. As a result, Canada has become something of an environmental pariah, and threats to expel the country from the Commonwealth have been made.

Australia's record is little better than Canada's. As the world's largest exporter of coal, Australia contributes massively to global warming. The coal lobby and both Labor and Coalition governments constantly talk about the development of 'clean coal': the idea is that greenhouse gases would be captured and stored as the coal is burnt. This technology is at least 10 years down the track, if it can ever be developed. The coal industry has no plan for what is to be done in the meantime. What is also clear is that the fossil fuel industry, aided by some newspapers and media interests, has supported a powerful campaign by so-called climate change sceptics to question and undermine the work of responsible climatologists and scientists. The tragedy is that this influences both public opinion and some politicians not to take climate science seriously.

It was in this extraordinarily difficult context that the UN Climate Change Conference met in Copenhagen from 7 to 18 December 2009. Because expectations were so high, many ended up seeing the conference as a disaster, an opportunity lost. Before Copenhagen it was widely accepted that a temperature rise of 2°C was the absolute limit if we were to avoid 'dangerous climate change'. Even at 2°C, Kiribati and Tuvalu would be drowned. To achieve even this, polluting countries would have to cut emissions by 25 per cent to 40 per cent by the year 2020, the year in which global emissions peak before they start their decline. By 2050 we would need an 80 per cent cut in emissions from every country. The aim at Copenhagen was to try to get a legally binding agreement on these issues.

The reality turned out to be very different. The key to the conference was the behaviour of China, now the world's biggest polluter. China has become increasingly assertive in international relations and this was very much on show at Copenhagen. For the Chinese the conference was more about geo-politics and putting the United States and Barack

Obama in their place than about saving the environment. China stonewalled its way through the process, which infuriated developed nations and led poorer countries to despair. After endless delaying tactics by China, India and other developing countries and a confusing scramble at the very end of the conference, with the whole process in jeopardy, a motion by the United States, China, India, Brazil and South Africa was jackbooted through, with the British Climate Change Secretary, Ed Miliband, describing the process as 'chaotic' and 'dogged by procedural games'. He described the negotiations as 'farcical', adding that 'we cannot allow negotiations on real points of substance to be hijacked in this way'.[23] He explicitly referred to China and its allies.

Essentially, the final motion recognises the need to keep temperature rises to 2°C, and promises to deliver US$30 billion to aid developing countries over the next three years. It also sets a goal of providing $100 billion per year to help poor countries deal with the results of climate change. This won't, of course, be much help to Kiribati, Tuvalu or the Maldives as they sink under the Pacific Ocean. But we also need to remember that when the small nations of the Pacific go under, so will the hundreds of millions who populate the low-lying parts of Asia. The agreement avoids setting a 2050 greenhouse target for the world and setting mandated limits for each country. However, while countries will set their own emission targets, a process was set up to verify reductions by industrialised countries such as China. This will give Obama leverage as he tries to get some type of emissions targets through the US Senate, which appears to remain very much in thrall to coal and oil interests and big polluters. The long-term result will probably be that a 3°C rather than a 2°C temperature rise will occur. This means that there is little incentive for even willing nations such as France, Germany and others in the European Union to increase their targets.

President Obama had told the lead-up Climate Change Conference in Poznan, Poland (1–12 December 2008): 'Now is the time to confront this challenge [global warming] once and for all. Delay is no longer an option. Denial is no longer an acceptable response. The stakes are too high. The consequences are too serious.' He put the best gloss he could on Copenhagen. He called it a 'foundation for international action', but admitted that 'we have much further to go'. The then UK Prime Minister, Gordon Brown, said, 'We have made a start ... we need to follow up on [it] quickly ensuring a legally binding outcome.' EU Commission President José Manuel Barroso was more direct: 'I will not hide my disappointment regarding the non-binding nature of the agreement ... In that respect the document falls far short of our expectations.' The head of China's delegation said his country had 'managed to preserve their bottom line', which he defined as 'our sovereignty and our national interest'. Putting a more positive spin on it, China's Foreign Minister, Yang Jiechi, described Copenhagen as 'not a destination but a new beginning'.

So was the conference a failure? From a scientific perspective it certainly was, as it sets the world on a path to 3°C warming, which is really dangerous climate territory. No framework has been established to continue the process. China, India, Brazil and other developing countries are simply unwilling to make commitments to binding targets, although they certainly recognise that they have to lessen their emissions, and that they have to be accountable to international verification. The best that can be said is that Copenhagen is the beginning of a new process which holds countries accountable. It also achieved some consensus on financing the poorer world to reduce emissions. The worst is that it was another wasted opportunity when time is very short. The problem was perhaps best summed up by John Sauven of Greenpeace UK. He described Copenhagen as a 'crime scene ... with the guilty men and women fleeing to the airport', and commented that 'there are too few politicians in this world capable of looking beyond the horizon of their own narrow self-interest, let alone caring much for the millions of people who are facing down the threat of climate change'.

Here it may be useful to imagine the possible long-term consequences of not acting at all, or of not acting decisively and quickly enough. One writer who has thought about this is the distinguished scientist James Lovelock. He predicts a descent into a new 'Dark Age'. Mention the Dark Ages and most people imagine a period a thousand years ago when central government had completely broken down and the population of Europe had reached its lowest ebb. It was a time when local thugs dominated whole regions through control of land and physical violence, when Vikings sailed up Europe's rivers and attacked monasteries and settlements with impunity, and when the weak could forget about justice and fair play. Natural disasters and pestilence constantly threatened a fragile subsistence economy, and food shortages and starvation weakened people already vulnerable to plague and every passing viral infection. Every pregnancy was a threat to the life of the mother. Life was hard, brutish and short. This picture of the 10th century is actually a caricature, but it does indicate what people think life might be like if good order and central government were to collapse in a world of acute weather events. For most people it is inconceivable that this could happen again: Dark Ages only happen to people in other historical periods.

Lovelock predicts that we are right on the edge of another Dark Age as a result of runaway global warming. He paints a picture of a mid to late 21st century world in which a few starving human stragglers struggle to eke out an existence in the last habitable places left on earth: Greenland and Antarctica. Thuggish warlords reign supreme, and they are armed with nuclear weapons. The earth is out of balance, and it is going to take 100,000 years for it to regain its equilibrium. Whether humankind will survive this process is doubtful. His book *The Revenge of Gaia* reads like apocalyptic science fiction or the Bible's Book of Revelation, depending on your taste. At the core of Lovelock's argument is the concept of Gaia, a vision of the earth as a single, living, unified organism whose geological structure and life forms have evolved cooperatively and delicately to maintain the right conditions for the survival of a multitude of species. Gaia is the earth's system of self-regulation, a complex symbiosis of diverse realities interacting to maintain the planet's equilibrium. The sheer complexity of this process requires altruism and cooperation.[24] Although it is certainly not Lovelock's interpretation, there is something almost purposive in the process he describes. Gaia seems to suggest that evolution is essentially a cooperative symbiosis, rather than a competition 'in tooth and claw' between organisms in which only the fittest survive. The concept of Gaia seems to contradict Richard Dawkins' notion of the 'selfish gene', and the Darwinian presumption that evolution is the product of random trial and error, a kind of meaningless, chance-produced meander through cosmic time that has resulted, by chance, in the world we know.

Lovelock argues that the earth is healthiest when it is in a glacial stage, as it was in the last ice age. However, such ages are neither stable nor permanent, and studies of the earth's climate over the last 130,000 years, and particularly over the last 11,500, show that it is liable to abrupt changes, with rapid warming or cooling. The consequences of these abrupt changes for life on earth have been considerable. As climate scientist Wallace Broecker has commented, 'The record of events that transpired during the last glacial period sends us the clear warning that by adding greenhouse gases to the atmosphere, we are poking an angry beast.'[25]

It may be an angry beast, but this interlocking network is also so complex and finely balanced that it is no wonder some have succumbed to the temptation to divinise Gaia, turning her into 'a vaguely personal goddess' as she was in the ancient Greek world. For instance, scientist Tim Flannery says, 'I believe that over the course of the twenty-first century we will again come to serve our Earth goddess, perhaps even revere her.'[26] While one might disagree with any attempt to invent a pseudo-theology or resurrect an ancient goddess, it is clear that our excessive burning of fossil fuels seriously threatens the delicate balance of the earth system. What really worries Lovelock, Flannery and others is that we could be fast approaching a series of tipping points which Flannery defines as points 'at which the greenhouse-gas concentration reaches a level sufficient to cause catastrophic climate change'.[27] This point of no return will so throw the system out of balance that a whole series of connected and irreversible collapses will occur. It's not that the scientific consensus is saying absolutely that a civilisation-ending repeat of the Dark Ages or worse is going to happen; it's that many scientists have a gut instinct that this is the direction we are heading in.

Apocalyptic scenarios stir up immediate responses, but whether they bring about the kind of long-term conversion and profound conviction that is going to be needed to deal with a crisis like global warming is questionable. Part of the problem with Lovelock's approach is that talk of 'Dark Ages' can be disempowering, depressing and counter-productive. As Monbiot notes, the danger of saying it is too late 'is to make it true. To suggest that there is nothing that can now be done is to ensure that nothing is done.' But he admits that 'even a resolute optimist like me finds hope ever harder to summon'.[28] Lovelock is certainly a fine scientist, but I agree with Monbiot; apocalyptic scenarios are disabling for many people. Appeals to idealism and ethics are more persuasive, and I will return to them throughout this book.

So how much time do we have? The answer: not very much. A continued increase of greenhouse gases up to 450 ppm will take us far beyond widespread species extinction and sea level rises that will displace millions of people. It will result in increasing desertification in Australia, southern Africa, the southern United States and Mediterranean countries, widespread forest fires, the drying-up of lakes, the destruction of coral reefs, increasing acidity in the oceans and the loss of all sea ice in the Arctic, major ice loss in the Antarctic and major melting of the Greenland ice sheet and most of the world's glaciers. In 2007 the

IPPC predicted a sea-level rise of up to 0.59 metres by the end of the 21st century, but the consensus in 2009 predicted rises by 2100 of between 1 metre and about 1.9 metres.[29]

This would wipe out, as well as the low-lying Pacific islands, the Ganges Delta in Bangladesh and India's West Bengal. These areas are already being heavily impacted from two sources. First, there is a greatly increased flow of water from the melting of Himalayan glaciers down the Ganges and the Brahmaputra Rivers. The confluence of these two enormous systems is just northwest of Bangladesh's capital, Dhaka, and the increased flow through the flat, fertile land of the delta is already causing severe erosion. Second, rising sea levels in the Bay of Bengal are causing flooding, and the cyclone-prone coastline is being battered by increasingly extreme storms caused by rising temperatures. Both these threats to the area, which is home to upwards of 125 million people, are caused by global warming. The situation is going to get worse. According to the UN Environmental Programs' newly released *2009 Year Book*, 'the planet is quickly approaching the tipping point for abrupt climate changes, perhaps within a few years'.[30] The situation has become so acute that some scientists are beginning to look at technological solutions such as the use of 'sodium trees' or sodium hydroxide to absorb carbon in the atmosphere. But, as I have said, extreme caution is needed with geo-engineering solutions.

So how do we persuade people, especially in democratic countries, of the importance of these issues? Although most reasonable people are aware of global warming, they somehow block out its consequence: widespread climate instability. The climate scientists and others who have had the courage to be prophets of doom act as though the populace is influenced by intellectual arguments; this only works with a minority of people. Despite the overwhelming evidence of global warming, most people will hide their heads in the sand. They admit it's happening, but refuse to accept that it will affect them. Psychologically, the science is complicated and abstract and the issues seem long term. Doubts can be reinforced by 'climate sceptics', whom the major polluters use ruthlessly and successfully. If you have children or grandchildren, it is very hard to face up to the kind of world that they might have to inhabit. It's too horrible to conceive, so you sweep the whole issue under the carpet.

This kind of logical disconnect is also manifested in the way most people in the developed West know that the planet's non-renewable resources are finite and that the supply of fuels such as oil must eventually come to an end, but lack the will to break their addiction to them. We are good at hoping against hope, trusting that somehow a solution that will not disrupt our comfortable way of life will be found. Democratic governments and the vested interests of polluting industries collude in this avoidance. For instance, the global financial crisis in September-October 2008 had scarcely hit when the coal, oil and resource industries hit the airwaves and newspapers to assure us that nothing could possibly be done about global warming until the financial crisis was past. It was too much of a threat to jobs. Economics still seems to dominate almost all policy decisions despite the humiliation of global capitalism, and superficial economic dogmas and nostrums are still accepted as gospel truth by many in positions of power, and many of the rest of us as well.

Economists talk as if there was no link between the economy and the environment. Many seem to be 'screen-jocks' who live in a world of abstractions and computer modelling where raw materials and energy sources are just numbers on a screen. Economics and finance have become detached from reality. The world financial crisis of 2008 grew out of massive financial losses resulting from irresponsible but widely accepted lending practices whose disastrous results were completely predictable. These practices were based on a combination of greed, dishonesty and econometric modelling that bore no relationship to what was actually happening in the world. Only someone lost in their own theories could imagine that you could safely lend a large sum of money to a person who had absolutely no ability to repay the loan. Interestingly, the only solution offered by so-called rationalist economics was, ironically, socialistic: governments using taxpayer funds to bail out the banks and the markets!

A striking example of an econometric approach to global warming can be seen in the report of economist Ross Garnaut, who was commissioned in 2007 by various Australian governments to examine the impact of global warming. We have already seen that CO_2 levels of between 450 ppm and 550 ppm would involve a temperature increase of more than 2°C which, in turn, would lead to massive extinctions, and to an unlivable situation for many people. Yet Garnaut's report seems to find 550 ppm an acceptable target for Australia. The reason, according to the report: no country should sacrifice economic growth until there is international consensus. He says that going it alone will cost too much. It is not that Garnaut is unaware of the consequences: he outlines them in detail, including the fact that Australia's iconic Great Barrier Reef and most other coral reefs will be lost, as well as the driest continent's major river system, the Murray-Darling. Nevertheless, he still argues that:

> Achievement of a comprehensive agreement of around 550 ppm objective would be *a step forward of historic dimension*. Such an achievement ... would avoid the worst outcomes from unmitigated climate change. It would give confidence to the international community that co-operation is possible in this difficult sphere. Once in effect ... it would unleash forces for innovation and structural change that would demonstrate that strong mitigation was consistent with continued economic growth, and bring more ambitious goals into the realm of the possible. It would bring the next step to 450 [ppm] closer to reach (emphasis added).

He admits that 'The difference in environmental outcome between successful achievement of a 550 ppm objective and of a 450 ppm objective is substantial for Australia ... But it is small compared with the difference between 550 ppm and the complete failure of mitigation.'[31] Sure, but who is proposing doing absolutely nothing about global warming except utterly irresponsible elements in the polluting industries and benighted climate sceptics?

But look at the response Garnaut's report received from the Australian Labor government – which had been elected on the back of the promise to do something about global warming. Even Garnaut was disappointed. To stabilise greenhouse gases at 450 ppm by the year 2020 Australia would have to reduce its emissions by 25 per cent from levels at the year 2000. In the end the Australian government committed to a miserly 5 per cent reduction; they will go up to 15 per cent if other countries come on board. This will place Australia's environment in the way of irreparable harm. So after promising at the December 2007 Bali Climate Conference 'robust targets ... fully cognizant of the science', all the then Prime Minister, Kevin Rudd, managed to deliver was a 5 per cent cut. The climate change minister, Penny Wong, said, 'we had to get the balance right, we had to support the jobs of today', even though setting such a course will utterly devastate the jobs of tomorrow, and, more importantly, the lives of our children.

So what can we do now? How do we motivate people and move them to action?

First, it will not be by drowning everyone in scientific or economic information. Discussion has to move to the moral sphere. We have to convince people that we are facing a massive, overarching *moral* problem, bigger than war, far more serious than financial meltdowns, closely linked to but transcending even social inequity, and certainly far outweighing our personal needs and preoccupations. It is only then that we will be able to engage the community at sufficient depth to change behaviour beyond recycling and reducing their carbon footprint. To use explicitly biblical and Christian language, global warming has to be seen within the context of good and evil, virtue and sin. We have to talk in a language that indicates that what we are doing to the natural world is evil, or, in the language of moral theology, sinful. We are committing what philosopher and theologian Thomas Berry calls 'biocide' (the killing of the life systems of the planet) and 'geocide' (the killing of the planet itself). We have 'a sensitivity to suicide, homicide and genocide', Berry says, 'but we commit biocide and geocide and we have no morality to deal with it'. This is because we have become completely 'absorbed with the pathos of the human'.[32]

But moral discourse in secular democracies is difficult, because we have neither the ethical apparatus nor the rhetoric necessary for it. Since the 18th century Enlightenment our culture has progressively whittled away the Christian foundation of morality, the roots of which go back to the New Testament as well as to Aristotle and the Greeks. To replace Christianity, John Stuart Mill proposed a utilitarian ethic, which he explained as the greatest good for the greatest number. In contemporary society utilitarianism has degenerated into a kind of subjective hedonism that says that if my way of acting doesn't hurt someone else, it is morally acceptable, and that my actions are my business and shouldn't be judged by anyone. This approach is unconcerned with the good of the whole community, let alone of the planet. It is focused on a kind of libertarianism whereby individuals shape their own meaning and goals with the sole caveat of not being a 'nuisance to other people', as Mill put it. This has resulted in crass individualism and the denial of any overarching, broadly embracing moral obligations and ethical norms. We have almost lost the ability to articulate a moral discourse that engages with the whole human community.

This kind of ethical relativism is compounded by neo-Darwinians such as Richard Dawkins, who contend that nature is purposeless. Things arise by pure chance and if they survive it is because the environmental conditions at the time happened to be right for them. Random variations explain their adaptations and mutations. Everything is blindly driven by the reproductive urge to pass on genes to succeeding generations. Thus the natural world is stripped of meaning and purpose, and becomes the product of a completely random process. In this context nature has no value because it has come from nowhere and is going nowhere. In fact there is no such thing as 'nature'; there is just an accidentally related, meaningless jumble of random beings and events. Views like these can lead people to jettison any care for the natural world except as a comfort zone for humankind. A meaningless, accidental world that is purposeless by definition cannot have intrinsic value. It simply is. The only value it can have is one we project upon it.

Not that the Catholic Church is a paragon of virtue on climate change. As Irish theologian and ecologist Sean McDonagh has pointed out, there is some window-dressing, but essentially the institutional church doesn't take this issue seriously.[33] McDonagh points out that the treatment of ecology and climate change in the *Compendium of the Social Doctrine of the Church* is 'one of the shortest chapters in the entire volume', and most of it is devoted to biotechnology. There are hardly any Catholic seminaries where Creation Theology is taught. Certainly, Pope Benedict XVI has often talked about the need 'to reflect upon the kind of world we are handing on to future generations', and during the July 2008 World Youth Day event in Australia he spoke clearly and passionately about care for the earth several times. But sitting beside him was Australia's best known 'climate change sceptic', the archbishop of Sydney, Cardinal George Pell. Pell's position is rather ironic in light of the fact that the 2002 *Social Justice Statement* from the Australian Catholic Bishops Conference said that:

> as the worst emitters per person of greenhouse gases on the planet, Australians are particularly challenged in justice to reflect on the plight of our Pacific Island neighbours. The cry of seven million inhabitants of these beautiful islands ... who fear that their lands will be battered and submerged by rising sea-levels and changing weather patterns, require us to take immediate measures to reduce greenhouse gas emissions.[34]

Catholic priest Dr Charles Rue has pointed out that climate change deniers have had influence in the church:

> [They play] on people's good will and Christian charity and can lead to confusion by appearing to show compassion: 'carbon taxes will rob the poor'; 'don't deny developing nations scientific agriculture such as genetically modified crops and bio-fuel production'. Even people of good will committed to social justice can be deceived by such ideas.[35]

In a way, the biggest problem the church has is to be true to its own tradition. Catholic-Christian ethics has always accepted the intrinsic value of the material world. Even at its most anthropocentric, Christianity sees the world as the context where God is revealed. But more than that, the Christian doctrine of the incarnation clearly supports the fundamental moral principle of this book: that the good of the planet must come before everything else. It is a radical belief that God has chosen to reveal God's inner self to us in and through matter, through the very stuff of the world. God comes to us in Christ's body, which is descended from and intimately genetically related to all other bodies and to the whole history of matter. The doctrine of the incarnation is uniquely Christian.

Arguing from the opposite perspective – from the material world back to God – the medieval theologian St Thomas Aquinas maintains that because God is the Creator of everything:

> you find traces of the Trinity in every creature … [Each creature] shows forth the personality of God the Father … and represents the Word [Christ] just as an artistic work represents the creativity of the artist, and reflects the Holy Spirit in so much as She is love.[36]

Aquinas is saying that everything in the natural world conjures up a reflection of its Creator and therefore the whole of creation is an icon or sacrament of God. So for the fullest possible vision of God we need all species, everything in the natural world. Thus the incarnation of God and the divinisation of matter become the fundamental Christian principles on which human ethics and values are built. Putting it another way, the good of the planet as the reflection and revelation of God becomes the foundation upon which we build our moral structure.

In Christianity matter really matters. In fact *materia* (matter) matters so much that Aquinas makes it the principle of individuation: it is my matter that makes me myself as distinct from every other creature. He uses an odd phrase, *materia signata quantitate*, matter signified by quantity, to explain how individuality is established. The exact meaning of the phrase is obscure, but what is clear is that it is 'matter' that constitutes each individual as an individual. It is my flesh that both separates me from all others of my species and quantifies and distinguishes my species from all others. I am who I am because of my body, my matter. For Aquinas it is not my 'soul' or 'spirit' that constitutes my individuality, but my body.

Matter provides a basis for individuality and a foundation for the moral imperative that the good of the planet must come before everything else. Berry argues that the ethical framework we need today must be provided by the larger context of the earth and the natural world:

> The human community is subordinate to the ecological community. The ecological imperative is not derivative from human ethics.

> Human ethics is derived from the ecological imperative. The basic ethical norm is the well-being of the comprehensive community, not just the well-being of the human community. The earth is a single ethical system.[37]

Berry insists that 'All human institutions, professions, programs and activities must now be judged primarily by the extent to which they inhibit, ignore, or foster a mutually enhancing human–earth relationship.'[38] The foundation for this is that the earth has a significance in itself that far outweighs the value of all of us. It existed for millions of years before us and could well survive our extinction, albeit with considerably diminished numbers of life forms.

This returns us to our central focus: the need for an overarching system of ethics. We seem to have created a moral vacuum in society, and to have replaced morality with political correctness. Ideas such as cultural diversity and minority rights, for instance, while of some importance, have assumed the status of unassailable, peak moral imperatives, while other, deeply established moral norms are ignored. We need to move from political correctness to genuine moral imperatives. We have to recover the operating principles that will help people begin to think about global warming *morally.*

Catholic-Christian morality is based on four operating principles. These principles are called cardinal virtues: they are prudence, fortitude, temperance and justice. The word 'cardinal' here is derived from *cardo*, the Latin word for hinge. In other words, these are the virtues upon which our moral lives hinge or depend. They are the qualities or characteristics that should govern our moral actions. At first sight they seem abstract, but they're not, particularly in the context of global warming.

First, what is prudence? Aquinas follows Aristotle in his interpretation of prudence as 'practical wisdom'.[39] Prudence is what we need to apply to discern the right course of action in any particular moral circumstances. It comes out of our experience, and we use it to make real, concrete ethical decisions. Its opposite is folly, stupidity and lack of judgment. In the second book of the second part of the *Summa Theologiae* Aquinas discusses prudence as the first and most important of the cardinal virtues.[40] 'Prudence,' he says, 'is reasoned regulation of conduct, reasoning well about the whole business of living well.' It is about applying universal principles to particular cases. It is an acquired virtue; it requires an alertness and shrewdness of mind, and these don't always come naturally.[41] Prudence demands that we always act cautiously and make sure that all our actions are appropriate to the demands of natural law, which is geared to protecting our planet. Aquinas says that prudence is cognitive rather than instinctive, in the sense that it requires 'memory, reasoning, understanding, docility' (by which he means a willingness to confront the evidence), and practical in that it needs 'foresight, circumspection and caution'.[42] He says that to live a good, moral life you not only have to know the moral law, but you also have to be able to apply that knowledge in complex ethical situations.

Significantly, he also sees prudence as a kind of foresight. 'Prudence,' he says, 'considers issues that are ahead of us in the distance in so far as they are a help or hindrance to what we decide at the present moment.'[43] He also quotes the 7th century theologian and bishop St Isidore of Seville, who says, 'A prudent man looks to the future. He is sharp-sighted and foresees uncertainties.' 'Prudence,' Aquinas says, 'is to know the future from the present and the past.'[44] Aristotle succinctly calls it 'the grasping of the right moment'.[45] All of this has clear resonance in the context of a world threatened by global warming. Prudence demands that we don't act in a way which may result in irreparable damage to the climate system.

Aquinas says that prudence has several elements.[46] The first, he says, is memory. We use memory to recollect and reflect upon the experiences of past moral decision making, and this teaches us what works in the majority of cases. Knowledge of history is important. In the context of global warming, climatologists have warned that warming and cooling events have occurred within time scales of just a few years. That is, we know that rapid and interconnected collapses can occur. Prudence dictates that we take these facts seriously. Second, Aquinas says, you need understanding, which he explains as 'right reason applied to action'. This is not so much an intellectual exercise as an astute assessment of all the elements of a situation. The third element is docility, which Aquinas says is the humility that allows inexperienced or ill-informed people to be 'taught by others, especially by older people who have acquired a sound understanding ... in practical matters'. In our context it means that the time has come to listen to climate scientists. Fourth, you need to be able to see connections and congruities between things. This is an ability many economic rationalists seem to lack entirely. They seem not to see that the world is not an infinite source of resources; nor can they figure out the connection between the burning of fossil fuels and global warming. The fifth element of prudence is closely related to this: the need to be able to engage in a logical reasoning process when applying universal principles to particular circumstances. In this case the general principle is that you can't constantly interfere with nature without repercussions. Pouring carbon into the atmosphere is abusive, and nature will respond. Sixth, Aquinas says, you need foresight, in order to be able to predict the consequences of your actions. The application of this to global warming is obvious. If you constantly use the atmosphere as a sewer for pollutants, you must expect that something is going to happen. Seventh, circumspection, or caution, is required. This means taking everything into account when making decisions: if we are going to open more coal mines, for example, we need to already have in place some method of containing the pollution they generate. Prudence would dictate that if we don't have those proven carbon sequestration or cleaning methods – and we don't – we are morally bound not to open any more coal mines, and in fact we are bound to progressively close down those we have.

The relevance of prudence to the global warming crisis is obvious. We have a great deal of knowledge about what is ahead of us. Politicians, business leaders and bureaucrats need to have the docility to listen to what experienced scientists say about this issue. Any prudent person can see the connection between what we are doing now in terms of burning fossil fuels and what will happen in the future if we don't scale back greenhouse gas emissions. Prudence binds us to take these issues seriously and demands that we act to prevent widespread destruction of the natural world and the creation of chaotic life situations for those who come after us.

What is actually happening is, of course, very different. Many politicians in many countries still refuse to act. Even the European Union has backed off the promises they made at Bali in December 2007, as a result of the global financial meltdown. This is proving a difficult issue for President Obama too, and we are yet to see real environmental runs on the board. The Australian government also has failed to fulfil its election promises, apparently because it would put too much 'pressure' on polluters and industry and therefore also on employment. Some politicians claim that scientists are making an ambit claim, just like the polluters, and that the two have to be 'balanced'. They seem not to believe that the scientists are trying to tell them what is actually going to happen if we don't act now. If prudence is the primary element of moral judgment, then politicians are clearly acting sinfully if they do nothing or just try to put a bandaid on a global crisis. This is a moral issue and we don't have time to mince words. We need to apply moral pressure to politicians. The science is clear. As Karoly says, 'The [climate] system can't cope now, and it's just going to get much worse.'[47]

The second cardinal virtue is fortitude. This is the courage to do the right thing no matter what the cost to oneself. It is the ability to rise above the self-doubt that often threatens those who take a stand for a just cause. It is the strength to oppose powerful opposition forces and vested interests that encourage compromise, mediocrity and surrender, and that ridicule good people who try to do the right thing. It is the strength to challenge the inertia of the political establishment and bureaucracy. Fortitude involves resistance, perseverance and, ultimately, a willingness to die if that is the price of standing up and being counted. Opposition to global warming certainly requires fortitude. Aquinas says that 'fortitude involves the removal of any obstacle that stops the will following reason'. By 'reason' here he means a considered assessment that what is happening – global warming – is evil and morally unacceptable. He says that it is fear that causes us to withdraw from tough decisions, such as opposing the polluters whose actions lead to global warming, and that 'Fear must be curbed.'[48]

Fortitude also involves endurance, which Aquinas defines as the ability 'to stand unmoved in the midst of dangers'. He says that 'The act of fortitude contains two elements, namely boldness or confidence, and endurance.' He goes on to quote the Roman orator Marcus Tullius Cicero (106–43BC), who talks about the kind of boldness which inspires people 'with the assurance and hope to [carry out] great and honourable undertakings'. Aquinas, with Cicero, links this nobility of purpose to patience and endurance: this is 'the voluntary and prolonged persistence in arduous and difficult things'.[49] He is also quite clear that a brave person can often be 'motivated to action by moderate anger'. Anger, he suggests, gives fortitude the assertive edge that it needs; it 'sometimes stirs up the aggression to attack'.[50] What we need nowadays is more anger at the people involved in producing pollutants and at the spin-doctors who act as spokespersons for those people.

However, while fortitude requires courage, it doesn't demand recklessness. As moral theologian Bernard Häring says: 'One must properly and prudently evaluate the whole situation, carefully appraising the merits and importance of the cause one is to serve, the magnitude of the effort required, and … the dangers involved.'[51] Here Häring is referring to the third cardinal virtue, temperance, which keeps life in balance. Temperance is about self-discipline and humility. The Latin *temperantia* means moderation or self-control. It is the education of the passions, emotions and desires. To achieve this one must undertake *askesis*, the Greek for exercise – what Christians call asceticism. This fits in perfectly with the attitude we need towards global warming. Temperance involves self-control, self-sacrifice and genuine asceticism: that is, a willingness to make sacrifices – in this context for the greater good. Although Aquinas sees temperance as a virtue that applies principally to individuals, rather than groups, in today's world we can perhaps broaden its application: we need, as a species, to reduce our use of resources, to lower our standards of living and to think of those coming after us. In an age when we still have people advocating endless increases in production, temperance is definitely a virtue with widespread application.

The last of the four cardinal virtues is justice, which is really love of others in action. It is, as Häring says, benevolence, a wishing-well, 'a right attitude of soul towards one's fellow men and the community'.[52] He points out that it is based on love and care for others, as individuals and societies. It is closely linked to the theological virtue of love, or charity, and involves the kind of benevolence that is also typical of Buddhist spirituality.

This perspective is important because justice easily becomes a cold, abstract virtue, a kind of punishment fitting the crime, to paraphrase W.S. Gilbert in *The Mikado*. The meaning of the word is too easily and quickly contracted to a kind of forensic process, to crime and punishment. Aquinas defines justice as 'a habit according to which each person, constantly and continuously, bestows on others what is due to them'.[53] In other words, justice is essentially social and communal. He also says that justice and morality demand that we cannot live in a way that denies to others 'what is due to them'. In the context of global warming, if there is one thing we owe to our children and grandchildren and people in the future it is a liveable world, a place of beauty and diversity in which other species flourish. Yet it is precisely this which is threatened.

Justice is usually divided into four parts: commutative justice, strict or legal justice, distributive justice and social justice. In fact this division is really a variation on a theme; it is looking at the same reality from four perspectives. In common parlance, when we use the word 'justice' we usually mean legal justice, the type handed down by the courts. But the other three ways of looking at justice are even more important, and all of them have practical application to the global warming crisis.

Commutative justice is perhaps the most straightforward. It is contract justice, whereby individuals or groups enter into an agreed compact: 'It forbids the violation of the right of another or any deprivation of his right. Principal violations of commutative justice are theft, fraud, unjust damage.'[54] In the context of global warming there is a real, or at least implied, contract between generations. Here we come back to the moral truth that we have no right to destroy the world and thus deprive coming generations of their rights. Commutative justice morally binds us to care for the future. Also, developed countries, as the biggest polluters, have a moral responsibility to help poorer countries adversely affected by global warming.

Legal justice is essentially about the common good of the community. In modern democratic societies elected parliaments legislate, citizens accept and obey laws for the common good of all, and the police and the legal system enforce and administer the law. In this context, while individual rights must be protected, the common good has priority over private needs and desires. However, in societies dominated by economic rationalism, it is the common good which has suffered most. We have become so self-obsessed that President John F. Kennedy's great challenge in his Inaugural Address on 20 January 1961 would be meaningless to many citizens of democratic countries today. His dared his fellow Americans to 'Ask not what your country can do for you – ask what you can do for your country.' Aquinas emphasises that 'the common good transcends the individual good of one person'. He then approvingly quotes Aristotle: 'The greatest virtues are those which are most beneficial to other people, because genuine virtue is the power to do good to others.'[55] It is precisely the ability to think beyond the parameters of the self that is most difficult for people today, obsessed as they are with their own needs and insecurities. This makes it particularly hard for us to realise that we have moral obligations to the future. It even blocks us from realising that care for the future actually involves our own children and grandchildren.

Distributive justice is the third element of justice. Essentially, this refers to the two-way movement of goods and services between the individual and the community. Distributive and legal justice are two sides of the same coin. As Häring says, 'In the measure in which the individual devotes his powers and resources to the common welfare, the community must show its concern for his particular welfare.'[56] In a way, distributive justice applies especially to those who have most. While wealth is not necessarily sinful in itself, the Bible is deeply suspicious of the rich. This is summed up in the words of Jesus: 'Truly I tell you, it will be hard for a rich person to enter the kingdom of heaven. Again I tell you, it is easier for a camel to go through the eye of a needle than for someone who is rich to enter the kingdom of God' (Matthew 19:23–4). Yet so often it is the rich who are the major opponents of moves to control greenhouse gas emissions; they have the most to lose.

The final variation on the virtue of justice is social justice. This has often been highlighted by the Christian tradition and the Catholic Church. It combines all the other three elements of justice. Perhaps the word which best sums it up is 'equity': it demands a fair, impartial and just distribution of the goods of society among all its members. In the context of global warming, equitable distribution has to be understood on an intergenerational basis. We have no right to use resources in a way that makes the planet close to uninhabitable for those who come after us. Social justice is not time-constrained; it is about obligations to the future as well as to the present.

So where does all of this leave us, morally speaking? The answer is, in a completely untenable ethical situation. What we are doing to the environment – and specifically to the atmosphere – is morally reprehensible and sinful. That is why I mentioned at the beginning of this book that we will be the most despised generation of history. We have consumed the world's resources for our own benefit, with complete contempt for those who come after us. We tend to think of sin in far too narrow and personalised a context. We see it as what individuals do. That view lets most of us off the hook. It allows whole communities to collude in utterly reprehensible behaviour: doing next to nothing to change our addiction to burning coal for power, and not curbing our use of fossil fuels by developing alternative forms of energy and finding other means of transport. Inertia is not an excuse. To do nothing involves us all in sinful situations. Note that here I have used the word 'sinful' when describing the situation in which we find ourselves as citizens of developed countries, and I have confined the word 'sin' to what individuals do. Thus individuals who deliberately and knowingly pollute commit sin because they have personally made immoral decisions and acted on them. It is more difficult when you are a member of a community caught up in a sinful situation. A crude way of expressing this is to say that the sin is spread across a much larger group of people. For instance, all Germans who lived between 1932 and 1945 were caught up in Nazism. Nowadays we are caught up in global warming. Perhaps it is not as obviously sinful as Nazism, but in the long term it will be far more destructive.

In these circumstances it is the role of the virtuous person to make a stand, to speak out. That is why fortitude is a cardinal virtue. Some very brave Germans risked their lives standing against Hitler, and some considered that the evil that the Führer brought to the world justified killing him. In democratic societies we are not risking our lives when we oppose the polluters or confront our governments. But we may be subject to ridicule and sneered at as 'extreme greens' and 'tree huggers', or laughed at as 'fairies at the bottom of the garden', or told we're stupid because we don't understand economic constraints. But even those who make a stand may be caught up in global warming because we also have vested interests, via shares or superannuation, in polluting industries. The problem is that once you are aware of an issue like global warming or environmental destruction, you become bound to act. Sinful collusion begins when you do nothing.

Ultimately, that is why we need virtuous people in the community, people for whom prudence, temperance, fortitude and justice are operating principles, and who are convinced that global warming is as much a moral as an ecological crisis. Shakespeare understood this clearly. In *Hamlet* he describes a society sick and rotten to the core as it sweeps under the carpet the murder of the legitimate king by his brother, and the crowning of the murderer, who then proceeds to marry the murdered king's widow. The guard Marcellus is absolutely right when he says 'Something is rotten in the state of Denmark' (*Hamlet*, Act 1, Scene 4). All the imagery of the play reflects this, with its constant emphasis on sickness and disease, on the secret, corruptive illness at the core of the state. It is much more difficult to conceal things in a modern, democratic state and we are increasingly aware of the lobbyists in the United States, Canada, Australia and elsewhere whose job is to protect the fossil fuel and polluting industries. We have to start naming and shaming these industries. Industries and corporations can be involved in sinful activities, just as individuals can sin. To pretend otherwise is to live in a moral vacuum.

The problem of global warming is widely recognised, but few make the connection between it and over-population. It is to this question that we turn now.

3 Population

The greatest threat to the environment is humankind. Since the advent of *Homo sapiens* almost all extinction scenarios are attributable, either directly or indirectly, to our pressure on the rest of nature – to our actions. This is because humans are, from an ecosystem point of view, an exotic species. If humankind has a natural environmental niche it is central East Africa, where our remote ancestors, the Australopithecines, who were the first hominids, originally evolved. This was followed by 5 million years of highly complex non-linear development. This process eventually produced our near-ancestors, *Homo habilis* and *Homo erectus*, two hominid species who seem to have existed parallel to each other for most of their existence, still in East Africa; they probably shared a common ancestor. They were able to exist together because they didn't depend on the same food sources.[1] So if there is a natural place for humankind it is the hot, moist climate of sub-Saharan East Africa, where tropical diseases and parasites kept population numbers low.

Somewhere between 250,000 and 130,000 years ago, *Homo sapiens* appeared. There are two main theories as to how humans spread across the world. One is that a group of already evolved *Homo sapiens* left Africa to spread out over Europe and Asia. The other is that *Homo erectus* left

Africa about a million years ago and evolved into *homo sapiens* across a number of regions. Whichever theory is right, Richard E. Leakey and Roger Lewin correctly point out that this whole period:

> was truly remarkable in the evolutionary history of humankind. Our African cousins the Australopithecines fell into extinction at the beginning of the period, perhaps succumbing to the ever tightening grip of competition for resources exerted by *Homo erectus* ... And the enormous evolutionary potential pent up in the populations of *Homo erectus* ... generated a dynamic state of biological development, a matrix of progression toward the *sapiens* state.[2]

As humans adapted to cooler, less tropical climates, their numbers increased because of the absence of diseases and pathogens.

Homo sapiens' greater brain capacity meant that humankind could transmit high-level knowledge and skills from generation to generation, and develop a sense of continuity and culture. As epidemiologist Tony McMichael points out, this has allowed 'successive generations to start progressively further along the road of cultural and technological development. By travelling that road, the human species has, in general, become increasingly distanced from its ecological roots.'[3] Humans have increased their ability to exploit resources and maintain a higher population. But there are real limits to the population-carrying capacity of all areas, especially when resources begin to be exhausted. Population increases are achieved 'at the cost of reductions in biodiversity', and always run the danger of over-exploiting the environment, which leads to the collapse of the offending civilisation. 'It is in the nature of ecological systems that debts are finally called in,' McMichael says.[4] This explains why the history of population is something that moves by fits and starts.

While there have never been so many people in the world as there are now, the actual dynamics of historical demography are still only partially understood. Estimates of human numbers for the past are, at best, informed guesses, and can vary widely. There may have been 1–4 million people on the earth around 10,000BC, and this might have increased to about 5 million by 5000BC. World population estimates for the time of Christ are anywhere between 150 and 300 million. The really dramatic increase in human numbers occurred after 1700AD, and this growth is exponential. It took the entire history of the human race to reach 1 billion in the 19th century, but only another century to reach 2 billion. By 1960 we had reached 3 billion, and by 1999, 6 billion. At the end of 2009 the world population was 6.8 billion.

Human population numbers really start to escalate with industrialisation, which was based on the increasing use of fossil fuels. Before this, useable energy came from wind, water and the muscle power of animals and humans. But in the late 18th century this constraint was broken by the steam engine, and we – at least those of us in first world countries – were gradually able to free ourselves from these limitations. As Will Steffen points out, this opened up:

> an era of far looser constraints upon energy supply, upon human numbers and upon the global economy. Between 1800 and 2000 population grew more than six-fold, the global economy about 50-fold, and energy use about 40-fold. It also opened up an era of intensified and ever-mounting human influence upon the Earth System.[5]

We are now reaching the stage when that growth has become so great that we could soon be facing unprecedented catastrophe.

Some people estimate that by 2100AD there could be as many as 10–12 billion people if nothing intervenes to stem population growth. Others believe that numbers will stabilise around 9 billion in the mid to late 21st century. Former US Vice-President Al Gore expresses the problem of current growth in a vivid comparison: 'To put these numbers in a different perspective, consider that the world is adding the equivalent of one China's worth of people every ten years, one Mexico's worth every year, one New York City's worth every month.'[6]

Despite its importance, population is a difficult issue to discuss in polite society. Mention it and you are soon accused of being 'anti-human', an 'extreme green', 'racist', 'anti-immigrant', or wanting to dictate to developing countries how they should behave. Or you are censured for being misinformed because the 'real issue' is not over-population, but lack of equity in the distribution of the resources of the world. Perhaps the reason for these sorts of responses is that people personalise the issue, and everyone thinks their own life is of inestimable value. Consequently it's hard not to sound misanthropic when discussing population. There is also enormous vested interest in maintaining high rates of growth and immigration, especially in those Western countries which have reached zero population growth, or have decreasing populations. The attempt to stifle discussion is often led by business leaders, who want to maintain the number of consumers for their goods and services without regard to the pressure this puts on the environment. In market-oriented thinking, new immigrants add to the pool of consumers; they are not seen as putting strain on fragile environments.

Another part of the problem is that discussion of population and the carrying capacity of particular ecosystems offends political correctness on both the right and the left. For the right it suggests that you favour abortion, contraception, fertility control and sterilisation, especially in developing countries, and that you want to limit the rights of couples to decide the number of children they wish to have. For the left, it smacks of neo-colonialism and paternalism; you are accused of dictating population size to developing countries and of distracting attention from social justice. As the colourful Conservative Lord Mayor of London, Boris Johnson, says, in the 1960s and 1970s people were interested in demography, 'and it was perfectly respectable to talk about saving the planet by reducing the growth in the number of human beings'. But now 'we are getting to the point where you simply can't discuss it'.[7] Anyone who tries can be subjected to vicious invective. As a result, political parties are often completely unwilling to discuss population issues or optimum population size for a specific nation or region and few have population policies. Immigrant countries such as the United States and Australia have never developed population policies or debated optimum carrying capacities. Only small groups, such as Sustainable Population Australia, have had the courage to try to keep these issues before the public, often at the risk of being called 'racist'. (Here I acknowledge that I'm a patron of Sustainable Population Australia.) The fear of breaching political correctness, particularly among the left, seems to have frightened even the Greens away from the issue.

Johnson puts the basic quandary bluntly: 'How the hell can we twitter on about global warming and reducing consumption when we are continuing to add so relentlessly to the number of consumers? The answer is … political cowardice.'[8] In 1992 Al Gore put the issue more politely: 'No goal is more crucial to healing the global environment than stabilizing human population.'[9] More recently, however, Gore has been more optimistic about population. He told an audience at Harvard University in December 2006 that this issue is now moving towards resolution, with the world population stabilising at about 9 billion people.[10] Gore said that the major problem now is the demand for ever-higher standards of living, not only in the West, but also in countries like China and India, where more people are using energy and resources at an ever-increasing rate.

In my view this emphasises only one side of the problem. The issue is double-headed: it is both absolute human numbers and the insatiable human demand for ever-higher standards of living. Also, there are a number of very poor countries, especially in Africa, where population numbers are not stabilising, but increasing dramatically. Niger, for instance, a land-locked country south of the Sahara, is four-fifths desert: the current population is 13.3 million. Fertility rates are exceptionally high: 7.29 children per woman. There is no family planning program and there are already serious food shortages. Even if fertility somehow halves, by 2050 there will be 50 million people in Niger, and this is an unsustainable number.

Serious discussion of population goes back to Reverend Thomas Malthus, who wrote his *Essay on the Principle of Population* in 1798. There has been debate ever since about the accuracy of his claims. Despite the optimism and economic growth of the decades between 1950 and 1970, pessimism about over-population and profligate use of resources was expressed by many, including the Club of Rome in their 1972 report *The Limits to Growth*, and by academics such as Paul Ehrlich, of Stanford University. The titles of Ehrlich's best-known books, *The Population Bomb* (1972) and *The Population Explosion* (co-authored with his wife Anne Ehrlich in the early 1990s) were deliberately designed to let readers know that we are heading for population catastrophe. Ehrlich and others argued that we must turn away from the high birthrate approach which has understandably dominated culture and religion for most of world history. I say 'understandably' because in the past high infant mortality and an early average age of death meant that human beings struggled to replace themselves.

But the discussion of population lost much of its respectability from the mid 1980s onwards following the sterilisation policies of successive Congress Party governments in India and the one child policy in China. While the need for some sort of population reduction policies may have been understandable given the population pressures India and China were and are facing, other countries, such as Thailand and Indonesia, have run successful population reduction programs for decades without using the measures introduced by China and India. Most countries in the Western world have seen their population growth fall to zero or below, with replacement coming largely from immigration.

There is uncertainty among experts as to the reasons for human population numbers rising and falling. Some elements are clear: longer life spans, a vast improvement in nutrition, public health and sanitation, and much better medical knowledge and procedures, especially in the area of childbirth. But the contradiction is that the developed countries, which enjoy the best public health and the most readily available medical services, are now at zero population growth or below, while the populations of underdeveloped countries, which lack these services, are still increasing. So while public health issues are part of the equation, they don't fully explain modern population growth.

Whatever the reasons, there are now simply too many of us. When thinkers such as Ehrlich (most of them biologists) first propounded their views in the 1960s and 1970s, they were criticised by many, especially economists, who argued that the earth could support a much larger human population and that that would in fact increase everyone's economic prosperity. Their belief was that human population growth would level out without interference as standards of living rose and education became universal. While both biologists and economists concede that the world is very crowded and there is enormous pressure on resources, most economists tend to be optimists about the future: they see each additional human being as an extra unit of production and consumption. Biologists generally tend to be pessimistic: they see every new baby as another mouth to feed and another human being taking space and resources.

Many technophiles also support the optimistic view. They argue that new ways of producing food, including through genetic engineering, will lead to even higher yields. So new technologies will allow humans to cope not only with the present population, but even with vastly larger numbers. The argument is that the more people there are, the more wealth there will be, and with more people will come more ingenuity and therefore new technical solutions.

Others, including Catholic and Christian groups concerned about the environment, are far less sanguine about genetic engineering.[11] They see it as a threat to biodiversity and to human health. They are also concerned about private corporate control of the world's food supplies and food research.

The assumptions that underpin the economists' and technophiles' optimism reflect the dominance and pervasiveness of technology in our culture. Many people see technology as a solution for all the problems we face. One of the profound intellectual fissures of the contemporary world is between those who believe that technology is a form of salvation, and those who place their trust in the rhythms and systems of the natural world. Those who trust nature are not Luddites who reject technology; they just see it in perspective, as a tool.

In most developing countries the increase in human population has had disastrous effects. As Gore correctly says:

> Societies that learned over the course of hundreds of centuries to eke out a living within fragile ecosystems are suddenly confronted – in a single generation – with the necessity of feeding, clothing and sheltering two or three times as many individuals within those same ecosystems.[12]

These countries now cannot afford to care for their environments. Insatiable and unstoppable human needs for food and energy put enormous pressure on ecosystems and lead to over-exploitation, resulting ultimately in droughts, famines and ever larger areas of desert.

It seems that population growth is beginning to slow down, but the number of people is still increasing at about 200,000 every day – 6 million per month. At that rate we reproduce the whole population of Australia in three and a half months. However, world fertility rates are dropping faster than expected towards replacement level, which is 2.1 children per mother. As a result, estimates of 12 billion people by 2200 are being reassessed, and some think that world population will reach about of 9.2 billion in 2050. As the United Nations reported in 2007, 'Realization of these projections is contingent on ensuring that fertility continues to decline in developing countries.'[13] The UN estimates that world fertility rates will decline from 2.56 children per woman in 2005–10 to 2.02 children per woman in 2045–50. However, population projections have often proved to be wrong, and there are sure to be many unforeseeable variables over the next five decades.

These are still enormous numbers, and a peak of 9 billion people doesn't mean we are somehow out of trouble. Since there is much that we don't understand about the dynamics of population, there is no room for complacency. Natural growth – that is, the number of births over deaths – is still very high in many countries that have recently experienced or are experiencing the trauma of war or genocide: Liberia, for instance, is estimated to have a population growth rate (births over deaths) of 4.50, Burundi 3.90, Afghanistan 3.85, Western Sahara 3.72, East Timor 3.50, Niger 3.68, Eritrea and Uganda 3.24, the Democratic Republic of Congo 3.22 and the Palestinian Territories 3.18.[14]

Population increase puts pressure on food supplies, and hunger is a reality for almost a billion people in the developing world. Grain harvests in 2006–07 fell well short of expectations, which means that the supply of food is not keeping up with demand. This has led to a large increase in the price of staples. Potable water is running short in some regions and the rise in sea levels resulting from global warming will take large areas of fertile coastal land out of production, as well as render some countries, especially coral atolls in the Pacific Ocean, uninhabitable. An increase in food production is not assured. Another issue is the impact of the escalating demand for biofuels on food supplies. Governments in Europe, Britain, the United States and elsewhere are encouraging the use of greenhouse-friendly biofuels derived from plants such as sugar, corn and maize to produce ethanol, or oil palm or soybeans to produce biodiesel, all in order to deal with global warming. Producing these plants uses large amounts of water. Yet we know that global warming means that water will be in ever shorter supply. At the same time, rainforests, which are very effective carbon sinks, are being cleared in many developing countries to grow grain for food and to supply the biofuel industry. This is the vicious circle that results from the combination of over-population and environmental destruction. These are interconnected and intractable problems that will not be solved easily.

While the population increase in developing countries is due to natural growth, the increase in first world countries is due to immigration. When you combine immigration with natural growth you get the overall growth rate: in the United States it is 0.97, in Canada 0.90 and in the United Kingdom 0.42. Most of that is from immigration. Australia currently has a very high overall growth rate, largely due to immigration. The Australian Bureau of Statistics reported that:

> a population growth rate of 2.1 per cent was recorded for the year ending 30 June 2009, up from 1.7 per cent recorded last year [2008]. This is the highest growth rate in 40 years (2.1 per cent in 1969). As at 30 June 2009, Australia's population had grown to 21,875,000, an increase of 443,000 people over the previous year. Australia's net overseas migration contributed more than half of this growth, at 64 per cent or 285,000 people. Natural increase (the excess of births over deaths) contributed 158,000 (36 per cent).[15]

This will have a very large impact on Australia's attempt to cut greenhouse gas emissions, because many of these people are coming from countries with a much lower standard of living and therefore a much lower contribution to global warming. These kinds of disconnections in policy formulation occur largely because immigration and population have become such taboo topics that policy makers fail to see, or are unwilling to tackle, the contradictions between their policies on these issues. Global warming gets lost in these discontinuities.

Although there is a fair amount of intra-European migration, most EU countries have very low growth rates, and some have moved into the negative zone. For instance, Russia's overall growth rate is –0.51, Lithuania's is –0.53, Romania's is –0.45, the Czech Republic's is –0.03, Croatia's is –0.09, Germany's is –0.07, Poland's is –0.15 and Italy's is 0.13. It is interesting that predominantly Catholic countries such as Italy, Lithuania, Poland and Croatia have now moved into negative population growth when Catholicism is often blamed for high birthrates. It is also interesting that Islamic Iran has a population growth rate of 1.35, and Indonesia, with the world's largest Islamic population, has a growth rate of 1.16, considerably less than its near neighbour Australia. Both Iran and Indonesia have had great success with family planning. Another example is Muslim Bangladesh, the world's most densely populated country, which has cut its growth rate from 7 children per woman in the early 1970s to 4.5 in 1990, to 1.67 in 2008. This too was achieved through a successful family planning program.

So the clichéd scapegoating by the media and commentators of Catholicism and Islam as being uncritically supportive of large families and high fertility is completely wrong. Reality is always complex and rarely conforms to such caricatures. However, the papacy and hierarchy of the Catholic Church, as distinct from most of the laity and many of the clergy, do still have a long way to go in confronting and dealing with the moral and ethical conundrums embedded in the questions surrounding population.

I will now try to deal with some of these issues.

*

First, the simple fact is that no one faith has yet developed the ethical apparatus necessary to assess the morality of population limitation. Most of the major religious traditions are divided over the question of fertility control and the means of achieving it. Many faiths have only the most rudimentary views on this question. Because the religious traditions have been largely absent from this debate, it has been mainly carried on in secular and economic terms by biologists, demographers and economists. The reason for religious people avoiding this issue is simple: it is a theological and moral minefield. It involves a whole range of acute ethical issues, as well as challenges to some ingrained attitudes within the various traditions. Perhaps the clearest of the moral conundrums we face are the ethical issues involved in intergenerational rights: if we consume so many resources now that the quality of life of future generations is compromised, are we acting in a morally responsible way? We have answered this question in the previous chapter: we clearly have serious and binding moral obligations to those who come after us. They have as much right to a quality of life as we do.

Linked to this is the moral issue of the imbalance between the living standards of developed regions such as North America, Western Europe and Australia and the 20 per cent of people who are starving or undernourished. Does this imbalance create an ethical demand that developed countries lower their standard of living and dispose of food surpluses to needy countries at concessionary prices? Is there a basic moral right, overriding the powers of nation states, to allow migration from countries of over-population and chronic shortage to those with apparent space and surplus food? And what about the right to reproduce? What limits can the community place on the rights of individuals to decide their fertility and family size? Are programs such as the one-child policy in China working? Is it racist or chauvinistic for developed countries that have already achieved zero population growth, or are close to it, to demand population control as a prerequisite for economic assistance to underdeveloped nations with growing numbers?

Even among non-religious people there are sharp divisions as to how population equilibrium or more moderate rates of population growth might be achieved. The basic spectrum of opinion ranges from Malthusian pessimism at one end to naturalistic optimism at the other. The pessimists believe that the population problem is intractable and will only be solved by draconian measures, while the optimists contend that humanity is very adaptable and that equilibrium will be reached through market forces without regulatory intervention – although it must be said that support for a lack of regulation has taken a severe battering since 2008, when we saw what uncontrolled free-market capitalism can do.

Sitting midway on this ideological spectrum is the notion of intervention. The interventionists maintain that it is only through some form of direct intervention that population stability will be achieved. They aim to achieve this through a more equitable distribution of the world's resources and the donation of resource surpluses to those most in need. This is the social justice solution that is favoured by many Christians and Catholics. It is not clear, however, how this, on its own, would stem population growth or protect the environment. The emphasis in this argument is not on the environment, but on social justice. A better environment is, at best, an accidental by-product.

A minority of interventionists favour compulsory limitations on reproduction, legally enforced by governments: this would mean sterilisation, contraception or abortion. This approach is opposed by those who place great importance on human rights, and by the churches and religious institutions. The most obvious problem with the coercive approach is that it sees the whole issue from a single perspective: cut back population by whatever means necessary and our problems will end. In fact, all the evidence points to things being more complex.

Most interventionists focus on the education and liberation of women in developing countries.[16] We already know that women will use any educational opportunities they receive to improve the living standards of their families; then, with a consequent reduction in child mortality, they are more willing to limit conception. Wherever women have been guaranteed rights and equality, the birthrate has been reduced. They also need employment and interests beyond the home. Ehrlich reports that 'when women have sources of status other than children, then family size declines'.[17] Access to reliable contraception and acceptance of it even in conservative societies is an important part of this process.

There have been real successes in improving the lot of women. Between the late 1960s and 2000 the total birthrate of developing countries reduced from 6 to 3 births per woman. While Catholicism is widely and at times viciously criticised for its opposition to contraception and abortion, the contribution of religious orders and Catholic care agencies to education and higher standards of literacy, health care, development aid and the breaking down of social and class barriers (such as its ministry to the *Dalits* – outcasts – in India) have been important contributions to improving the lives of women. While religions such as Catholicism and Islam are often blamed for imposing oppressive conditions on women, the actual oppression that they experience in Latin America, Africa, and Islamic countries such as Saudi Arabia and Afghanistan is just as much the result of tribal and patriarchal cultural attitudes as it is of religious conviction or teaching. Religion is used in the enforcement of social mores of male control, lack of education and high fertility. It is, of course, difficult to sort out which comes first, religion or culture, but there is no doubt that they reinforce each other, so it is unfair to blame religion for the whole problem.

These various opinions about population control are not mutually exclusive, and it is clear that it is only by combining parts of all of them, and then making adjustments appropriate to the local area, that we will begin to stem population growth. In the end nothing will be achieved if we do not reduce economic growth and attempt to lower the expectations that people have about standards of living. This will be the most difficult task we face. How do you persuade people in the West to lower their standards of living and how do you set limits on the expectations of those in developing countries? Even if the world population stabilised or began dropping by the year 2050, it would be of no use if everyone continued to expect to live at the same level as people in the developed world do now. Yet that is what the burgeoning middle classes in India and China expect as their expenditure spreads from basic needs to wants. The fact is that expectations will have to be trimmed by both Westerners and the emerging middle class in developing countries: the earth is finite, and we cannot continue to use resources at the present rate.

India is an interesting case. In fact, the Indian 'middle class' is rather difficult to define. About 60 million people (6 per cent of the Indian population) earn between US$4000 and $21,000 per year, which means about $20,000 to $120,000 in purchasing power in the West. However, the category 'middle class' is often expanded in India to include those earning between $5 and $10 a day:

> A recent study … suggested a 'simple consumer-based criterion' for membership of the middle class: ownership of a telephone, a two or four-wheel (motorized) vehicle, and a color television. Under this definition the middle class makes up nearly 20 per cent of the population – 200 million people.[18]

In March 2009 the Tata motor company announced that it was building the 'world's cheapest car', the Tata Nano, a petrol-powered car that will market for about US$2000. Targeted at India's young middle class, it will add enormously to the country's already highly polluted atmosphere; in greenhouse gas terms it is a disaster. The result is that 6 per cent of

India's population is more polluting than the country's entire underclass – the 840 million people who live on less than $5 a day.

Another issue that needs to be faced is the possibility of a pandemic – perhaps an avian flu pandemic of some sort, such as the highly infectious and lethal H5N1 variety – that wipes out large numbers of people. There is a real sense in which nature is a self-correcting system, and disease is one method it uses to restore balance. If there are too many of us, if we have become a pest species, then we run a real risk that nature will restore the balance forcefully. Virologists are expecting a pandemic outbreak sooner rather than later, and estimates of casualties are as high as 150 million.

Pandemics are a historical reality. The best known pandemic in European history is the 'Black Death' of 1348–49, which wiped out more than a third of Europe's population. The other well-known pandemic is the 'Spanish Flu' (influenza) pandemic of 1918–19.[19] This pandemic, which originated in the United States immediately following the end of World War I, caused an estimated 40–50 million deaths worldwide (some estimates are as high as 100 million), more than the war itself. It was particularly bad in countries such as India.

Developed countries are, to some extent, prepared for the next pandemic. But as the World Health Organization says, 'the impact of the next pandemic is likely to be greatest in low income countries because of different population characteristics and already strained health care resources'.[20] A pandemic occurs when a new strain of a virus, a strain that can be passed on through contact with the respiratory secretions of an infected person, appears. Authorities agree that the next pandemic is likely to be a flu pandemic, and will probably be an entirely new virus derived from a form of avian flu that crosses from birds to humans and can then be passed on by contact. Because of modern travel, it will spread faster than ever before, and because it will be completely new, we will have no immunity to it and no vaccine to deal with it. While the flu may not kill all victims directly, complications (such as those that result from pneumonia and sinusitis) will increase mortality enormously, as happened in the 1918–19 pandemic.

Pandemic or no pandemic, how are we going to set ethical limits to population? Some say that living 'sustainably' will set the limits. The usual definition of sustainability comes from the 1987 report *Our Common Future*, chaired by the then Norwegian Prime Minister, Gro Harlem Bruntland. It says, 'Sustainable development is development that meets the needs of the present without compromising the ability of future generations to meet their own needs.' This definition says nothing about protecting nature. It is all about humans. Perhaps that reflects the fact that it was written two decades ago. Loggers destroying old-growth forests claim that their actions are 'sustainable' because the forest will probably grow again. Perhaps, but it won't be an old-growth forest for another 400 years, if ever. It will be monocultural. Many of the species that depended on the complex interlocking system of the old-growth forest will be gone. Some people in conflagration-prone countries claim that constant preventive burning to lessen the intensity of wildfires is 'sustainable', even though this endless cycle of burning accentuates the vegetation conditions that encourage wildfires in the first place. Essentially, then, sustainability is in the eye of the beholder. It is very difficult to define and is often little more than window-dressing.

What does sustainability mean in terms of population? How many people constitute a sustainable population? The UK-based Optimum Population Trust has calculated countries' carrying capacities by comparing actual population numbers with how many people a specific country could sustain with a 'modest footprint carrying capacity'. It defines this as a lifestyle broadly related to European standards of living with a reduction of about three-fifths of present consumption of fossil fuels. In this scenario several countries, such as Canada and New Zealand, could actually carry slightly larger numbers.

However, by this standard most countries are already living well beyond their carrying capacity:[21]

COUNTRY	POPULATION	CARRYING CAPACITY
Australia	22 million	18 million
United Kingdom	60 million	23 million
United States	280 million	254 million
Israel	6 million	1 million
Italy	58 million	16 million
China	1.3 billion	168 million
India	1 billion	103 million
Egypt	67 million	6 million
Bangladesh	135 million	6 million
Nigeria	111 million	10 million
Pakistan	138 million	26 million

If we calculate the total numbers for these countries, their carrying capacity is approximately 630 million, but their actual population far exceeds this: 2.9 billion! These statistics vividly illustrate how unsustainable our present population situation is. So even if rich countries lowered their standard of living and the poor achieved this 'modest' lifestyle, the earth's carrying capacity would still be far exceeded. So unless development goals, equity and social justice for the third world are linked to reduction in population numbers, the situation is impossible. Human numbers are now so far beyond sustainability as to render the concept of sustainability irrelevant.

A major part of the problem is that we lack an overarching moral framework to deal with population. For decades demographers have been warning us about over-population. But as we saw with global warming, facts and statistics lack persuasive power. They don't engage people at a deep enough personal level to change their behaviour.

The great religious traditions have had little to say about over-population. Generally all of them have been officially characterised by a pro-reproduction stance, especially when it applies to their own members. I say 'officially' because there is and always was a real difference between what church or religious officials taught and what ordinary believers actually did. For instance, Catholics in countries such as the United Kingdom, the United States and Australia have always been accused of having lots of children. However, the historical evidence does not show this. In Australia, for instance, census data shows that Catholic fertility has remained almost in lock-step with national fertility since the late 19th century, and is now slightly below that of the rest of the population. In Ireland the population was 8.5 million in 1845, but by 1960 it had fallen to half that number. The Irish achieved this partly by emigration of more than 1 million people, but also through what Thomas Malthus called 'prudential restraint' which involved late age of marriage and a strong emphasis on sexual restraint.[22]

Let us now turn to the teachings of specific religions regarding reproduction and population. At the core of the Jewish view is the command to 'be fruitful and multiply and fill the earth' (Genesis 1:28). Given the terrible losses that the European Jewish population suffered in the Holocaust, some modern Jewish thinkers have encouraged an increase in the Jewish birthrate. However, there is no explicit theological or rabbinical reflection on the population problem as such. Nowadays the 1.66 per cent increase in Israel's population of 7.28 million, 5.5 million of whom are Jews, comes largely from births rather than from immigration, which now constitutes only 12 per cent of the country's population increase. High fertility rates are more common in the conservative Jewish groups.

The theology of Martin Luther emphasised the importance of individual salvation and of each person's right to respond to a free and conscientious relationship with God. It is out of this theological matrix that the Western notion of individual human rights emerged. Because of this notion of personal autonomy, the Protestant tradition has not had a great problem confronting the issue of artificial contraception. Certainly, puritan evangelicalism in the Victorian era was utterly opposed to any form of sexual licence, and birth control was viewed as opening the way to promiscuity. But in 1930 the Lambeth Conference of the Church of England approved the limited use of contraception. This position spread throughout Protestantism, and by the 1960s, with the introduction of the pill, discussion of the morality of contraception had been superseded by reflection on the ethics of population. For instance, the 1958 Lambeth Conference said:

> Family planning ought to be the result of thoughtful and prayerful Christian decision. Where it is, Christian husbands and wives need feel no hesitation in offering their decision to God and following a clear conscience. The means of family planning are in large measure matters of clinical and aesthetic choice, subject to the requirement that they be admissible to the Christian conscience.[23]

In fact, the most creative thought on the population question in the Christian tradition has come from Protestant ethicists. However, even here the focus has been on broad statements such as responsible individual freedom and the maintenance of equity so that the burden of reducing population should not fall exclusively on certain groups. The general Protestant view is that the individual's right to make their own fertility choices ought not be denied, and there is considerable suspicion of government-endorsed coercion. There is agreement that an individual can voluntarily seek sterilisation, but this should never be imposed.

The traditional Protestant emphasis on the conscientious, autonomous exercise of individual moral responsibility continues. Eastern Orthodox thought has followed Protestantism in a slow liberalisation of its stance against contraception, but the strong tradition of the importance of extended family among Orthodox believers doesn't encourage family limitation. Orthodoxy has very little to say on the population question as such.

The Muslim response to population is two-edged. First, the large majority of the world's Muslims live under governments that have officially adopted family planning projects. Islam is not traditionally opposed to fertility control. However, the religious position is that the right to apply the ethic of limitation is exclusively vested in individual couples. As Basim F. Musallam writes: 'Muslims are free to control births, and governments are not. As long as compulsion is avoided, the provision of information, clinics, services, and devices can all be accommodated within the dominant interpretation of religious law without damage to its spirit.'[24] However, there seems to be a gulf between rhetoric and practice. In many Muslim countries, especially in fundamentalist circles, the whole business of family planning is seen as a Western plot to reduce the Muslim population. As a result, it is as difficult for many Muslims as it is for Christians and Jews to take the population question seriously. In the 1990s an odd link between the Vatican and some Muslim countries – such as Iran and Libya – seemed to have formed around UN policy on population control; however, at the Cairo Population Conference in 1994 the predicted 'holy alliance' between the Vatican and fundamentalist Muslims did not materialise, and support for the Holy See's position came mainly from smaller Catholic countries, such as Malta and Honduras.

Where does the Catholic Church stand on the question of population? First, the church has had many admirable things to say about equity and social justice. Second, recent popes and some national bishops conferences, religious orders and many laity have shown increasing concern for the environment. Nevertheless, official Catholicism has a poor record in developing an ethical approach to the issue of population. It has said little on the question and what it has said is inadequate. Its approach has been distorted by the question of contraception and the implications of this teaching for papal authority. It is not only the Vatican that is to blame for this. With few exceptions, there has been no serious Catholic ethical or theological reflection on the issue of population control in the English-speaking world over the last five decades.

Historically, the Catholic Church has been pro-reproduction. This makes eminent sense if it is seen within the context of its theological view of marriage, which developed over a 1500-year period from the time of St Augustine (354–430AD) until the 19th century. Until the 1950s Catholic moralists consistently argued that the purpose of marriage was the reproduction and nurture of children. The relational aspect of the union was usually mentioned, but in practice it was accorded a secondary place. Indeed, for much of human history marriage has principally been about the maintenance of the social – and economic – status of the family and clan through reproduction. This was a genetic and cultural imperative that was reinforced by religious sanction. But from the pontificate of Pope Pius XII (1939–58) onwards the change of attitude that had been going on in the wider world for several decades started to permeate Catholic thought. After considerable theological debate, a more contemporary view of marriage emerged, in which the mutual fulfilment of husband and wife was recognised as being as important as, if not more important than, the reproduction and care of children. Just as this debate was being resolved in the Catholic Church in the early 1960s, the contraceptive pill appeared. While this complicated things for Catholic moralists, after a lot of resistance, the mutual fulfilment of the spouses was accepted, along with procreation, as an equally important part of marriage by the Second Vatican Council in 1965.

When the pill came on the market in 1960, the whole context of the Catholic debate about marriage changed. For the first time in history an accessible and reliable contraceptive gave women freedom from the biological consequences of intercourse. The relational aspect of marriage became more and more important in church discussions and the wider community. But there was still very little connection made between the debate about contraception and the issue of world population. The moral battle over contraception which raged in the church throughout the 1960s and 1970s remained very much at the level of personal ethics. This came to a head in 1968 with the publication of Pope Paul VI's encyclical *Humanae Vitae*, which condemned artificial contraception. In the decades that followed an enormous amount of ministerial and moral energy was consumed by this debate. The question of population hardly ever appeared on the Catholic moral horizon.

However, there were exceptions. During the papacy of John XXIII and the period of the Second Vatican Council (1962–65) there was a consciousness of the population problem in countries such as Belgium and the Netherlands. As with many of the 'hot-button' issues at Vatican II, it was the Belgian Cardinal, Leon Josef Suenens, archbishop of Mechelen-Brussels, and the then-87-year-old Lebanese-born Melkite Patriarch, Maximos IV Saigh, who confronted the population question at the Council. Speaking on 29 October 1964 in the debate on the document 'The Church in the Modern World', the document that was to become *Gaudium et Spes*, Suenens referred to:

> the immense problem arising from the population explosion and over-population in many parts of the world. For the first time we must proceed with such a study in the light of faith. It is difficult, but the world, whether consciously or not, waits for the Church to express her thought.

He was immediately followed by Patriarch Maximos IV, who said that:

> demographic pressures in certain countries of particularly heavy population prevent any increase in the standard of living and condemn hundreds of millions of human beings to unworthy and hopeless misery. The council must find a practical solution. This is a pastoral duty.[25]

The context in which both men spoke was the section on marriage in *Gaudium et Spes*. Even the most progressive churchmen still saw population as a subset of questions about marriage and reproduction.

One outstanding exception to this was English priest Father Arthur McCormack. After time as a missionary in West Africa and as an expert at Vatican II in the 1960s, McCormack worked for six years in the Pontifical Commission for Justice and Peace in Rome, until 'it became painfully clear that his views of the problems of world population were an embarrassment to the Holy See'.[26] After leaving the Vatican he worked for the United Nations and other international organisations between 1971 and 1984, publishing five books, including *The Population Problem* (1970) and *The Population Explosion. A Christian Concern* (1973). McCormack's opinions were actually quite conservative: he argued that the church had to confront the issue of population and that population growth would only be slowed through the elimination of poverty and the introduction of natural family planning. He also argued that population growth should be taken into account before the church condemned artificial contraception. In a 1982 article in the English Catholic weekly *The Tablet*, he said that the church 'overlooked or ignored' scientific alarm about population, and complained that:

> Even in the slums of the Third World, where there have been plenty of warnings about 'immoral' methods of birth control, there has been no

> suggestion of a population problem of the magnitude I have indicated, or of realistic efforts to deal with it.[27]

Over the last 50 years McCormack has remained a lone voice. Perhaps many Catholic moralists have avoided the issue of population because they fear punitive and repressive interventions in their academic life and pastoral care if they are seen to disagree with the official Vatican line on contraception. Whatever the reasons, this has meant that there has been no development of Catholic social doctrine that might have offered something constructive to the population debate. As the US Catholic ethicist J. Bryan Hehir succinctly puts it, 'The detailed discussion of contraception in Catholic moral theology has at times conveyed the impression that this one issue constituted the whole Catholic position on population ethics.'[28] While Hehir is correct, the popes have very occasionally addressed the question of population. Paul VI (1963–78) mentions the issue in his encyclical on development, *Populorum Progressio* (1967):

> It is true that too frequently an accelerated demographic increase adds its own difficulties to the problems of development: the size of the population increases more rapidly than the available resources ... From that moment the temptation is great to check the demographic increase by means of radical measures.[29]

However, he admits that:

> It is certain that public authorities can intervene, within the limits of their competence, by favoring the availability of appropriate information and by adopting suitable measures, provided that these are in conformity with the moral law and that they respect the rightful freedom of married couples ... It is for parents to decide ... on the number of their children.[30]

John Paul II often discussed sex, marriage and the family, and was regularly critical of the modern descent into hopelessness, selfishness and consumerism which he called an 'an anti-life mentality'. In the 1981 Apostolic Exhortation *Familiaris Consortio* he was also critical of 'a certain panic deriving from the studies of ecologists and futurologists on population growth, which sometimes exaggerate the danger of demographic increase to the quality of life'.[31] This led him to denounce:

> as a grave offense against human dignity and justice all those activities of governments or other public authorities which attempt to limit in any way the freedom of couples in deciding about children. Consequently, any violence applied by such authorities in favor of contraception or, still worse, of sterilization and procured abortion, must be altogether condemned and forcefully rejected.[32]

In the encyclical letter *Solicitudo Rei Socialis* (1987), John Paul II's treatment of what he calls the 'demographic problem' is woefully inadequate. He almost grudgingly admits that 'One cannot deny the existence, especially in the southern hemisphere, of a demographic problem which creates difficulties for development.' But he turns immediately, and without further comment, to the northern hemisphere where, he says, 'the nature of this problem is reversed: here the cause for concern *is the drop in the birthrate*, with repercussions on the aging of the population, unable to renew itself biologically' (emphasis in original). He again repeats his alarm at 'systematic campaigns against birth', which he describes as 'a tendency toward a form of racism, or the promotion of certain equally racist forms of eugenics'.[33] However, he was sensitive to the criticism that the aim of the papacy was to get Catholics to out-breed everyone else, particularly Muslims. In a speech on 17 July 1994, as part of his attempt to oppose the emphasis on abortion in the lead-up to the UN Population Conference in Cairo, he said:

> Catholic thought *is often misunderstood* … as if the church supported an ideology of fertility at all costs, urging married couples to procreate indiscriminately and without thought for the future … In deciding whether or not to have a child [couples] must not be motivated by selfishness or carelessness, but by a prudent, conscious generosity that weighs the possibilities and circumstances (emphasis in original).[34]

While Pope John Paul might not have denied the existence of a demographic problem, he had no suggestions about how the problem might be confronted, except to caution that it could not be through contraception, abortion, or a program of sexual education that included contraception. The tragedy of Catholicism is that throughout his 26-year papacy the whole discussion of population was sidelined, even ridiculed. There were passing and superficial references to the importance of protecting the environment, but no attempt to relate that to the problem of population. The papal emphasis seemed fixated on sexuality. Veteran BBC Rome correspondent David Willey reported that on one South American visit 'the Pope used the word "contraception" no less than sixty times in ten days of public speeches'.[35] Willey also described the 1988 Vatican conference on the 20th anniversary of the encyclical *Humanae Vitae*, when Western countries were accused of a form of 'contraceptive imperialism' which imposed on developing countries 'vast contraception and sterilization programs, thus harming family life, threatening women's health and violating human rights'.[36] It makes little sense for John Paul II to talk about couples exercising 'a prudent, conscious generosity that weighs the possibilities and circumstances' of limiting fertility while excluding virtually all effective forms of achieving that except abstinence.

One might have hoped for something better in John Paul II's encyclical *Veritatis Splendor* (6 August 1993), which focused specifically on fundamental questions concerning the church's moral teaching. The opening line of the encyclical seemed promising: 'The splendor of truth shines forth in all the works of the Creator.' It seemed that the encyclical was going to base Christian morality on creation. But as the Irish priest-environmentalist Sean McDonagh pointed out in *The Tablet*, there is no discussion whatsoever of the ethics of environmentalism in the letter. The moral principles outlined in *Veritatis Splendor* never move beyond the anthropocentric.[37]

Benedict XVI has a reasonable record on environmental questions, but his views on population are extraordinarily myopic. In his 2009 encyclical *Caritas in Veritate* they seem almost to mirror those of the church of the 1930s, a time when there was deep concern about 'population suicide':

> formerly prosperous nations are presently passing through a phase of uncertainty and in some cases decline, precisely because of their falling birth rates; this has become a crucial problem for highly affluent societies. [This puts] a strain on social welfare systems, increases their cost, eats into savings and hence the financial resources needed for investment, reduces the availability of qualified laborers, and narrows the 'brain pool' upon which nations can draw for their needs.

He claims that 'smaller and at times miniscule families' impoverish social relations and are 'symptomatic of scant confidence in the future and moral weariness'.[38] No evidence is offered for any of these assertions.

Even at the best of times Catholic moralists think of population within too narrow a context. What is lacking is reference to the bigger moral picture, the picture that transcends the preoccupations of the human. The question of population impacts directly on the future of the natural world and its myriad species. Linked to climate change, it is the most important issue facing humankind. It is not just about a so-called personalist ethic. If anything, it is about a universalist ethic, a morality focusing on how humankind relates not just to itself, but to the whole world around it. Catholic ethics has viewed population only within the context of marriage, reproduction and social justice. A broad, integrated approach is required for all complex problems, and as Hehir points out:

> The population problem is one strand of a larger fabric involving questions of political, economic, and social structure at the national and international level. While acknowledging the existence of a population problem, this view asserts that it is morally wrong and practically ineffective to isolate population as a single factor, seeking to reduce population growth without simultaneously making those political and economic changes which will achieve a more equitable distribution of wealth and resources within nations and among nations … At both the national and international levels the categories of common good, social justice and freedom of choice for individuals and families in society are used to define the population question.[39]

But there is a problem here: for all the discussion of justice and equity, important as they are, Catholic theorists never actually get to the question of population. What happens is that more conservative Catholics stop at the issue of contraception and those of a more progressive bent stop at social justice and the equitable distribution of wealth and resources. Certainly there is genuine sympathy for environmental questions in the church. Many recognise that they are important, but an unconscious anthropocentrism still dominates the Christian scene, and for most believers humankind rather than the created world remains the primary image of God. In other words, the emphasis is still on humans first and foremost, with nature running a poor second.

However, for those concerned about population pressures, the questions are not primarily about individual reproductive or social justice rights. The reality we confront now is that a billion people are undernourished or starving. So we cannot feed the people on earth now, let alone those who will be born in the future. And the more of us there are, the greater the effects of climate change and environmental destruction are going to be. It is true that there must be redistribution, and that there are dreadful inequalities. Nevertheless, as the number of human beings continues to grow enormous pressure is put on the environment, more greenhouse gases are produced, whole ecological systems are destroyed and more and more species slide into extinction. There are clearly profound, broad-scale ethical issues embedded in these scenarios, but the anthropocentrism of most religious-ethical systems prevents people of faith from bringing their moral reflection and persuasion to bear on the problems of environmental destruction and species extinction. The population question remains trapped in the realm of the human and most people seem unable to take a step beyond that and grasp the fact that the pressing moral needs of nature and humankind must override personal reproductive rights or papal teachings about such issues.

Six point eight billion people and rising is already completely unsustainable. We're now way beyond the earth's physical carrying capacity and are already facing acute food shortages. UN Secretary-General Ban Ki-Moon warned a food summit in Rome on 3 June 2008 that food production would have to rise by 50 per cent by 2030. We might be able to achieve this if we approved genetically modified crops, more irrigation and an even greater use of fertilisers and chemicals. But those advocating these technological fixes, which may or may not be successful, turn a blind eye to the loss of biodiversity, water shortages and the collapse of river systems, land degradation and increasing salinity. Australia, one of the great food producers of the world, is already experiencing all of these. Sure, we could eliminate all the other species we think are not useful for our survival, and only keep those needed for food production and human needs. In that type of feed-lot world we might just survive, at least physically. But what an awful survival it would be, with every bit of fertile land turned over to industrial agriculture. It would be a monochrome world without anything to stimulate our imaginations. So what we face is not just a matter of more equitable distribution; it is a question of absolute numbers and carrying capacity.

Humanity has never been in this kind of situation before. This means we have to rethink some of our moral presuppositions. At the core of the population problem is a conflict of rights: the right of individuals to reproduce, and the right of other species and whole ecosystems to continue to exist. For some this is no problem at all: the human right to reproduce is overwhelming. The whole earth system exists for us and has no meaning outside humankind. This is not a view I share.

Aquinas said the world and its species are icons of God. Everything that exists shows something of the image of God, and to lose any of it is to lose something of our contact with God. To reduce the natural world to a kind of human feed-lot is to destroy the possibility of experiencing transcendence and to drive out whole aspects of the divine presence. This is the clear implication of the Catholic theology of creation. This is not invalidated by those who ask how viral infections, blowflies, plague-carrying rats or mosquitoes show the glory of God. They are part of the whole ecological system and have their part to play, even if that role is not attractive to us. Essentially, the moral task we face is balancing human reproductive rights with the rights of other species and ecological systems.

So what are we to do? What can be recovered from the Catholic tradition to help us develop a population ethic? And how should this relate to a more broadly Christian ethic? Is it possible to develop a genuine Christian response to the question of population? I think it is.

The majority of the world's 1.2 billion Catholics now live in developing countries – in Latin America, sub-Saharan Africa, the Pacific, and parts of Asia. Fertility is an issue for all of them, so Catholicism cannot escape this problem. One of the positives of religious faith is that it helps people think, at a personal and community level, about the moral issues involved in having children. Because it was distracted for so long by the contraception issue, the Catholic Church has largely failed to do this, for which it is rightly criticised. What Catholicism has to do is focus other elements in the tradition on the moral question of population.

Clearly the cardinal virtue of prudence, combined with responsibility to coming generations, comes into play here. Given the already known impact of an out-of-control population, prudent moral action demands that we act to bring human numbers back under reasonable control. In Chapter 2 I argued that prudence is the ability to discern the right course of action in particular moral circumstances, and noted that it is focused on concrete ethical decision making. It is an acquired virtue, and calls for alertness and shrewdness. Its opposite is folly, lack of judgment and stupidity. To ignore the situation we're in now would be stupid folly.

Prudence, as we saw, is intimately linked to temperance and justice. Temperance involves self-control, self-sacrifice and genuine asceticism. In this specific moral context it imposes on developed nations a demand to reduce their use of resources, and lower over-the-top standards of living in order to help poorer nations now, and those who come after us. Social justice is also a key part of moral decision making here. Perhaps the word which best sums it up is 'equity'. Justice demands an equitable, fair, impartial distribution of the goods of the world among all its members. This also applies on an intergenerational level. From a Catholic moral perspective, equity for the poor of the world is an essential element in any moral position on population. At the same time we need to recognise that in developed countries, which have contraception readily available and growth dropping to zero or even below, population is less of a pressing question. For developed countries the fundamental moral issue is equity and social justice, a self-sacrificing asceticism that is prepared to lower standards of living so that people in poor countries and future generations will be given a fair share of the goods of the world.

While the moral demands on the Western world are clear, things are more complex in the developing world. Let us begin with the question of basic reproductive rights. Any prudent discussion of human reproduction must include the full circumstances into which the child will be born. A key element in that equation is the question of the demands that human fertility places on the ecological system into which a child is born. To decide to have a child is not a purely subjective act by an individual couple or woman. It involves broader social and environmental issues. Socially, the moral question is: can this child be nurtured, cared for and fed? Can the family and the community support it? Certainly, high fertility rates are understandable in poor, work-intensive societies, because children provide labour in rural areas and urban slums: 'Children are economic assets in poor countries, not liabilities like their middle class counterparts [in developed countries].'[40] And it is true that population numbers in some poor countries are dropping, as a result of improvements in living standards, basic economic security, education, health care and voluntary family planning. The reduction of social and gender-based inequalities usually leads to a lowering of the birthrate. But this is not true everywhere.

Environmentally, the moral question is: what demands will meeting the child's needs place on the local environment? Can these be met? Is there evidence that the particular area where the child is to be born is already over-populated? Is this leading to environmental destruction? If the region's ecology is already compromised, what is the prognosis for its ability to support human life at all if present degradation rates continue? Another relevant issue here is that excessive fertility leads to a youth bulge in populations – the resulting large numbers of unemployed young men can in turn make violence and civil conflict more likely. Internecine strife can be particularly vicious, as the 1991–2002 civil war in the West African state of Sierra Leone showed. There are many other examples in Africa and elsewhere.

Until now, both the Catholic Church and almost all democratic states considered all these issues as non-questions. They have maintained the very recently developed notion that reproduction is a purely private decision, one in which the community and the state have no say. But this not true historically. Certainly, before the mid 19th century reproduction was not a purely personal matter, a choice made by consenting adults. Children were needed by the tribe, clan, or community: to maintain its numbers, contribute to its common wellbeing and extend its ability to protect and develop its territory. Throughout human history, reproduction has always been a social as well as a personal act, endowed with religious and ethical connotations. It is not just a private decision. Of course the personal and relationship aspects are important, but the *right* to reproduce must be resituated in the context of the common good, broadly understood. The community has rights with regard to reproduction. Deciding whether or not to have a child must be thought about in the context of the ability of the couple and the community to care for and support the child. It must also take into account the present population crisis and the rights of other species.

Second, it is women who bear children, so their social, educational and economic position must be a key issue in reproduction. All of the evidence from the WHO, UNESCO (the UN Educational, Scientific and Cultural Organization), the OECD (the Organization for Economic Co-operation and Development) and other international organisations, as well as from scholars who have examined this issue, is that the status and education of women is centrally important. Their personal freedom, literacy and security from familial or spousal violence are essential to their ability to make decisions about their fertility. As the Ehrlichs note, 'The number of children that women choose to have is usually lower when they are educated, have equal rights to property and equal access to work with equal pay.'[41] Paul Ehrlich also points out that in Cuba, China, Thailand and the state of Kerala in India, women have the right to inherit property, and in all of these areas the birthrate has been reduced. This is confirmed by work done by demographers at the Australian National University.[42] Access to cheap and efficient contraception is also crucial.

This is where religion plays an important educational role. In many developing countries churches provides a supportive and caring community where information is available, and where women and couples can talk the issues through with informed people. Both women and men can be helped to understand that high fertility is not necessarily 'natural' or the 'will of God'. This needs to be accompanied by practical medical help, including contraceptive advice. In fact this is precisely what is provided in many Catholic communities in the developing world, despite the official stance of the Vatican. It is why the 1968 papal condemnation of artificial contraception was such a tragedy: it was a chance to use the church's moral authority and persuasion to change attitudes, especially in developing countries with large Catholic populations. Instead the official church rendered itself all but useless, although many courageous lay Catholics, sisters and priests have used their ministries to offer moral, educational and medical services to help poor women make their own decisions about fertility.

Another role that the church should undertake is to educate boys and men in patriarchal, hierarchical, honour/shame societies to respect women's freedom and basic rights. Parts of Latin America and Africa are examples of this. The fact that Mediterranean Latin-Italian culture is still dominated by an honour/shame culture after almost two millennia of Catholicism points to the complete failure of the church to instil genuine Christian values. As historian David G. Schultenover comments:

> One effect of male-female polarization in Mediterranean society is emotional distance between men and women, even between husbands and wives. The distrust of women in general extends to wives in particular, and since love is seldom a motivating factor in marriage, love cannot overcome the distrust.[43]

While religions such as Catholicism and Islam are often blamed for imposing harsh conditions on women in order to maintain a high fertility rate, the oppression that women experience in the Latin world and in parts of Africa is just as much the result of cultural attitudes as of religious conviction or teaching. Religion is used as a confirming element in the enforcement of male control, lack of female education and high fertility.

So a fundamental element in a morality of population is the education and liberation of women: giving them control of their fertility. The second element is that the church must focus on women's rights as a moral issue and be prepared to confront unequivocally the abuse of women by men. Violence towards women can never be justified. The church must be intimately present within the structures of a society, but it also has to act as a strong countercultural force.

The third moral element is making fertility control and family planning as accessible as possible. There are real problems here, as birth control and family planning are sometimes seen as a Western plot to impose a set of values favouring smaller families. Most Latinos and Africans have traditionally seen fertility as a blessing. This has been reinforced by Catholic bishops claiming that they are protecting cultural traditions in countries such as the Philippines and Kenya, both of which have high fertility rates. But the present circumstances demand that these cultural traditions be judged in a broader ethical context. It is precisely the failure of Catholicism to confront the causes of unsustainable population increases in countries such as these that has led to devastating environmental degradation.

This is never going to be an easy issue. Part of the problem is that there has been considerable analysis of the mistakes that were made in birth control programs in the past, especially in India. Columbia University historian Matthew Connolly has catalogued these in relentless detail.[44] There has also been a concerted push from some quarters, including from a minority of powerful Catholics, to discredit family planning by linking it to oppressive population control programs such as that of India.

But the core of the problem is much deeper. As Harvard Divinity School professor emeritus Ralph B. Potter points out, public debate about these issues is divisive because deeply held philosophical and religious convictions underlie all approaches to the question of population. Given that the debate is about the control of fertility, it touches everyone. Potter comments that because 'population policies entail the restraint of accustomed liberties, they require explicit justification'. He points out that the impact is different on different groups: 'Policies many be seen to favour one way of living and handicap another … Deep aspirations and anxieties touching upon questions of identity, self-perpetuation, prosperity, and survival may become engaged.' So those who argue for fertility restraint have to 'deal with rejoinders that insist upon the value of "freedom and autonomy" or "self-determination in procreative matters"'.[45]

It is precisely these issues that I have attempted to address in this chapter. I would be the first to admit that they are not only difficult, but explosive. It is no wonder politicians in democratic countries avoid such questions like the plague.

PART III

THE BEST AND THE WORST

4 Environmental thugs

If American historian Lynn White is right, the greatest environmental thugs in history are Christians. In a brief but influential article in *Science* in 1967, White accused the Judeo-Christian tradition of being largely responsible for the dichotomy between humankind and nature. White's view was that Christianity was the most important element in the resistance of Western culture to the development of environmentalism. He held that the Judeo-Christian insistence on the supremacy of humankind over the rest of creation caused a disjunction in human thought that made Christianity 'the most anthropocentric religion the world has seen'. He contended that in the Christian understanding of the cosmos the whole of nature was created exclusively to serve humankind, the only true image of God. He argued that the biblical assumption was that human beings have the right to subdue and use the whole of creation, and that that assumption was taken up strongly by Christian theology. As a result, he claimed, no real change in human–cosmic relations would occur 'until we reject the Christian axiom that nature has no reason for existence save to serve man'. Following his article a fascinating controversy broke out. White's views would still find considerable sympathy among many secular environmentalists today.[1]

So what truth is there in White's arguments? How much is Christianity to blame for contemporary exploitative attitudes towards the cosmos and the environment? Are Christians environmental thugs?

Many historians have concluded that White's views are far too simplistic, as theologian H. Paul Santmire has shown.[2] Environmental damage began long before Judaism, let alone Christianity. Since the advent of agriculture in the Fertile Crescent 10,000 years ago, the exploitation, exhaustion and erosion of soil, as well as deforestation, have characterised much human interaction with the natural world. As historian Simon Schama puts it, 'the entire history of settled (rather than nomadic) society, from the irrigation-mad Chinese to the irrigation-mad Sumerians, is contaminated by the brutal manipulation of nature.[3]

Cosmologist Rupert Sheldrake (cosmology is the study of the way in which we understand the world and the position of human beings within it) has also argued that White's approach is too generalised. Sheldrake traces humanity's antagonism to nature and need to manipulate and sometimes destroy it back to the ancient Greeks, and even further:

> Cultures differ in the strength of their impulse toward mastery and in the countervailing sense of kinship with the natural world. But the whole of human history – ever since fire was first tamed, tools first made, metals first used, animals and plants first domesticated, cities first built – has involved man's domination of nature to varying degrees.[4]

Even those cultures that lived in harmony with nature inevitably altered their environments. This concurs with Thomas Berry's argument that humankind has been dominated since Neolithic times by 'exploitative anthropocentrism'. He points out that China, for instance, though it had an exalted theoretical view of nature, destroyed much of its forest cover long before the Christian era.[5]

In fact all humans, Christian or otherwise, ancient or modern, are exploitative and anthropocentric. Harvard biologist Edward O. Wilson doesn't mince matters in his book *The Future of Life*. He describes *Homo sapiens* as a 'serial killer of the biosphere', and says that wherever new settlers have entered a pristine environment their impact has been disastrous:

> Humanity, when wiping out biodiversity, eats its way down the food chain. First to go among animal species are the big, the slow and the tasty ... Most of the megafauna soon vanish. Also doomed were a substantial fraction of the most easily captured ground birds and tortoises.[6]

From the beginning, *Homo sapiens* interacted with the environment. At first, human beings were almost completely dependent on it. It determined how they lived. But slowly people gained the ability to modify their surroundings. As their technological expertise increased and they were able to manipulate their environment, the more the belief that the earth existed for the nurturing of humankind gained ground. Certainly the development of agriculture, the domestication of animals and then urbanisation all indicate a distinct sense of separation and alienation from nature. Towns and cities are essentially artificial environments which cut human beings off from nature.

However, attempting to discuss the role of indigenous peoples in the environmental destruction of North America, Australia or New Zealand often leads to heated arguments. The conversation can become mired in a form of political correctness that romanticises all indigenous people as environmental saints. It is true that most indigenous people did live in a reasonably sustainable way before the arrival of Europeans, but that doesn't mean their ancient ancestors didn't do damage to what had been pristine environments. Wilson, for instance, cites Australia,

Madagascar and New Zealand as examples of biodiversity destruction.

New Zealand is the most recently settled of these countries. Wilson describes it as a 'vast biological wonderland' before human settlement. The exact date of Maori arrival is still being debated. Originally thought to be in the 10th or 11th centuries, it is now placed in the late 12th or early 13th century. The Maori came to New Zealand from further east in the Pacific. Their impact was immediate. Wilson says that 'the somber archaeology of vanished species has taught us the following lessons. The noble savage never existed. Eden occupied was a slaughterhouse. Paradise found is paradise lost.'[7] Also referring to New Zealand, historian John Man comments:

> There is a belief among urbanized romantics that idealizes hunter-gatherers as the embodiments of ecological wisdom, carefully preserving their food sources from overuse. It is hard to find evidence to support this belief. On the contrary, many pre-urban societies exploited their resources to the limit of their ability.[8]

Another example is Australia. Australia was home throughout the late Pleistocene (about 45,000 to 10,000 ybp [years before the present]) to the megafauna, giant marsupials that were much larger than any of their surviving present-day relatives. Examples include *Thylacoleo carnifex*, a leopard-sized marsupial carnivore, *Megalania prisca*, a large flesh-eating lizard, the massive kangaroo, *Procoptodon goliath*, several species of large emu-like flightless birds, and *Diprotodon optatum*, a marsupial herbivore the size of a modern rhinoceros which was widespread in dry inland Australia. According to the distinguished historian John Mulvaney and his co-author Johan Kamminga, in their *Prehistory of Australia*, the megafauna and humans co-existed 'for at least 10,000 years and probably considerably longer'.[9] In other words, humans were probably not directly responsible for their extinction. Having said that, there are three variables here: first, the actual date that humans arrived in Australia (estimates vary between 40,000 and 60,000 ybp); second, when and how the megafauna became extinct; and third, the relationship between these two events.

One of the first to tackle these issues was the archaeologist Josephine Flood. She says that 'directly or indirectly, Aboriginal occupation of the Continent had as great an impact on Australian flora and fauna in the Pleistocene as European settlement was to have in recent times'. She concedes the possibility that the 'huge browsers that survived the initial impact of man the hunter finally seem to have met their end during the Great Dry at the end of the Pleistocene', an intense ice age that began about 20,000 ybp and lasted until just after 10,000 ybp. She maintains that while this was probably the last gasp for the megafauna, the main period of extinction preceded this. After examining available evidence against human agency as the major cause of megafaunal extinction in Australia, Flood concludes:

> The main period of extinction precedes the main late Pleistocene climatic change. The only new element in the equation was man, who may have caused the extinctions by a combination of hunting and his use of fire, which drastically altered the animal's habitats. The weight of … evidence favors human hunters as the decisive factor.[10]

Elements of the Flood argument have been restated by evolutionary biologist Tim Flannery in *The Future Eaters*.[11] His contention is that a kind of 'blitzkrieg' occurred when humans first arrived on the continent. Like everyone arriving in an alien landscape, he claims, the first Australians went through a stage of overkill during which they consumed their future, until the extinction of their food sources forced them to live more harmoniously with their environment. Mulvaney is far more cautious. He says, 'no single cause is sufficient to explain the disappearance of a large and diverse range of animals adapted to such a wide range of habitats. Least evident is the part humans may have played in the process.'[12] This indicates just how complex the interaction between humankind and the environment is. Human impacts in Australia were lessened by the small population of Aborigines, the massive size of the continent and the diversity of the landscape and environment. All these factors meant that the consequences of human arrival were only gradually felt. These arguments aside, there is no doubt that human settlement in Australia had a significant effect and that humans modified the flora and fauna.

So the notion that the earth exists for humankind predates the Bible by thousands of years, and blaming the Judeo-Christian tradition for the entire history of alienation from nature, while superficially attractive to some, does not survive scrutiny. Nevertheless, White's claims are not without some truth. In terms of Europe particularly, Christianity has had its fair share of environmental 'thugs', and has become much more anthropocentric than it need have been. The dominant tradition of Christian theology has taken an unnecessarily negative approach to the natural world. The core reason for this is that Christianity for centuries failed to deal positively with the human body. There is an intimate connection between our feelings about our bodies and our attitudes towards nature. It is our bodies that tie us most closely to the materiality of the earth. If we devalue and despise our own bodies, there is little hope that we will value nature.

There is now, however, a growing realisation in the churches of the importance of the environment. Anxious to respond positively to this, and with the best will in the world, many Christians feel that all they have to do is change their attitude. They think that they can gloss over the dominant tradition and move on quickly to recover and articulate what they see as the more positive aspects of the Christian tradition in this area. However, this is premature, and the past is not so easily abandoned. For almost 1600 years many Christians denigrated the body and the material world. We can't just take one quick side-step and pick up a new approach that is more ecologically friendly. We have to first recognise that the Christian tradition, at its core, is deeply compromised by body–soul dualism. It is not just a matter of articulating a more ecologically sensitive attitude, nor of highlighting the views of Christians such as Sts Hildegarde of Bingen or Francis of Assisi. The task for Christian theology and the church is much harder.

As we have already noted, there is increasing sensitivity to environmental issues in mainstream Christianity. However, in reality the various churches' actual commitment ranges from genuine concern to green window-dressing. This new commitment to the environment will remain superficial until there is a decisive shift in theology from anthropocentric dualism to what might be called 'cosmocentrism'. I will argue later that what is required for a genuine environmental theology is a profound inner change, something akin to religious conversion, and that this change will not be achieved merely through the articulation of another attitude. Change can only occur when both the positive and negative aspects of the old way of thinking are understood fully; only then can we jettison it. In order to come to this, some historical perspective is needed.

For most of its history Christianity denigrated the body. At the core of this ethos was a profound suspicion about matter; materiality was seen as antithetical to spiritual growth and the search for God. The source of this suspicion originates in the answer to the question: What is the human person? For centuries, popular Christian belief answered this question by defining the person as a body enlivened by a soul. The soul is identified with the spiritual and higher faculties of the person and the body with its lower animal and material aspects. In popular belief, the soul has been seen as the life-source that gives shape, individuality and life to each human being; the material body is merely the repository for the spirit. This identification of the body with the 'lower' functions leads to a deep ambivalence about matter and sexuality. The Hebrew Scriptures (the Old Testament), however, had never heard of this distinction; it only entered Hebrew religious thought in the 1st century before Christ.

The ancient Jews were not interested in defining the human person in a philosophical or psychological sense. For them a person was 'enspirited' flesh. The word 'flesh' meant the totality of all that a person was: a conscious, emotional, individual self. The word also suggested close relationship with others. This is what St Paul meant when he said that 'a man will leave his father and mother and be joined to his wife and the two will become one flesh' (Ephesians 5:31). In other words they were not soul mates; they were body mates. In biblical theology, to be in the flesh was to be a person; it was our flesh that both made us individuals and rooted us in society and in relationship with others. Flesh and spirit were one and the same; the flesh was as much spiritual as material.

So what happened to Christianity when it moved out of its Jewish milieu into the cosmopolitan world of Greece and Rome? In order to interact with this international culture, the church had to discover new ways of articulating Christian belief and thought. It had to adopt the language and cultural patterns of the people of this world, and develop a coherent explanation of its belief in a way that made sense to them. Bear in mind that early Christianity was neither sectarian nor fundamentalist. From very early in its history the church attempted to be part of the culture and evangelise the late-Roman world through the use of the religio-cultural and philosophical tools that were at hand. In this context the Hebrew notion of human beings as animated bodies quickly transmuted into the Greek notion of incarnated souls.

The religious milieu of the late Greco-Roman world – in the 2nd and 3rd centuries – was deeply permeated by Gnosticism. Gnosticism was a complex of teachings and movements, a veritable subculture, somewhat like the New Age movement today. Its origins are obscure and pre-Christian, but it had considerable interaction with the early church. There is a sense in which Gnosticism is the primal heresy: it attempts to disembody religion and spiritualise it. Historian J.N.D. Kelly has described Gnosticism as a 'bizarre mixture of speculation, fantasy and mysticism'.[13] It taught that there was a chasm between the spiritual and material worlds. The latter, the Gnostics said, was not the creation of God and was intrinsically evil. Human beings yearned to be free of materiality and to ascend to their true heavenly home, far away from matter. Applying these notions to early Christianity, the Gnostics rejected the Old Testament's depiction of a God involved in time, history and people's daily lives. They argued that Jesus had only the appearance of a body, and that redemption could only be achieved by a form of esoteric knowledge which he had supposedly secretly taught. Salvation certainly didn't come through his death on a cross. Through contact and osmosis, the church absorbed elements of Gnosticism's otherworldliness.

Just when ordinary Christians were attempting to resist Gnosticism's blandishments, theologians were seeking a meaningful philosophical underpinning for their theology. The earliest Christians stuck more or less to Jewish theological patterns, but by the middle of the 2nd century Christian theologians had begun to borrow from other philosophies: Stoicism, Neo-Platonism and Epicureanism. Christianity absorbed elements of all these philosophical systems, and all were, at best, ambivalent about matter and life in the body. Theologian Rosemary Ruether correctly sums this up:

> Late antique culture [was] obsessed with the fear of mortality, of corruptibility. To be born in the flesh is to be subject to change, which is devolution toward decay and death. Only by extricating mind from matter by ascetic practices, aimed at severing the connections of mind

> and body, can one prepare for the salvific escape out of the realm of corruptibility to eternal spiritual life.[14]

For the philosophers of the late Roman world, the dualism of body and soul was a central theme: the fullness of life was to be found in the soul, which had been captured, dragged down, and degraded by contact with the body. Asceticism was construed as the way of escape. Thinkers such as the Emperor Marcus Aurelius (121–80) saw the natural world as a place of illusion, a joke, a dream, delirium. Historian E.R. Dodds observes: 'Much the same feeling underlies the long and splendid passage where Plotinus in his last years, drawing on both Plato and the Stoics, interprets the grandeurs and miseries of human life in terms of a stage performance.'[15] Of all the philosophical currents in the late Roman world, the most important was Neo-Platonism, and Plotinus (204/5–70), who conducted a philosophical school in Rome, was the most important of its thinkers.

Philosopher Arthur O. Lovejoy has distinguished two conflicting major strains in Platonism: 'other-worldliness and this-worldliness. It is the other-worldly strain that has affected Christian theology and spirituality most.' For Plato, other-worldliness is 'the belief that both the genuinely "real" and the truly good are antithetic in their essential characteristics to anything that can be found in man's natural life, in the ordinary course of human experience'.[16] So for Platonists, the passing reality of this world has no real substance. The good, which is sought by human reason and will, can be found only through contemplation of a higher realm.

The other-worldly aspect of Platonic philosophy centres on the question: How can we have true knowledge? Plato argued that true knowledge subsists in universal forms or ideas and these cannot be apprehended by the senses. These forms alone are truly real. They can be perceived only through the soul, which exists prior to the body. While the soul is in conjunction with the body it has to struggle to remember the forms and thus to know truth in any genuine sense; the body and the senses simply cannot apprehend what is really real. As Platonic thought developed in the late Roman world, the body came to be viewed as more than just a hindrance to the soul; it actually weighed it down and prevented it from attaining knowledge of the truth. It was the prison of the soul and prevented it from attaining the supreme form – the One. As Christians gradually adopted Platonism as a theological underpinning, the One became identified with God. Many in the philosophical and religious élite of the ancient world tried to live as if they did not have a body. Dodds comments:

> Pagans and Christians (although not all pagans or all Christians) vied with each other in heaping abuse on the body … Plotinus appeared ashamed of having a body at all. [The desert hermit] Saint Anthony blushed every time he had to eat or satisfy any other bodily function. Because the body's life was the soul's death, salvation lay in mortifying it.[17]

Neo-Platonism thus created a dualism between soul/spirit on the one hand and body/world on the other. The unity of human reality was lost.

Lovejoy notes that other-worldliness has been, in one form or another, 'the dominant official philosophy of the larger part of civilized mankind', but also makes the penetrating observation that despite this, most ordinary people have never really believed it, 'since they have never been able to deny the things disclosed by the senses'.[18] Thus the notion that the visible world is fake and the real world is eternal and invisible became accepted in Christianity. The source of this is not the Bible or the words of Jesus; it is Plato, mediated by Plotinus. Their thought has in fact become more normative than the Bible. Asceticism rooted in the denial of sexuality and ultimately in a profound fear of death became endemic in Christian theology and, through the leaders of the church – the clergy and members of religious orders – flowed into the Western European cultural tradition. Thus, in one sense, Lyn White is right.

While dualism has been part of the theological tradition from early on, the key figures in introducing it into Christianity were St Gregory Nyssa (335–c.395), who applied Neo-Platonic thought to Christian spirituality and mysticism, and St Augustine (354–430), who confirmed its position in Western theology. Gregory Nyssa was profoundly unworldly; he almost questioned the reality of the physical world. He is recognised as a powerful and original thinker, and his influence is especially strong in Eastern Christian spirituality.

St Augustine of Hippo has been blamed for the entire Western tradition of rejection of the body, and especially for an excessive rigidity in sexual morality. I know that caricaturing him as an environmental 'thug' will annoy some readers, but I think he did turn Western Christian theology in an excessively anthropocentric and dualistic direction. Historian Margaret Miles shows that Augustine was profoundly ambiguous about the human body.[19] In the years immediately after his conversion to Christianity in 386, he seems to have been preoccupied with overcoming the body, but in the final 15 years of his life he was profoundly occupied with the theological question of the resurrection of the body. This was the Christian teaching that most disturbed him: How can you reconcile a philosophy which sees the body as evil with a theological belief that it is in and through the body that human beings experience ultimate transcendental union with God? As both a Platonist and a Christian, Augustine could not shy away from dealing with this puzzle. The result was paradoxical: at the very time that he strongly asserted the dignity of the human body in resurrection, he was most negative towards a primal expression of bodily existence – sexuality. As Miles points out, it is easy to isolate passages from his work that are pejorative about bodily existence without remembering the reason for this prejudice. Given his

Neo-Platonic framework, it is inevitable that he stressed a mystical union with God that is only possible by a withdrawal of energy inward to the central core of being where, he believed, the soul was united with God. Augustine's ambiguity about the resurrection of the body was ultimately resolved through his belief in the transformation of ordinary human bodies into, as Paul says in the Jerusalem Bible translation, 'copies of [Christ's] glorious body' (Philippians 3:21).

Christianity in the late Roman world also strongly believed in the superiority of virginity over marriage. The exaltation of virginity and a life of sexual abstinence arose out of Neo-Platonic religiosity. The growth of the ideal of virginity was influenced by the idea that the prayer of virgins was especially efficacious. The early theologians Tertullian (c.160–c.225) and Origen (c.185–c.254) argued that purity gave the virgins a unique intimacy with the Christian mysteries and sacraments. The late Roman period saw the initial demands for celibacy of the clergy. While this emerged from the prevailing emphasis on virginity, it is also rooted in the Jewish and pagan notion of ritual purity.

The most important study of early Christian attitudes to the human body is historian Peter Brown's *The Body and Society.*[20] The book shows how the élite of late Roman Christianity, deeply influenced by a Platonised theology, came to see sexual renunciation as the profoundest symbol of Christian commitment. Slowly their views permeated down through pastoral teaching to ordinary Christians, but it seems they were by no means universally accepted. Brown also shows how committed Christians developed ambivalence about sexual relations, and:

> a change in the perception of the body itself. The men and women of later centuries were not only hedged around with a different and more exacting set of prohibitions. They also came to see their bodies in a different light.[21]

The practical consequence of this was that the nude male body was no longer something to be displayed when the young men of the Greco-Roman world went to the baths to enjoy the years of bisexual play before commitment to marriage, with its responsibilities to the emperor and the state. The gradual growth in the influence of Christianity meant that 'No longer were the body's taut musculature and its refined poise signs of the athlete and potential warrior, put on display as marks of upper class status.'[22] Instead, Christians were filled with a yearning for the coming of the kingdom of God, for the transformation of the decay that was inherent in bodily existence. For them the human body existed primarily to be transformed through the sacramental rites of the church, and through the exercise of the will on the always wayward passions, which would allow them to 'take on the lineaments of the risen Christ'.[23]

Brown points to the glorious mosaics of the period around the start of the 5th century, especially those that can still be seen in Ravenna in the churches of San Vitale, San Apollinare Nuovo, San Apollinare in Classe, the Arian Baptistery and the Mausoleum of Galla Placidia. All of these show Christ and the saints with 'risen' bodies of exquisite grace and proportion. They seem lighter than air as they stand 'effortlessly alive' on the green grass of paradise. 'The dull weight of death has been lifted from them and, with that, their physicality.'[24] So the beautiful male body which had been the boast and ideal of the classical world was now transformed, through sexual renunciation, into the body of the risen Christ and his followers.

This diversion into the importance of Greco-Roman and ancient Christian ideas about the body is important, because it set a pattern for subsequent Christian spirituality and theology. It also profoundly influenced the development of Western European ideas about nature and the natural world. There is a sense in which the whole Western tradition is merely a footnote to this early period in the formation of Christianity.

There is a contrasting theme that also runs through Christian history. This is the idea that nature is a kind of book in which we read something of the purpose of the Creator. It was the Stoics who first expressed this notion. In Stoic philosophy nature is arranged according to a divine order which shows humankind the meaning and purpose of the world. The eclectic Roman philosopher Marcus Tullius Cicero took up this idea and developed it in his dialogue *De natura deorum* (*On the Nature of the Gods*). Cicero argues that nature 'progresses on a certain path of her own to the goal of full development' unless interfered with by human agency.[25] Humankind can contemplate the world and discern order and purpose within it. Cicero's view is strongly anthropocentric: the world was created primarily for those beings that have the use of reason – it was made for the gods and humankind to use. We are caretakers of the world and our work in nature adds to its beauty and purpose. There is also what today we might call a 'developmental mentality' permeating his thought: 'Man cooperates with nature and ever improves on its pristine condition; the changes which he has made and is to make are in fact part of the divine purpose in creating the world.'[26] These ideas are also found in the Roman writer Apuleius and in the thought of the philosopher and statesman Seneca. Stoic ideas were influential during the Roman Empire, throughout the medieval period, the Renaissance, and up to the 18th century.

The Ciceronian argument also attracted theologians such as Augustine, who believed that the order of nature revealed God's plan at work on earth. The notion of nature as a second book, backing up the Bible, emerges as a common theme here. St Athanasius (293–373) says that the creatures revealed in the book of nature proclaim the glory of God who is the Creator of the ordered world. St John Chrysostom (347–407) says that the illiterate Christian, and the unbeliever, can read the book of nature.

However, the collapse of the Western Roman Empire in the early 5th century and the chaos which followed the collapse of the Carolingian

Empire in 870 led to a negative view of the natural world permeating Christian attitudes. The rough and unsophisticated conditions of the Dark Ages led writers such as Odo, the second abbot of Cluny (878–942), to declare that the end of the world was approaching, that the earth was foul with sin and that the deepest human anguish lay in the loss of the sense of the presence of God. There was a subtle change of attitude in the medieval period. Historian Clarence Glacken says that the dominant idea in the Middle Ages was that humankind 'assisted God ... in the improvement of an earthly home even if the earth were, in Christian theology, only a sojourner's way station'. This shows the continuing influence of Ciceronian ideas of nature. He goes on:

> The most compelling reason for the observation and study of nature ... was that it led to a greater understanding of God. It was part – but only part – of the proof of the existence of God, of God's plan for a designed world, and of the truth of the Christian religion.[27]

This is hardly a ringing endorsement of the value of the world in itself, but it shows that the medieval period didn't have quite as negative a view of the world as earlier theologians had had. But world weariness and the concept of the earth as a vale of tears was still the dominant view in monastic circles. This is reflected in the popular monastic hymn *Salve Regina*: *Ad te suspiramus, gementes et flentes, in hac lacrimarum valle* – To thee do we send up our sighs, mourning and weeping in this valley of tears.

Sheldrake has argued that a more positive attitude towards nature could be found among the rural masses, who saw nature as 'animate and mother-like'. He links this with the medieval teaching that all living creatures had souls.[28] Here he is emphasising the ongoing influence, especially in popular medieval religion, of ancient pre-Christian views rooted in the idea of the earth mother and the sacredness of nature.

While there is truth in his observations, historians of medieval religion would probably note that popular medieval religion was complex, focused around the role of Mary, mother of Jesus (as mediator with God), images, saints, relics, statues linked to miracles, and pilgrimages to shrines such as Canterbury or Compostela.

Sheldrake also argues that these notions of nature as mother-like and animate were finally destroyed in the 16th century by Humanism and Protestantism which, he argues, released the dual forces of scepticism and iconoclasm. Both saw an apparently instinctive religion in touch with nature as nothing more than superstition and idolatry. He is right to blame Protestantism for iconoclasm and the elimination of the notion of natural revelation, at least to the extent that it focused on the question of the salvation of the individual through personal faith and emphasised the centrality and uniqueness of the biblical word and the disembodied intellect rather than sacramental, instinctive natural symbols. Protestantism effectively lost all contact, especially in its Puritan Calvinistic forms, with nature. It is significant that Calvinism is the crucible from which modern capitalism and industrialism emerged.

But the question becomes more complex when it is focused on Renaissance Humanism. Certainly it was anthropocentric, intellectualist and self-referential, as much of its art reveals. But in Italy, especially in the 16th century, it quickly transmuted into the baroque. There is an instinctive, dramatic – almost operatic – quality in baroque Counter-Reformation Catholicism, with its simultaneous emphasis on the formalistic and the sensual. The baroque is characteristic of Latin and especially Italian Catholicism. It bespeaks a certain psycho-spiritual attitude to life which, while difficult to define, is characterised by 'a feeling of anticipation, of something yet to come, of dissatisfaction and restlessness rather than fulfillment'.[29] While today the baroque seems over the top – just look at the façade of St Peter's Basilica – and its almost gaudy use of colour seems showy and superficial, it actually uses the material and the sensual to draw the viewer into a world that points to something 'beyond'. In this sense it is a materialisation of the spiritual rather than a spiritualisation of the material.

The former is closer to the true Christian doctrine of the incarnation than the latter. Nature seems to be much more at home in this baroque milieu than in the exaggeratedly bibliocentric view of reality that is characteristic of the Calvinistic Protestantism which is so influential in the English-speaking world. The baroque leaned much more towards naturalistic symbols, such as the Sacred Heart and the passion and death of Jesus.

The scientific revolution gradually brought about a further change of attitude. During the Renaissance the idea of nature as God's book, which human beings could read, was still popular. The English philosopher Francis Bacon (1561–1626), for instance, saw the book of nature as elucidating and clarifying the Bible. While early modern scientists and astronomers such as Nicolaus Copernicus (1473–1543) and Johann Kepler (1571–1630) saw the world as an interactive cosmic organism, a radical change came with the French philosopher René Descartes. Descartes' ideas created the context in which modern environmental thuggery flourishes. Nature was secularised – or, more accurately, mechanised – by Descartes, and then by Isaac Newton (1643–1727). Descartes' intellectualism set the pattern for the relationship between science and religion that has dominated until today.

In order to find the certainty for which he longed, Descartes proved himself the proto-modern man by deliberately plunging himself into systematic philosophical doubt, by questioning everything:

> Thus I will suppose not a supremely good God, the source of truth, but rather an evil genius, as clever and deceitful as he is powerful, who has directed his entire effort to misleading me. I will regard the heavens, the air, the earth, colours, shapes, sounds and all external

> things as nothing but the deceptive games of my dreams ... I will regard myself as having no hands, no eyes, no flesh, no blood, no sense, but as nevertheless falsely believing that I possess all these things. I will remain resolutely fixed in this mediation.[30]

He rejected 'as absolutely false everything in which I could imagine the least doubt' in order to discover if 'anything in my set of beliefs remains that is entirely indubitable'.[31] Descartes recovered from his systematic doubt to discover the first, basic, indubitable proposition: 'I think, therefore I am' – *Cogito, ergo sum*. Descartes saw human beings as minds or souls at work in bodily machines. He claimed that consciousness was the starting point upon which true knowledge can be built. Thinking, rather than feeling, sensing, or intuiting, is the primal reality. Everything begins with subjectivity. Modern narcissism is born.

When Descartes looks outward from the depths of his subjectivity, he sees a mathematically ordered world with the whole of reality operating as a vast system of matter in motion. As Sheldrake puts it:

> Everything in the material universe worked entirely mechanically according to mathematical necessities ... Although the details of his system were soon superseded by the Newtonian universe of atomic matter moving in a void, [Descartes] laid the foundation for the mechanistic world view in both physics and biology.[32]

As the tag end of Platonism, Descartes created a massive dislocation: he split mind and spirit from the material world, which he saw as lacking any intrinsic value. The natural world is a machine, he said; all its interactions can be explained by the laws of physics. Animals are simply instinctive machines. Nature is governed by laws which can be understood and predicted. He was fascinated by mathematics and by the clarity and certainty it offered; he was also an important figure in the development of differential calculus. His philosophy was essentially a footnote to Platonism, evolved within the context of early modern science. Descartes, rather than Christian theology, set the scene for the modern assault on nature. An environmental thug indeed!

Isaac Newton took both Cartesian mechanism and natural theology seriously. As an anti-Trinitarian monotheist, he argued that God was more concerned with creation than with personal salvation. By discovering the laws of nature, Newton hoped to give glory to God. While there is a real sense in which he applied Cartesian notions to describe the mechanics of the natural world, he himself never lost his interest in alchemy and esoteric science. These expressed the flipside of his personality; he was never a mechanist in the crude sense that was later to become the norm. The mechanistic view of nature has achieved a great deal for science and still dominates contemporary thinking. It sees nature as a vast storehouse of resources that are there to be exploited for the short-term advantage of humankind. It is this attitude that has brought us to the disastrous environmental impasse that we face today.

Yet paradoxically, many today feel that they don't have a grip on their lives. Philosopher Theodore Roszak says – correctly, in my view – that people today feel they have no answers to questions about the meaning of existence. He says that secular society has excluded religious and spiritual responses to this existential vacuum, and that members of the helping professions (such as social work and psychotherapy) have little to offer. The same is true of science. 'Both science and technology,' writes Roszak, 'move toward esotericism and professional exclusiveness', and this alienates people. When pushed to provide a deeper ethical and metaphysical meaning structure, scientists and the helping professions simply opt out. The result is that our society has 'entered an intellectual vacuum'.[33] This alienation leads to a loss of our sense of community; people have no feeling that they are contributing to society. The atomised self has become the norm.

Consumerism is used by some as a substitute for meaning; others fill this intellectual vacuum with a kind of absolutisation of technology. The problem with technology is that it distances us from the natural world and from others. It creates a wall of abstraction between the real world, in which none of us is in control, and the virtual world, in which we can all feel in control. The German philosopher Martin Heidegger said that technology is now so pervasive in our culture that it is part of the very structure of our being. Nature is something out there, an object to be used and exploited, rather than a reality to be experienced and reverenced.

This type of atomised individualism has been loosely characterised as postmodernism. For postmodernists, all that is possible for each of us are subjective, parochial visions and experiences. Modernity, the roots of which go back to Renaissance Humanism, Descartes, the scientific revolution, the 18th century Enlightenment, and the liberal bourgeois culture of the 19th century, was marked by four significant characteristics: a passionate commitment to progress; the relegation of religion to the sphere of the private and personal; the importance and the rights of the individual; and the conviction that technology will solve all our problems. The industrial society that we've inherited was built on the notion of unending progress, an idea that came into its own in the bourgeois, liberal, commercial and intellectual culture of the mid 19th century. Its roots go back to Calvinism and Protestantism.

It is a good rule of thumb never to expect consistency in historical and cultural processes, and that is certainly true of the modern era. While the majority of modernism's most obvious cultural presuppositions seem reasonable and rational, they are actually based on unquestioned beliefs about the place of humanity in relationship with the rest of reality. For instance, the paradox of modern 'rationalist economics' is that it is largely the product of a 19th century myth – the myth of infinite progress. At the core of this myth is the belief that the liberalism, capitalism and individualism that had dominated European culture and industry since the 18th century would keep leading to an ever-fuller life. The belief was based on several things: the presumed limitless abundance of the earth; Darwin's theory of evolution; and the idea that science and technology would lead to material happiness, and would be able to solve all human problems.

The idea of eternal progress is materialist and utopian, as is Marxism. For the last 150 years these two intertwined myths have dominated the West's thinking, and its economic, political and social arrangements. Both have been extremely environmentally destructive. Because both these myths are based on the same presuppositions and emerge from the same intellectual history, there is probably a close link between their rise and fall. We have already seen the collapse of Marxism in the old Soviet Union and Eastern Europe. With the global capitalist crisis of 2008–09 we may well be seeing the initial stages of the death the neoliberal economic dream of market forces determining everything. In fact the notion that the market is benign and always works for the best perfectly illustrates the mythic nature of this theory. To refer to greed as 'rational' is a complete misnomer, for greed is no more based on fact and reason than were the conclusions of an ancient Roman 'reading' the entrails of a slaughtered bull.

This dream of limitless resources has had disastrous environmental consequences in the new worlds of North and South America, Africa, Asia, Australia – and all the other countries that export resource commodities. In Australia, for instance, the myth of unlimited development inspired the white settlers to explore and settle the land and 'conquer the wilderness' and, in the process, destroy 75 per cent of the rainforests and old-growth forests of the continent; the latter, despite the evidence of their usefulness as carbon sinks to counter global warming, continue to be logged for export as woodchips. It also drove to extinction many Australian species of flora and fauna. It has left many others endangered. It degraded much of the land through clearing of native vegetation and bred attitudes of contempt that led to the dispossession and widespread massacre of Indigenous people. At best, they were seen by whites as obstacles to the expansion of 'civilisation'; at worst, as mere pests to be exterminated, like the local fauna.

In the United States a similar development occurred. The 17th-century Protestant quest for the establishment of the 'new Jerusalem' in North America was secularised in the 19th century to become, in the words of historian Frederick Jackson Turner, the United States' 'manifest destiny'. The tangible result of both the religious and secular theories of destiny was the constant westward expansion of the frontier and the destruction of the traditional lives of the Native Americans. By 1890, the white occupiers had destroyed the last vestiges of their resistance, at Wounded Knee in South Dakota.

The modern myth of progress has several sources. Starting most remotely, there is the Judeo-Christian apocalyptic notion of cosmic and human history as a constant progression towards the fulfilment of all reality in God. Tied up with this is the idea that the rest of reality derives its meaning, structure and purpose from its connection to humankind and its destiny. Most Jewish and Christian commentators interpret the Bible as saying that it is humankind alone that is the image of God. This leaves the rest of the animate and inanimate world to attain worth only through its connection with whatever destiny or use humankind might bestow upon it.

More recently, another source is the scientific revolution of the 17th century. This was the age when, as historian Geoffrey Barraclough says, 'technological progress, introducing a new spirit of inquiry into all branches of knowledge, led with revolutionary suddenness to the perfection and dissemination of a new cosmology and a new outlook on the world'.[34] Barraclough is right. The notion of unlimited development and progress is a cosmology: a myth based on a philosophical belief about the nature of the world and our place in it.

The cosmology of the modern age of development is both anthropocentric and materialistic, and it is profoundly underpinned by Darwinian notions of the evolutionary spiral towards ever-greater complexity and perfection. The mythic and religious status of evolutionary developmentalism is made clear by Herbert Spencer, Darwin's immediate predecessor as an evolutionary theorist. With the lack of self-doubt characteristic of most Victorian thinkers, he argued that progress was not an accident, that evil and immorality would disappear, and that humankind would reach perfection. For Spencer, Europeans, and specifically British males, were the human ideal and norm by which other peoples, such as the Australian Aborigines and the Native Americans, were to be judged. Embedded in this view was an unashamed racism, vividly expressed in the concept of 'the white man's burden', which was to bring the advantages of European culture to the world.

The liberal notion of development included an important element of the 18th-century Enlightenment: the idea that the decisive characteristic that distinguished civilised European humankind was reason. As Barraclough says:

> Reason is the faculty that enables one generation to learn from another; it permits the accumulation of knowledge and is thus the postulate behind the idea of perfectibility.[35]

The idea of evolutionary perfectibility and the cult of limitless development became the dominant mode of thought in Western culture in the late 19th century and continued for much of the 20th. The myth was spread, over the last 150 years, through secular education.

Barraclough stresses that the notion of progress did not really take over as the dominant Western ideology until the advances made in science and technology in the middle of the 19th century. He argues that the turning point was London's Great Exhibition of 1851. A similar exhibition was held in Paris in 1855. In subsequent years international exhibitions such as the Chicago World's Fair in 1893 became popular theatres for the ideas of progress and economic nationalism. The theme was taken up by historians of the liberal Whig tradition and found full expression in J.B. Bury's *The Idea of Progress* (1920) and H.G. Wells' *Outline of History* (1920). We have now reached the tail end of this cosmology.

The truth is that those of us who live in industrial or post-industrial societies are the worst environmental thugs in history. This is vividly illustrated by the refusal of governments and polluters to genuinely confront the issue of global warming. Capitalism and Marxism have done much more in a century to destroy the natural world than Judeo-Christianity did in three millennia. Sure, both capitalism and Marxism can be said to be derived in a broad sense from Christianity, but why should the churches take the blame for movements that are essentially secular, and in the case of Marxism, explicitly anti-religious? The myth of progress, plus our complete modern dominance over all forms of life, even over the structures of the earth itself, has led to a destructive anthropocentrism that is unique in human history.

What is the result of our anthropocentrism? The earth is dying at an ever-quickening rate. What Berry calls the 'slaughter of the innocents' is occurring as animals and plants are simply wiped out; whole species are becoming extinct at an ever-faster rate. We don't really know how many species there are on earth: between 1.5 and 1.8 million have been named, and estimates of the total number range from 3.6 million to 100 million.

Wilson warns that 'If present trends continue … we will lose half the plant and animal species on Earth by the end of the [21st] century.' He also described at least some of the consequences of this:

> The loss is forever, and these species are hundreds of thousands of years old, in many cases millions of years old, and exquisitely well adapted to their environment. Each species is a masterpiece of evolution that humanity could not possibly duplicate even if we somehow accomplish the creation of new organisms by genetic engineering … we lose living libraries of genetic information that could be enormously useful to humanity in the future. Finally there is the moral argument: that there is something dreadfully wrong about destroying the creation.[36]

He sees this as an ethical question, one on which we will be judged by the people who follow us.

An example of species loss is the destruction of tropical and cool temperate rainforests. These highly diverse paradises, which double as carbon sinks, are being rapidly destroyed. Areas equal to the size of England are being hacked down every year in Amazonia, West Africa, Madagascar, the Philippines, Malaysia, Indonesia, Brunei, Sarawak, Papua New Guinea, the Pacific Islands, and even in developed countries such as Canada, the United States, Australia and Chile. About 11 million hectares are disappearing each year. If this rate continues, all the world's major rainforests except those in the west Amazon and West Africa will be gone by 2020, and only small cool temperate rainforest enclaves in Australia and parts of southern Chile will remain. The destruction and burning of rainforests is responsible for more than a fifth of the world's greenhouse gas emissions. With the continuing loss of habitat, thousands of species of animals, birds, plants, and insects are becoming extinct. The diversity of rainforest life, which took millions of years to establish, is threatened with destruction in decades.

That is why the pledge of US$3.5 billion over 3 years to help developing countries protect endangered rainforests – the Reduced Emissions from Deforestation and Degradation (REDD) initiative, involving six developed countries (the United States, the United Kingdom, Japan, Norway, Australia and France) – at the UN's Copenhagen Conference is significant. This was one of the few bright spots there. However, it remains to be seen what is actually saved.

The problem is that industrial-scale destruction of rainforests is not primarily caused by the poor; it is caused by large corporations and wealthy individuals. Yet nothing is done to prosecute these ecological vandals, many of them from countries such as Malaysia and Taiwan, operating with covert and sometimes overt cooperation from governments across the Pacific and Asia. In many countries environmental law is either subverted or non-existent, and international law is especially weak on issues such as logging. Nothing is done and the environmental thuggery goes on.

Environmental destruction has accelerated markedly since the end of World War II. Part of this is due to population pressures, but the most important component is the vast increase in the use of fossil fuels and raw materials in developed countries. This is also the period when petrochemicals began to be used on a much larger scale, with little regard for the consequences for the natural environment. While this increase has been amply documented in economic and social terms, it has rarely been commented on in historical terms. There is no comparison in previous history. It was not the two world wars that were the most destructive events ever experienced by humanity. It has been the developmental binge of the last 65 years. Even in human terms this has only benefited a small proportion of people. For the non-human world, it has meant disaster.

Two of the most vivid modern illustrations of human contempt for the natural world are to be found in Central Asia under the Soviet Marxist regime and in Australia under a capitalist regime. Both involve water.

The Aral Sea in Central Asia borders three countries: Uzbekistan, Kazakhstan and Turkmenistan. It was the fourth largest inland sea in the world in 1950. It is a salt water lake that was created by two rivers, the Amu Darya and the Syr Darya, both of which flow down into the Central Asian desert basin from the western end of the Pamir Mountains, a continuation of the Himalayan chain. The fresh water from these rivers kept the highly saline bed of the sea in perfect balance. For centuries the sea supported a rich fishing industry and the marshes a rich flora and fauna, including a subspecies of the Siberian tiger. Then, in the 1950s and 1960s, in a monumentally stupid act of central planning, the Soviet government decided to divert most of the water from the rivers into a vast irrigation scheme in one of the driest places in the world. The purpose: to grow cotton and rice. The scheme involved a series of dams and irrigation channels in which most of the water was lost to evaporation. In addition, large amounts of highly toxic pesticides and chemicals were used on the crops. By the 1970s it was clear that the Aral Sea was in serious trouble. But only desultory attempts at remediation have been made by the post-Soviet government of Kazakhstan. By 2008 the volume of water in the Aral Sea had been reduced by 75 per cent. All native endemic species have completely disappeared; the area is now an arid, toxic desert, the result of a combination of salt, sand, chemicals and pesticides. Drinking water has disappeared and the climate has become more extreme. So in less than half a century a rich local ecosystem which took millennia to evolve was not only completely destroyed, but was in fact turned into a poisonous wasteland.

But monumental stupidity is not confined to Soviet central planners. Australia, a highly developed capitalist society, faces a disaster equivalent to or even worse than the Aral Sea. Australia's problem is spread over a whole river system. Like Central Asia, inland Australia is essentially a dry landscape. But in the eastern and southern sections of the continent there is a marvellous network of rivers, the Murray-Darling Basin river system. Marvellous, that is, until irrigation arrived. Settlers began diverting river water into agriculture in the late 19th century, but the real problem period began with the Snowy Mountains Scheme, which started in the late 1940s.

Seen at the time as a vast nation-building exercise, the scheme aimed to divert water from melting winter snow on Australia's highest mountain range, the Snowy Mountains, inland, to irrigation projects. In the process the diverted water would also create hydro-electricity. There was no concern expressed for the environmental consequences. It was seen as a 'bold' scheme and the labour force required to carry it out was made up primarily of post-World War II European refugees and immigrants. At the core of the scheme was the diversion of an enormous volume of water from the Snowy River, which eventually flowed into Bass Strait, through a series of tunnels and hydro-electric generators, into the westward-flowing Murray River, where the water was used for irrigation. This has led to a serious degrading of the Snowy River. Recent efforts to restore even 27 per cent of the original flow to the Snowy have failed completely despite government promises.

The Murray-Darling system is also in terrible trouble. So much water is being taken out of the Murray that the river's lower lakes, the Coorong wetlands, are seriously endangered, and the mouth is dry. The other major eastern Australian river, the Darling, drains a vast inland area of plains and hills – more than 1 million square kilometres – west of the Great Dividing Range, which runs down the east coast of Australia dividing the costal areas from the inland. The Darling River is 2740 kilometres long and it flows from south-central and southwestern Queensland through western New South Wales to eventually join the Murray. The Darling River has been dammed all along its length, and vast quantities of water are extracted for irrigation. This whole river system has been so abused that it is now virtually running dry. Agriculture is the dominant economic activity in the basin. As with the Aral Sea, cotton and rice are again major culprits, but they are not the only ones: for decades the state governments involved have handed out far too many licences to extract water from the system.

An early sign of trouble occurred in 1992–93, when there was an epidemic of blue–green algae that for a period destroyed the life-systems of the rivers flowing into the Darling. This algal outbreak was the direct result of run-off from agricultural chemicals and cattle waste, and the use of the river system as a sewer by the towns next to it. Climate change has exacerbated the situation, but the essence of the problem is the complete contempt that state and local governments have shown for the environmental needs of the river systems. The environment is the last value to be respected. Another major part of the problem is interest groups that have consistently worked to stall any action by government. They aim to protect their own interests by working against any limits being placed on the amount of water they can extract. Some of them maintain massive privately owned water storages. In Australia, environmental thuggery, both governmental and private, is alive and well in the Murray-Darling Basin.

In October 2008 a government-commissioned CSIRO report on the state of the Murray-Darling Basin was completed.[37] Essentially, it shows that the situation is dire. The flooding that kept the basin's flood plains and wetlands in good ecological health has broken down almost entirely. This has been made worse by the drought which began in 1996. The impact of climate change on all this is uncertain, but according to the CSIRO report it will probably result in an 11 per cent decline in the amount of water in the system. The decline in the amount of surface water available for irrigation means that groundwater is increasingly being used instead. As the report notes, 'Current groundwater use is unsustainable in seven of the twenty high-use groundwater areas in the Murray Darling Basin.'[38] As I write, all the governments and private interests involved continue to play territorial games and ignore the desperate state of the ecology of the largest river system on the driest continent on earth.

In other words, it's the same old story: economic development without any regard for ecosystems. The basin produces 40 per cent of the gross value of Australian agricultural production. Australia is a very large exporter of food, but at extraordinary cost to the environment. The driest, least arable continent is exporting enough agricultural produce to feed three or four times the continent's own population of 22 million. At the same time there has been a steady refusal by state and federal governments to try to ascertain the actual carrying capacity of the continent. If they did this, Australians might have to acknowledge what many already know: their country is not infinite and its capacity to produce is being pushed far beyond sustainability.

But the earth is beginning to respond to our barbarism. Global warming hangs like the sword of Damocles over the entire world. All of this is the result of our lifestyles and the demands we make on our ecosystems. Berry puts it bluntly:

> We are the generation when the day of reckoning has come. In this disintegrating phase of our industrial society we see ourselves not as the splendor of creation but … [as] the most pernicious mode of earthly being. We are the termination, not the fulfillment of the earth process … We are the affliction of the world, its demonic presence. We are the violation of the earth's most sacred aspects![39]

Even allowing for a degree of prophetic hyperbole, the truth of Berry's statement is becoming obvious to those who break out of the willed blindness that afflicts so many people today.

If Lyn White were writing today, perhaps he would have to modify his accusations about Judeo-Christianity and environmental thuggery: now, almost all of us, particularly those of us who live in developed countries, are environmental thugs.

5 Bible

I must admit that when I first started thinking about religion and the environment 20 years ago the Bible was not the first place I thought to look. Perhaps that's because I'm a Catholic and, despite the renewed emphasis on scripture in Catholicism nowadays, I still look first to theology and the Church's tradition of worship and spirituality for inspiration. It is Protestants who tend to look to the Bible first. But then I discovered *The Earth Bible* and the work of Australian biblical scholar Dr Norman Habel. Essentially, *The Earth Bible* approaches scripture from an ecological perspective, which is very different from our usual anthropocentric interpretation. Habel argues that there are really three grand narratives in the Bible: about God, about humankind and about the earth. The aim of *The Earth Bible* is to focus the reader's attention on the relationship between the Scriptures and the natural world and thus help readers approach the Bible from an eco-justice perspective.[1] (*The Earth Bible* should be distinguished from *The Green Bible*, which is a version of the New Revised Standard Version [NRSV] with verses that have environmental connotations highlighted in green.[2])

Before I encountered *The Earth Bible* one of my biggest obstacles was that, though the early chapters of the Book of Genesis focus on God's creativity in the process of creation, there is still the 'dominion/subdue' text, which poses difficulties for developing an environmental theology. This text reads:

> Then God said, 'Let us make humankind in our image, according to our likeness; and let them have dominion' ... So God created humankind in his image ... God blessed them, and God said to them, 'Be fruitful and multiply, and fill the earth and subdue it; and have dominion' (Genesis 1:26–8).

No text has caused more discussion and dissension than this one, especially in the context of Lyn White's accusations that the Judeo-Christian tradition is responsible for our excessive anthropocentrism; this, in turn, justifies the view that the world exists for human exploitation.

However, before tackling this intractable problem, we should survey the whole of the first chapter of Genesis. We need to remember that this wonderful epic of creation recounts the Hebrew myth of origins with such verbal economy and vivid imagery that it needs to be read as a piece of literature not as a historical or scientific account. The story begins with *Erets* (earth), which, together with *Ruach Elohim*, the breath of God, is the primary focus of Genesis 1:1 to 2:4.[3] In the beginning 'the earth was a formless void and darkness covered the face of the deep' (1:2). The primordial earth is there from the start. It is, as Habel says, 'the primary subject of the story, the main character of the plot'.[4] Earth and the waters existed long before anything else was created. The word for the appearance of the earth is the same word that is used when God appears. In this sense the earth itself is a kind of theophany, a manifestation of God.

The breath of God quietly hovers in the darkness, waiting 'over the face of the waters' which cover the earth: 'No negative verdict is pronounced on these waters – there is no indication that they are threatening powers or turbulent forces of chaos.'[5] And then, almost as if in a stage play, light is created: 'Then God said, "Let there be light", and there was light' (1:3). Day and night were born (1:4–5). During the two days that follow, God creates the heavens and separates the waters so that earth may at last appear (1:6–9). This too is almost theatrical, as though the curtain of waters is rolled back or lifted and the Earth is revealed, just as God or an angel appears or is revealed in a theophany.[6] 'And God saw that it [the earth] was good' (1:10). Earth then becomes the source of all living things: all plants and animals. The sky is filled with birds, the seas with fish, and they procreate and multiply. Genesis depicts the earth 'as both the source of life and the home of all living creatures'.[7] It is primary matter, the source of everything. When humankind is created on the sixth day God's work is completed, and all the potentiality of the earth is revealed.

'And on the seventh day God finished the work that he had done, and he rested ... So God blessed the seventh day and hallowed it' (2:2–3). This is the so-called Sabbath text, and it refers to a day of blessing and rest. The Jews celebrate the Sabbath on Saturday, Christians on Sunday. For both faiths the symbolism is the same: it is the day when we reflect on and celebrate God's achievement in creation. As theologian Jürgen Moltmann puts it:

> In the Sabbath stillness men and women no longer intervene in the environment through their labor. They let it be entirely God's creation. They recognize that as God's property creation is inviolable; and they sanctify the day through their joy in their existence as God's creatures within the fellowship of creation.[8]

But the account of the story of creation is not complete. A disjunctive note is introduced when God creates humankind. In the Genesis story humans don't emerge from the earth in the way that all other creatures do; they emerge in a different way, apparently on a whim. God says:

> 'Let us make humankind in our own image.' So God created humankind in his image, in the image of God he created them; male and female he created them … and God said to them, 'Be fruitful and multiply and fill the earth and subdue it; and have dominion … over every living thing that moves upon the earth' (1:26–28).

The two key phrases here are 'have dominion' and 'subdue the earth'. The meaning of the original Hebrew is inescapable and the English translation is accurate. 'Dominion' is derived from the Hebrew verb *radah*, which means to subject or subdue another, to force or to keep them under control. It is what happens to slaves. The word is clearly used in Genesis to indicate human power and control over the world. The word 'subdue' has a similar range of meanings: it is derived from the verb *kavash*, a word that is even more forceful than *radah*. It refers to the actual act of subjugation, the act of putting the foot of the master on the head of the slave or the subdued enemy. It also refers to the occupation and plundering of the territory of a conquered enemy and is used, for instance, when the Hebrews invade Canaan (Numbers 32:22). It can also refer to rape. So any attempt to water down the text or to suggest that it doesn't mean what it says is wrong. The text unequivocally refers to human domination and use of the environment.

After conceding this, many biblical scholars try to get around it by arguing that humans are bound to act towards the world in the same way as the Creator, and in subordination to God's plan. That is, we must act as stewards, reigning over the world with restraint and benevolence. As God's vice-regents we are called to act as God has acted. I don't accept this interpretation; it simply side-steps what the text clearly says. I believe the 'stewardship' reading, while widely accepted today, is essentially wrong. In the text the earth is unequivocally relegated 'to a secondary status', and this creates real problems for our contemporary environmental approach.[9] It can and is endlessly used as a justification for extractive industries, for the rape and pillage of the earth and for all kinds of 'bulldozer theologies'.

The English Anglican Bishop David Atkinson tries to shift the discussion from stewardship to what he calls 'royal service'. He reads the dominion text in the context of service to the people by Israelite kings such as Solomon (c.961–922BC). 'Solomon,' Atkinson says, 'was the leader, but not exploitative.' In my view this is an overly benign assessment of Solomon's reign. Despite his enormous building program, Solomon's wealth didn't percolate down to the general population or to the poor.[10] Nevertheless, Atkinson argues that in the Genesis text humanity acts 'on behalf of God the Creator, exercising the role of a servant–king as a partner with the community of creation – not dominating, but enabling'.[11] This is a misreading of the dominion text.

There are two interconnected issues here: the first is the context in which the dominion verses were written, and the second is the history of their interpretation. Of the two, the second is more important.

Certainly we need to place Genesis 1:26–28 back into the religious, politico-social and environmental context from which it first emerged. There is still debate regarding the origin and provenance of the materials that go to make up the text of Genesis as we have it. Generally speaking, the creation stories were originally in oral form and dated from different periods. The Hebrew people were well aware of other Middle Eastern creation myths. Many of these stories were quite seductive. Clearly the Hebrew creation stories as recounted in Genesis served a theological purpose: they set up a monotheistic belief about God to compete with the polytheism and fertility myths of their neighbours. The Hebrews were trying to convey that their God, unlike the gods of the surrounding peoples, was supremely creative, not dependent on the struggles of cosmic forces to bring about creation.

Also, the creation account is not a scientific document. To assign a scientific meaning to it, as the creationists do, is not just bad science; it is also very bad scriptural interpretation. American Jesuit biblical scholar John L. McKenzie says:

> The author [of the first chapter of Genesis] was as ignorant of the natural sciences as any man of his time, and it is idle to speak of a conflict between Genesis and science when Genesis says nothing about the objects of science ... It is manifestly absurd to think that Genesis tells us anything about the [scientific] structure of the visible universe, or exhibits the faintest notion of the processes of its development.[12]

Nowadays there is widespread agreement among scholars that the Book of Genesis is made up of several text sources woven together. In Chapters 1 and 2 we have accounts of creation from two distinct sources. These are called the priestly and the Yahwist traditions. The term 'priestly' is used because the redactor – the final editor – was thought to be a temple priest, and the word 'Yahwist' is used because the redactor constantly uses the very ancient Hebrew word *Yahweh* to refer to God. The dominion text, Genesis 1:26–7, comes from the priestly source. The redactor took ancient material and used it for purposes that suited his own time – probably between 587 and 537BC, around the time of the Exile. The priestly tradition always arranges everything hierarchically. In this scenario God seemingly informs the heavenly court, saying, 'Let us make humankind in our image, according to our likeness.' The text then goes on to make humankind the climax of creation, to give it/us 'dominion'. It is the priestly redactor who isolates humankind as the only thing created in God's image. As such, humankind shares in God's authority and thus is able to rule over all creatures.

However, the context of the ancient material is more complex than this. The tradition the priestly redactor worked with arose from an earlier oral tradition: from when the Israelites were occupying the land of

Canaan (between Syria and Egypt), after the exodus, which was sometime around 1250–1200BC. These verses may have originally reflected Judaism's relationship with its new land: barren, dry, rocky and arid desert, quite a contrast to the 'fleshpots' of Egypt. In this land the Hebrews' very survival depended on subjugation of their neighbours and very hard work in subsistence-level agriculture. The early Hebrew farmers must have felt almost powerless in the face of an apparently antagonistic nature. There is a sense of their resentment of the natural world and their feeling that the environment had to be overpowered and subdued, just like their Canaanite enemies. Hebrews working the land could well have felt it appropriate to use harsh words such as *radah* and *kavash* when talking about the difficult landscape in which they had to eke out their existence.

Then there is the second, more ancient and succinct account of creation in Chapter 2 of Genesis (vv. 4–21). This material originally comes from the Yahwist tradition, and dates from around the 10th century BC. The style here, as biblical scholar Eugene Maly notes, 'is more vivid and concrete; the presentation of God is more anthropomorphic; the perspective is earthly and human rather than cosmic and divine'.[13] It seems likely that the Yahwist redactor has not changed the ancient material much at all, as the account describes God creating the heavens and the earth, but the waterless land has no plants. 'Then the Lord God formed man from the dust of the ground and breathed into his nostrils the breath of life; and the man became a living being' (2:7). Here humankind is actually created from the soil, thus establishing an intimate biological and spiritual connection with the earth itself. Then 'the lord God planted a garden in Eden, in the east; and there he put the man whom he had formed … A river flows out of Eden to water the garden' (2:8–9). This river becomes the source of four others, including the Tigris and Euphrates. In verse 15 God takes the man into the garden and asks him 'to till it and keep it'. In other words, he is called to work in harmony with the earth. There is a bucolic feel about these verses, perhaps reflecting an established peasant–farmer world. The plants are already domesticated: 'Out of the ground the Lord God made to grow every tree that is pleasant to the sight and good to eat' (2:9).

However, the emphasis in the Yahwist text is still on the separate and unique significance of humankind: 'So out of the ground the Lord God formed every animal of the field and every bird of the air, and brought them to the man to see what he would call them; and whatever the man called every living creature, that was its name' (2:19). The act of naming all other creatures gives humankind a special sharing in the divine nature, for to name something implies that one is part of the definition of that thing and so has power over it. Thus the second account of creation is essentially ambivalent about humankind's relationship with the landscape, and both accounts set us above the rest of the natural world.

The underlying theological notion in both these texts is significant: we have dominion over the earth precisely because we share in the life of God. We are, in a unique sense, the icons or images of God. (Actually, despite the gender-neutral language of the NRSV, in the biblical view only men are 'like God'.) The reason for this emphasis on the human is the early biblical writers' preoccupation with the dangers of idolatry: conceding that anything other than human beings could reveal something of God could set that other thing up as an idol to be adored and worshipped. This fear is revealed vividly in the second of the Commandments: 'Thou shalt not have strange gods before me.' At the core of these writers' consciousness was the fear that people would adopt aspects of the fertility religion of the Canaanite people who surrounded them.

A further disjunction between humankind and the earth appears in Chapter 3 of Genesis. Because of their disobedience the man and the woman are cast out of the garden. They lose their innocence, and their fate is particularly hard: 'By the sweat of your face you shall eat bread until you return to the ground, for out of it you were taken; you are dust and to dust you shall return' (3:19). Again, there is a note of antagonism towards the natural world, even though humankind is made from the dust of the earth.

While the Yahwist account of creation is certainly an improvement on the priestly tradition, neither account recognises animals, plants, birds, and even the earth itself as mirroring the Creator and therefore also being icons of God. The natural world is seen largely as inert and mute, and its only true value is in its relationship to humankind. Its connection with God can only be achieved through humankind. At best this is an ambivalent view of the natural world.

Also, the image of God that is presented in the creation accounts is deeply anthropomorphic, in that God is seen as a person like us. Genesis is right, of course: the nature of God is personal, but theology correctly emphasises that God is personal in a transcendent, divine sense. Popular belief tends to obliterate the theological view that our knowledge of God is, at best, partial and analogical, an extrapolation from our own personhood and human experience.

The Genesis text leads directly to Judeo-Christianity's fear of idolatry, to its view that humankind alone can be the image or icon of God, and that nature's value is derived entirely from its relationship to human beings. Thus our needs and preoccupations become the arbiter and norm of ethical judgment about everything related to nature. While Genesis certainly doesn't exhaust the Judeo-Christian understanding of the relationship between humankind and nature, and there is much more about the natural world in the rest of the Bible, mainstream Christianity, especially since Renaissance Humanism and the scientific revolution of the 17th century, has interpreted the creation accounts in ways that support these attitudes towards nature.

It is often forgotten that the interpretation of biblical texts is actually far more significant and influential than the texts themselves. This most certainly applies to the creation accounts in Genesis. Clarence Glacken has commented that the Genesis account of creation is characterised above all by brevity:

> Words are used so sparingly in describing the successive acts in the creation of the cosmos that, with the growth of Christianity and the continuing strength of Judaism, an enormous exegetical literature was inevitable ... The intense otherworldliness and rejection of the beauties of nature because they turn men away from the contemplation of God are elaborated upon far more in the theological writings than in the Bible itself.[14]

As the Bible is a collection of different pieces, in varying styles, written over a very long period, it is hardly surprising that there is no overall view of the natural world in it. The most general thing that can be said about the scriptural view of nature is that the text is not abstract, but rather geographically particular. In other words, the biblical writers were not interested in 'nature' or 'cosmos' as abstract notions; just like most ancient peoples, they were interested in specific places in the landscape. And here I emphasise that my treatment is not exhaustive; I have dealt only with the texts I think are significant.

The psalms are seen by many as environmentally friendly, but I don't believe this is entirely true. Several psalms – for example 18, 74 and 93 – revert to a kind of *Chaoskampf* (chaos battle) scenario in which God as orderly Creator is pitted against the chaos created by 'the seas', 'the dragons in the waters', and 'the heads of Leviathan' (Ps 74). In other psalms God is cast as a kind of storm God who thunders over the mighty waters, who smashes the cedars of Lebanon, who 'flashes forth flames of fire', or who 'shakes the wilderness and strips the forest bare'. The God of the psalms is not an unalloyed blessing for the earth and its creatures.

Before we deal with this image of God, let us examine the psalms in which the natural world is seen in a more positive light.

Take Psalm 19, for example. This hymn of praise is evenly divided into two parts; originally it may have been two separate psalms. The first part lauds God's glory in the heavens and the second praises His wisdom. The psalm proclaims the paradox of the beauties of day and night, declaring the glory of God in silence: 'There is no speech, nor are there words; their voice is not heard, yet their voice goes out through all the earth, and their words to the end of the world' (19:3–4). The verses allude to that silent change from day to night and night to day as the sun falls and rises. The psalmist is saying that this daily change voicelessly yet unambiguously proclaims the beauty and glory of God from one end of the earth to the other.

Psalm 104 is a hymn of praise of God as Creator. Scripture scholar Roland E. Murphy describes it as 'one of the most remarkable songs in the Psalter'. It is a beautiful psalm, closely related to the account of creation in Genesis 1–2. It also reflects ancient Hebrew cosmology. God dwells in a palace above the heavens, which stretch out over the earth 'like a tent'. The clouds are God's chariot and He rides 'on the wings of the wind'. 'You [God] make the winds your messengers, fire and flame your ministers. You set the earth on its foundations so that it shall never be shaken' (104:3–5). It is God who brings order to the waters, and He sets 'a boundary that they may not pass, so that they may not again cover the earth' (104:9). As a result of the order brought about by God, the chaos of the waters now provides springs and streams that 'flow between the hills, giving drink to every wild animal; the wild asses quench their thirst. By the streams the birds of the air have their habitation; they sing among the branches' (104:10–12). In this psalm the earth and everything above, in and on it have a voice and all creation sings God's praise. The peaceful relationship between animals, plants and humankind is emphasised in verses 12 to 23, but the ultimate purpose of creation 'is to bring forth food from the earth and wine to gladden the human heart, oil to make the face shine, and bread to strengthen the human heart' (104:14–15).

Certainly in this psalm the earth has a real voice, but the underlying message is unequivocal: creation exists 'for people to use' (104:14). There is no escaping the underlying anthropocentrism. Humankind is integrated into a peaceful, benign natural world continuously created by *Ruach Yahweh*, the breath of God, which 'renews the face of the earth' (104:30). Acknowledging this, the psalmist praises God: 'I will sing to the Lord as long as I live; I will sing praise to my God as long as I have being' (104:33).

A different note is struck in Psalms 65 and 148. Psalm 65 begins with a song of praise from the Hebrew people (65:1–4), those 'whom you chose and bring near to live in your courts … your house, your holy temple' (v 4). The first verse of the psalm introduces the notion of *dumiyyah* (contemplative silence) as a form of praise. We saw this also in Psalm 19, where the silent sequence of night and day gives praise to God. Here the psalmist says: 'To you [God] silence is praise.' It is only in genuine silence that humankind can attain the state of attention required to begin to contemplate the beauties of the world and the cosmos, and to perceive the transcendent presence of God in nature. The phrase 'To you [God in Zion] all flesh shall come' (65:2) is particularly interesting. 'All flesh' (the Hebrew word for flesh is *basar*) seems to refer to the whole of material reality: *basar* usually refers to the earthly condition of creation, including humankind, in its vulnerability and the fact that it is destined for death. The tonality changes in verses 5 to 13 with a shift in focus on the temple in Jerusalem to the universal cosmos, where God 'is the hope of all the ends of the earth and of the farthest seas … Those who live at earth's farthest bounds are awed by your signs' (65:5, 8). God silences 'the roaring of the seas, the roaring of their waves and the tumult of the peoples' (65:7). Verse 8 ('Those who live at earth's farthest bounds are awed by your signs; you make the gateways of the morning and the evening shout for joy') seems to suggest that humankind is awed into silence by God's sheer power.

The last part of the psalm focuses on the relationship between the earth and God. 'The river of God is full of water' (65:9); God is the living water that brings life and fertility. The last third of the psalm is a song of sheer praise of the whole of reality.

Psalms 146 to 150 are the last psalms in the Psalter. They are songs of thanksgiving and praise: in theology, doxologies. It was Psalm 148 that inspired St Francis of Assisi near the end of his life, in 1226, to write 'The Canticle of Brother Sun', which we sing today as the hymn 'All Creatures of Our God and King'. Francis would have frequently recited Psalm 148 as he prayed the church's daily prayer. This psalm is a doxology of pure praise which gives priority to the created world. In vv. 1 to 6 it is the heavens that praise God; in vv. 7–10 the earth joins in; vv. 11–13 bring in 'the kings of the earth and all peoples'; and then suddenly the focus is narrowed in v 14 to the people of Israel. While the underlying cosmology is, understandably, that of the ancient Hebrews, there is a real feeling of universality in this psalm.

Why is the vision narrowed in the last verse? Here the psalmist says, 'for the people of Israel are close to him, Praise the Lord!' (148:14), as though contradicting everything that had gone before. Old Testament scholar Mark David Futato asks: 'In a psalm so focused on the global, why shift to one nation?' His answer: 'It is because God has chosen this one nation as the vehicle through which he will make his entrance into the world in order that his blessings might flow to all and to the whole.'

The kind of universalism manifested by some strands of ancient Hebrew theology during and after the exile (597–39BC) – especially in the psalms and the prophets – is remarkable. For the earliest Hebrews who invaded the land of Canaan, foreign people were either enemies or irrelevant. During the period of the kings in Israel (c.1000–c.600BC), foreigners were the instruments of God's judgment and punishment on

Israel, or they were nobodies. But with the deportation of the Hebrews from their traditional lands and the exile, a new universalism began to emerge, with God seen as the saviour of all peoples: if foreign peoples come to understand Israel's vision, they too will come to know God and share in the knowledge and spirituality that God conferred on the Jewish people. So a vision developed of all nations coming to Jerusalem as the locus for the worship of the true God on earth. With that comes a theological breadth that was previously lacking. But a sense of universalism is hard to maintain even for the most theologically broad-minded. What I suspect happened at the end of this psalm is an example of this kind of failure: it's as though the psalmist said: 'Yes, the whole of creation and all of humankind will praise God, but don't forget in all this openness that we, the Hebrews, are the ones who are really close to him. Praise the Lord!'

In several of the psalms (29 and 97, for example) God is presented as a kind of 'storm God'. 'The voice of the Lord is over the waters; the God of glory thunders … The voice of the Lord flashes forth flames of fire. The voice of the Lord shakes the wilderness' (Ps 29:3, 8). The same kind of image is found in Psalm 97: 'Fire goes before him [God], and consumes his adversaries on every side. His lightnings light up the world; the earth sees and trembles' (97:3). What is most interesting in Psalm 29 is the close identification between God and the storm; the storm is the visible manifestation of God, the voice of God.[15] The human response is clear: 'And in his temple all say, "Glory"' (29:9).

I mentioned earlier that some psalms place God and aspects of the cosmos in conflict.[16] Here we run up against the problem of interpretation again. As our knowledge of the cosmologies of the peoples surrounding the Hebrews expands, we find that their creation myths focus on a heroic deity's battle against chaos, often identified with the ocean, the sea, or rivers, and the great creatures that dwell within them. These are represented by Leviathan, an imaginary or real sea creature of enormous size, often identified as a whale (see Psalm 74:13–17). This kind of representation has implications for a harmonious God–earth relationship. The Bible largely avoids this kind of *Chaoskampf* scenario, but it was hard for the Hebrews to exclude it entirely because of the pervasive influence of these myths in the ancient Middle East.

I want to turn now to the story of the earth in the prophetic literature of Israel. The best place to start is the greatest of the prophets, Isaiah, and the famous vision from Chapter 6, where two Seraphim (six-winged creatures in human form) cry out to each other in the temple in Jerusalem: 'Holy, holy, holy is the Lord of hosts; the whole earth is full of his glory' (Isaiah 6:3). The word 'glory' here refers to the visible presence of God, so the text is saying that God is manifestly present in 'the whole earth', not just in the temple. Here we have an unequivocal assertion of the earth as a theophany, a living presence of God. In Isaiah 11 we come upon another vision of a kind of paradise restored, where 'The wolf shall lie down with the lamb, the leopard shall lie down with the kid, the calf and the lion and the fatling together, and the little child shall lead them' (11:6). This peaceful kingdom will come about when the *Ruach Yahweh*, the breath of God, restores a king who will rule with righteousness and justice, especially towards the poor, and 'decide with equity for the meek of the earth' (11:4). This kind of cosmic reconciliation later becomes a staple of both the Hebrew and Christian visions of the entire world sharing in God's salvation.

A quite different note is struck in Isaiah 24. Here we come upon a kind of apocalyptic scene as 'a curse devours the earth' (24:6). It is as though chaos ruled supreme: 'The earth shall be utterly laid waste and utterly despoiled' (24:3). The reason is because humankind has 'transgressed laws, violated the statutes, broken the everlasting covenant' (24:5). Isaiah's vision could resemble what the future might hold for us if global warming really takes hold, or if plague and infection devastate the human population, if judgment day comes:

> Terror, and the pit, and the snare are upon you, O inhabitant of the earth! Whoever flees at the sound of the terror shall fall into the pit and whoever climbs out of the pit shall be caught in the snare … The earth is utterly broken, the earth is torn asunder, the earth is violently shaken (24:17–19).

This apocalyptic vision makes sense if you examine the political background to the first 39 chapters of Isaiah's prophecy. The power of an aggressively expansionist Assyria under King Sennacherib (704–681BC) was supreme, and the northern kingdom of Israel was swept away in 701BC, in the prophet's own lifetime. (After Solomon's death in 922BC, two weak and divided kingdoms had emerged, Israel in the north and Judea, centred on Jerusalem, in the south.) The opening line of Lord Byron's poem 'The Destruction of Sennacherib' expresses the vulnerability of Israel vividly: 'The Assyrian came down like a wolf on the fold'. Judea was equally threatened, but it survived by temporarily accepting vassal status. This political context explains Isaiah's apocalyptic tone.

The prophets who lived through the destruction of the northern kingdom and who foretold the coming doom were Hosea and Amos. Amos was particularly concerned about the social injustice which reigned supreme in the period before the Assyrian invasion, particularly during the reign of Jeroboam II (786–46BC) and the kinglets following him. As Scripture scholar Phillip King puts it, 'An oppressive social pyramid had been constructed and class inequalities were having drastic consequences, the poor being victimized by the predatory rich. Religious decay was one root of these social crimes.'[17] For Amos, the natural world reveals the sheer power of God:

> For lo, the one who forms the mountains, creates the wind, reveals his thoughts to mortals, makes the morning darkness and treads the heights of the earth – the Lord, the God of hosts, is his name … The

> one who made the Pleiades and Orion, and turns deep darkness into morning, and darkens the day into night, who calls for the waters of the sea, and pours them out on the surface of the earth, the lord is his name (4:13; 5:8).

Hosea, who lived a decade or so after Amos, is equally concerned with the coming judgment on the Israelites' infidelity. This is symbolised by the prophet's wife's infidelity: 'I will punish her for the festival days of the Baals, when she offered incense to them and decked herself out with her ring and jewellery, and went after her lovers, and forgot me, says the lord' (Hosea 2:13). But Hosea was not pessimistic about the future of Israel. He had hope, and he presents this in terms of a renewed covenant with the land itself:

> I will make for you a covenant on that day with the wild animals, the birds of the air and the creeping things of the ground ... On that day I will answer, says the Lord, I will answer the heavens and they will answer the earth; and the earth shall answer the grain, the wine and the oil, and they shall answer Jezreel; and I will sow him for myself in the land (2:18–23).

The Assyrian empire was swept away in 609BC, and the equally expansionist neo-Babylonians, under King Nebuchadnezzar (605–562BC), seized power. Caught between Egypt and Babylon, the southern kingdom of Judea sought safety as a vassal of Egypt in 609. But in 605 the Egyptians were defeated by Nebuchadnezzar and in 602 Judea became a vassal of Babylon. In a disastrous error of judgment, Judea revolted against the Babylonians in 601. In 597 the Babylonians laid siege to Jerusalem and took the city. The first deportation occurred. In 589 there was another ill-considered revolt against the Babylonians, motivated by what historian John Bright calls 'fierce patriotism [and] ... headlong confidence'.[18]

After a long siege the Babylonians took Jerusalem, in July 587. The city and temple were destroyed, the countryside was laid waste and the exile began, as almost the entire population was deported to Babylon.

In the midst of these political convulsions Jeremiah was called to prophesy in Jerusalem. He was utterly frustrated with Judea's leaders putting their trust in political manoeuvring and ham-fisted diplomacy, trying to play the Egyptians against the Babylonians rather than trusting in God. Jeremiah's prophecy is dominated by deep pessimism, because he was called to proclaim that the city would be destroyed because of the infidelity of leaders and people. As Bright says:

> No braver or more tragic figure ever trod the stage of Israel's history than the prophet Jeremiah … It was his lot … to say … that Judea was doomed and that that doom was Yahweh's righteous judgment upon her for her breach of covenant.[19]

Everything came to a head in 588–87BC, 'the tenth year of King Zedekiah of Judea … when the army of the king of Babylon was besieging Jerusalem' (Jeremiah 32:1–2). As noted above, the siege was successful, the city was destroyed and the people taken into exile. What Jeremiah prophesied came to pass:

> Disaster overtakes disaster, the whole land is laid waste … I looked on the earth and lo, it was waste and void, and to the heavens, and they had no light … For thus says the Lord: 'The whole land shall be a desolation … the earth shall mourn, and the heavens above grow black' (4:20,23,27–28).

The exile created more than an environmental crisis in Judea, for the Jews saw the land as an inheritance left to them by God. It was not just a question of the ownership of property; each clan and family had a relationship with a specific place. Now they were exiles in a foreign land and Judea was in the hands of their conqueror. But Jeremiah was not without hope for the future of the Jewish people, even though he died in Egypt in the years after the fall of Jerusalem. Since nothing was impossible for God, he looked forward to a new beginning in the future. The return to the chosen land was to be the symbol of their hope:

> See I am going to gather them from all the lands to which I drove them … I will bring them back to this place, and I will settle them in safety. They shall be my people and I will be their God … I will plant them in this land in faithfulness, with all my heart and all my soul (32:37–41).

While Jeremiah held onto some sense of hope, a more tragic fate for the earth is sketched out in the prophecy of Ezekiel, who was probably active among the first-generation exiles in Babylon. In his prophecy the earth gets a terrible battering, not because it has done anything wrong, but because the Hebrews have been totally disloyal to God and broken the covenant through their worship of idols and their trust in international politics rather than the power of the divine presence: 'I will stretch out my hand against them, and make the land desolate and waste … Then they shall know that I am the Lord' (Ezekiel 6:14). The connection between land and 'desolation' and 'waste' recurs constantly in Ezekiel: 'I will make the land a desolation and a waste … and the mountains of Israel shall be so desolate that no one will pass through. Then they shall know that I am the Lord, when I have made the land a desolation and a waste because of all their abominations that they have committed' (33:28–29).

These are the kind of stark environmental images that make sense to us today; we are used to images of deforestation, erosion, dried-up rivers, erosion, drought and pollution.[20] This imagery is even more focused when Ezekiel speaks 'against the forest land in the Negeb' (20:46). Nowadays this is a desert area, so it is hard to know how to interpret this verse; perhaps in the pre-exile period there were forests on the edge of the southern wilderness. However, the text is very appropriate for today, when we lose rainforests at the rate of 0.4 hectare (1 acre) per second all across the world, even in developed countries like Australia, where woodchippers, with government connivance, are still permitted to tear into old-growth forests. 'Say to the forest of the Negeb, Hear the word of the Lord … I will kindle a fire in you, and it shall devour every green tree in you and every dry tree; the blazing flame shall not be quenched, and all faces from south to north shall be scorched by it' (20:47). This is the kind of bushfire imagery that makes sense in places like Australia, California and in the Amazon, where forests have been decimated for land for cash crops.

But it was not just Judea that was to be destroyed by God. It would also be foreign countries: 'I will make the land of Egypt a desolation among desolated countries' (29:12). Both the evil and the good would be struck down: 'Thus says the Lord, "I am against you and I will draw my sword from its scabbard and hew down both righteous and wicked from within you"' (21:3). Mountains particularly take a beating from God in Ezekiel, partly because it was on the mountains that the worship of idols was carried out; the term 'high place' usually indicates a pagan shrine or altar:

> O mortal, set your face toward the mountains of Israel, and prophecy against them and say. You mountains of Israel, hear the word of the Lord God! Thus says the Lord God to the mountains and the hills, and to the ravines and the valleys; I, I myself will bring a sword upon you, and I will destroy your high places. Your altars shall become desolate, and your incense stands shall be broken (6:2–4).

So what are we to make of these texts in which God seems to be at war with the environment? You can always say Ezekiel was a crank. But as biblical scholar Kalinda Rose Stevenson argues, 'the book not only radiates violence, it radiates urgency'.[21] She says that just as Ezekiel adopted 'highly exaggerated figurative speech to dramatize the dangers' facing the Hebrew people, so 'many Ezekiels in our own era', for whom the crisis is environmental, use the same kind of exaggerated speech to highlight the terrible danger we face. Perhaps with issues such as global warming and the disaster in the Gulf of Mexico from the BP oil rig, we have already gone beyond the time for moderate and rational speech, and now need a much more confronting form of prophetic utterance to confront the complete inaction of governments, polluting corporations and, ultimately, ourselves.

A much more optimistic note about the earth is struck in Deutero-Isaiah (Isaiah 40 to 55). This prophet was writing just before the end of the exile. Around 550BC the Babylonians were weakening, and the Persians under Cyrus, who were seen by the Jews as God's instrument, were on the rise. A very hopeful note is struck in this prophecy. This is reflected in the verses used in the opening tenor aria of Handel's *Messiah*:

> The voice of him that crieth in the wilderness, prepare the way
> of the Lord, make straight in the desert a highway for our God.
> Every valley shall be exalted and every mountain and hill made low;
> the crooked straight, and the rough places plain (Isaiah 40:3–4, King
> James Version).

God will manifest his love and care for the Hebrews through the natural world:

> I will open rivers on the bare heights, and fountains in the midst of the valleys; I will make the wilderness a pool of water, and the dry land springs of water. I will put in the wilderness the cedar, the acacia, the myrtle, and the olive; I will set in the desert the cypress, the plane and the pine together … the hand of the Lord has done this, the Holy One of Israel created it (41:18–20).

This will not be just confined to the flora; the fauna join in too: 'The wild animals will honor me, the jackals and the ostriches; for I give water in the wilderness, rivers in the desert' (43:20).

Turning to Wisdom literature, to the biblical books that describe how a wise, shrewd, moral, socially aware person should act, the Earth Bible team concedes that 'Wisdom literature, in its present form, tends to elevate the elite class, encourage subjects to be loyal to their ruler – usually male – and provide education for the privileged ruling classes.' The voice of the earth seems to be lacking. However, they do discern an element of deconstruction of 'what it means to "rule"', and 'an alternative way of maintaining social order'.[22] They refer specifically to Proverbs 30:

> Four things on earth are small, yet they are exceedingly wise: the ants are a people without strength, yet they provide their food in summer; the badgers are people without power, yet they make their homes in the rocks; the locusts have no king, yet all of them march in rank; the lizard can be grasped in the hand, yet it can be found in kings' palaces (Proverbs 30:24–28).

The text seems to be saying that the wise man can learn from the natural world; these small, weak creatures are not under human control, yet they are 'exceedingly wise'.

However, it is when the Book of Proverbs comes to consider Sophia, 'woman wisdom', that we get a really integrated link between wisdom and ecology.[23] Sophia essentially means 'feminine Wisdom'. I have used a capital 'W' because Sophia is so closely identified with God. She is there 'on the primordial stage, where acts of creation are being formed'.[24] Because she is there at the beginning, Sophia understands how things 'work'; she alone can reveal earth's mysteries. She is simultaneously co-creator, midwife and mother of the cosmos:

> The Lord created me [Sophia] at the beginning of his work, the first of his acts of long ago. Ages ago I was set up, at the first, before the beginning of the earth. When there were no depths, I was brought forth, when there were no springs abounding with water. Before the mountains had been shaped, before the hills I was brought forth – when he had not yet made earth and fields, or the world's first bits of soil. When he established the heavens I was there, when he drew a circle on the face of the deep, when he made firm the skies above, when he established the fountains of the deep, when he assigned to the sea its limit, so that the waters might not transgress his command, when he marked out the foundations of the earth, then I was beside him like a master worker, and I was daily his delight (Proverbs 8:1, 22–30).

The Christian reader will, of course, immediately identify Sophia with the Holy Spirit, the third person of the Trinity. But Sophia can also be identified with Christ, because he also was there when the world was created. In a text reminiscent of the one above from Proverbs, St Paul, in the Letter to the Colossians, says that 'He [Christ] is the image of the invisible God, the firstborn of all creation; for in him all things in heaven and on earth were created … all things have been created through him and for him' (1:15–16). I will return to a more detailed consideration of this text in the chapter on Christ.

*

The last book I'll consider in the Hebrew Scriptures is the book of Job. McKenzie rightly maintains that Job 'is perhaps the most profound and original literary work of the entire Old Testament'.[25] Probably composed somewhere between the 5th and 3rd centuries BC and set in an indeterminate period, the book is neither a philosophical reflection on the problem of evil, nor a theological treatise on an absent and seemingly vindictive God. It is about lived human experience and 'the problem of unmerited evil, the suffering of the innocent and its corollary, the prosperity of the wicked'.[26] The story is simple: it opens with Job, a 'blameless and upright man who feared God and turned away from evil' (1:1). He is very rich and blessed by God. But suddenly he loses everything and is infected with 'loathsome sores from the sole of his foot to the crown of his head' (2:7), probably a reference to leprosy. What is most scandalous, however, is that what happens to Job is the result of two bets between God, who appears as a kind of oriental potentate, and Satan, who is not yet identified as the devil, but is a kind of a 'prosecutor who spies on men's wrongdoing and reports it to his master'.[27] Job finds himself sitting among the ashes of his former wealth when along come three of his old friends who had 'heard of these troubles that had come upon him' (2:11). These 'comforters' provide the conventional ancient religious answer to the problem of evil: because God awards the just and punishes sinners, there must be sin somewhere in Job's life.

Utterly dissatisfied with their responses, Job treats their pious nostrums as complete tosh. He knows that he has acted with righteousness. In essence, Job's argument against God treating him so badly is that while 'the tents of robbers are at peace, and those who provoke God are secure' (12:6), he finds that he has become 'a laughing-stock to his friends if he cries to God and expects and answer. The blameless innocent incurs only mockery' (12:4, Jerusalem Bible translation). In a foreshadowing of the final theophany in which God mysteriously answers him, Job says that even the earth itself knows that he has been treated dreadfully and unjustly by God:

> Ask the animals and they will teach you; the birds of the air and they will tell; ask the plants of the earth and they will teach you, and the fish of the sea will declare to you. Who among all these does not know that the hand of the Lord has done this [to me]? (12:7–9).

God's treatment of Job is appalling, and Job finds himself a trapped human victim in this mad game between God and Satan. He finds himself *in extremis*, utterly confounded; wisdom and human reason are meaningless. He cannot make any sense out of it.

It is important to recall here that belief in immortality, and life after death, was not part of the belief system of the Hebrews when Job was written. This only came with the influence of Greek thought, first on Diaspora Judaism in the 2nd century BC, and even later among Jews in the homeland. Even in Jesus' time many Jews, such as the Sadducees, did not believe in immortality. This meant that Job could not hope for justice after death. In Job's theology, the most that anyone could expect after death was a kind of meaningless shadow existence in a dark, undifferentiated underworld called Sheol. But given his dreadful treatment by God, death and Sheol became very appealing to Job. 'Death means a return to Earth, to a peaceful domain where the hand of God can no longer intrude or trouble humans … [Here] it seems divine surveillance is limited.'[28]

The importance of the book of Job for environmental theology is that the earth and environment play an important role in Job's quandary.[29] There is a deep consciousness of close human connections with the earth: 'A mortal man, born of woman, few of days and full of trouble, comes up like a flower and withers, flees like a shadow that does not last' (14:1). Yet humankind has even less permanence than a tree – and anyone who has lived in a dry climate with eucalypts will understand these verses:

> For there is hope for a tree, if it is cut down, that it will sprout again, and that its shoots will not cease. Though its root grows old in the earth, and its stump dies in the ground, yet at the scent of water it will bud and put forth branches likes a young plant. But mortals die, and are laid low; humans expire, and where are they? (14:7–10).

Job frequently uses the dynamics of the earth as a symbol of a scarcely perceptible God, as this extraordinary passage illustrates:

> He it was who spread the North above the void, and poised the earth on nothingness. He fastens the waters in his clouds – the mists do not tear apart under their weight. He covers the face of the moon at the full, his mist he spreads over it. He has traced a ring on the surface of the waters, at the boundary between light and dark. The pillars of the heavens tremble ... With his power he calmed the sea ... His breath made the heavens luminous ... All this but skirts the ways he treads, a whispered echo is all that we hear of him. But who could comprehend the thunder of his power? (26:7–14).[30]

In Chapters 38 to 42 God purports to respond to Job's complaints, but the answers just don't address the issues that Job raises. The divine answer is that God's wisdom is found in his management of the universe. Despite all the paradoxes embedded in creation, the cosmos doesn't fall apart and return to chaos. Essentially, God tells Job that the task of humankind is to learn to live with reality and evil rather than try to explain it. As McKenzie puts it, 'the book of Job ends with the conviction that only faith makes evil tolerable, faith which brings insight through the experience of God which is within the reach of one who desires it'.[31]

Speaking in the whirlwind, God puts Job and all humankind in perspective. As Habel correctly points out, 'God virtually ignores humans in the larger scheme of things; there is nothing anthropocentric in this design of the cosmos.'[32] The God we meet in these chapters is not the pop-psychology God of 'healing' spiritualities, the psychobabble God of 'feeling good about yourself'. This is a God who begins by telling Job that he is an ignorant upstart who should mind his own business: 'Who is this obscuring my designs with his empty-headed words? Brace yourself like a fighter; now it is my turn to ask questions and yours to inform me' (38:2–3). This is the kind of robust, unsentimental, confrontational spirituality that seems to be peculiarly appropriate to our world. Humankind needs to know its minor and short-lived place in the greater scheme of things. God's challenge is to confront Job with the age and magnitude of the cosmos, and then to demand that Job know his significance in this context. This is exactly the conundrum that we face: who are we to be the ruination of the earth when we have been here for so short a time and are so insignificant? Who are we within the context of God's enormous creativity? Who are we to demand answers? Our task is to learn humility and to know our place.

We need to apply God's questions to Job to ourselves:

> Where were you when I laid the earth's foundations? Tell me, since you are so well informed! Who decided the dimensions of it, do you know? Or who stretched the measuring line across it? What supports its pillars at their bases? Who laid its cornerstone when all of the stars of the morning were singing with joy, and the Sons of God in chorus where chanting praise? Who pent up the sea behind closed doors when it leapt tumultuous out of the womb, when I wrapped it in a robe of mist and made black clouds its swaddling bands; when I

> marked the bounds it was not to cross and made it fast with a bolted gate? Come thus far, I said, and no further; here your proud waves shall break (38:4–11).

Job, and by implication, all humankind, is placed firmly in his place with a series of questions that provide our true context:

> Have you ever in your life given orders to the morning or sent the dawn to its post? … Have you ever journeyed all the way to the sources of the sea, or walked where the abyss is deepest? Can you fasten the harness of the Pleiades, or untie Orion's bands? Can you guide the morning star season by season and show the Bear and its cubs which way to go? (38:12, 16, 31–32).

As if that's not enough, God then moves on to the animal kingdom, with a whole series of questions about humankind's control over the fauna of the world. Then comes the punchline: 'Then Yahweh turned to Job, and he said: Is El Shaddai's opponent willing to give in? Has God's critic thought up an answer?' (40:1–2). Job is rendered speechless: 'My words have been frivolous: what can I reply? I had better lay my finger on my lips. I have spoken once … I will not speak again … I will add nothing' (40:30–5). God then refers to 'Behemoth' the hippopotamus and 'Leviathan' the whale. These enormously strong creatures place humankind in context; beside them we are weaklings. The modern tragedy is, of course, that because of our technology, these very animals have been driven close to extinction by our voracious lust to control the world, a desire often justified by whaling nations' specious 'cultural' reasons.

Job offers us a unique perspective on anthropocentrism and the real role of humankind. No other book in the Hebrew Scriptures has such a contemporary ring. Job's God is a God who makes sense in the world of the 21st century by placing humankind in perspective and highlighting our nothingness within the context of the cosmos. This is the kind of challenging, bracing God that contemporary spirituality needs to recover.

I will now turn to a treatment of the environment in the New Testament. The Christian Scriptures are a small collection of books, just a quarter the size of the Jewish Scriptures. The largest part of the New Testament is the four Gospels. The first thing that strikes me is how little the New Testament has to say about nature; as Moltmann says, 'the New Testament does not seem to add anything new to the understanding of the world as creation'.[33] So to discover the New Testament's attitudes, we must tackle the issue obliquely.

From the beginning of the Gospels it is clear that Jesus has a real affinity with 'wild places', and it is in these environments that he uncovers more and more about the meaning of his life. It is from the wilderness that the first proclamation of the 'good news' comes: 'A voice of one crying out in the wilderness: "Prepare the way of the Lord"' (Mark 1:3). It is to a wilderness area that Jesus goes to initiate his ministry, beginning with his baptism in the River Jordan. The Jordan runs through a narrow, arid, wild valley, and the site of the baptism was probably just south of the Sea of Galilee. The area is extremely hot in summer and even today it only supports a small population. The river carries a large amount of silt, so the water is not clear.

It was here that Jesus came to be baptised by his cousin, John the Baptist, a figure very much part of the Jewish prophetic tradition. 'And when Jesus had been baptized, just as he came up from the water, suddenly the heavens were opened to him and he saw the Spirit of God descending like a dove and alighting on him. And a voice from heaven said, "This is my son, the Beloved, with whom I am well pleased"' (Matthew 3:16–17).

This was immediately followed by Jesus' journey into the desert wilderness. He spent a period of prayer and fasting there, and was tested and tempted by Satan. Here he began the process of spiritual maturity. In the biblical tradition, the desert is the place where life is stripped right down to its essentials and where a primal encounter with God can occur, particularly in a crisis. For Jesus it served as an initiation to his public life.

Jesus then begins his ministry in Galilee, his home province. He preaches his best known sermon, the Beatitudes, far away from human habitation, on a mountain: 'Seeing the crowds he went up on the mountain, and when he sat down his disciples came to him. And he opened his mouth and taught them' (Matthew 5:1–2). In a variant reading, Luke's Gospel says, 'Now during those days he went out onto the mountain to pray; and he spent the night in prayer to God' (Luke 6:12), and that it was only after this experience that he preached the sermon on the mount – except Luke places it on a plain! There are many allusions to the natural world in Jesus' sayings, but they are particularly focused and relevant when he talks about human anxiety and suggests a way to deal with it. 'Look at the birds of the air; they neither sow nor reap nor gather into barns, and yet your heavenly Father feeds them … Consider the lilies of the field, how they grow; they neither toil nor spin, yet I tell you, even Solomon in all his glory was not clothed like one of these' (Matthew 6:26–30). A similar theme is taken up a little later in the same Gospel: 'Are not two sparrows sold for a penny? Yet not one of them will fall to the ground apart from your Father … So do not be afraid' (10:29–31).

All three Synoptic Gospels (Matthew, Mark and Luke) tell the story of Jesus calming the storm. In Mark's account this storm occurs at night. After a day of preaching to the crowds Jesus asks the disciples to sail him across to the eastern side of the Sea of Galilee:

> They took him with them in the boat just as he was. Other boats were with him. A great windstorm arose, and the waters beat into the

> boat, so that the boat was already being swamped. But he was in the stern, asleep on the cushion; and they woke him up and said to him, 'Teacher, do you not care that we are perishing?' He woke up and rebuked the wind, and said to the sea 'Peace, be still!' Then the wind ceased, and there was a dead calm (4:35–39).

There is a related story when Jesus walks on the water. Again he has been teaching the crowd and is exhausted. He clearly wants to get rid of his disciples, so he sends them by boat to Bethsaida in the northeast corner of the Sea of Galilee. He meanwhile 'went up on the mountain to pray' (Mark 6:45). The boat runs into a contrary wind, and:

> When he saw that they were straining at the oars ... he came toward them early in the morning, walking on the sea ... When they saw him walking on the sea, they thought it was a ghost and cried out; for they all saw him and were terrified. But immediately he spoke to them and said, 'Take heart, it is I; do not be afraid.' Then he got into the boat and the wind ceased. And they were utterly astounded (6: 47–51).

These two incidents are found in all Synoptics; clearly they were seen as significant, because they revealed Jesus' ability to influence the natural world and calm the elements.

However, these Gospel episodes have ambiguous connotations for the natural world. It seems Jesus can suspend the order of nature at will. Biblical theologian William Loader correctly points out that these actions 'subordinate the natural processes of the Earth to manipulation that benefits human beings. No harm is done, but the approach is symptomatic of a world view that can disregard natural processes.'[34] While not denying that miracles are possible and conceding that both stories remind us of the parting of the Red Sea and the crossing of the River Jordan in the Exodus of the Jews from Egypt, there is a tendency among some Christians to want to suspend the laws of nature and declare miracles which subordinate the natural world to the needs of the human; this essentially enhances anthropocentrism and trivialises the non-human world.

Even more environmentally problematic are a series of New Testament texts that discuss the end of the world with images of cosmic collapse and disintegration. An example of this kind of text is found in Mark 13. Jesus is speaking: 'There will be earthquakes in various places; there will be famines ... But in those days, after that suffering, the sun will be darkened and the moon will not give its light, and the stars will be falling from heaven, and the powers in the heavens will be shaken' (13:8, 24–25). These texts have been used by fundamentalists and some Evangelicals to justify treating the natural world as nothing more than a place of trial for humankind. One fundamentalist American web page puts it bluntly:

> Christianity claims that the universe is not eternal, but was created by God as a temporary abode to house God's spiritual creatures. After God's purposes are accomplished, He will destroy the entire universe in a cataclysmic apocalypse, and create a new universe with entirely different laws of physics. This universe is the best possible for the purpose for which it was created, which is a place in which spiritual beings can choose to love or reject God.[35]

It is this kind of crass literalism which the George W. Bush administration used as a reason to ignore global warming and concerns about the environment. At least in St Matthew's version of the end time, when Jesus will come to 'separate the sheep from the goats' (25:31–46), the grounds for judgment are a serious commitment to social justice and the service of others.

However, the apocalyptic world destruction scenario is only one of several used in the New Testament. In the Letter to the Romans (8:18–23), Paul paints a very different picture. In this fascinating but difficult text Paul links our fate to that of the whole of creation, and says that all of material reality is struggling through a birth process that will lead to 'the redemption of our bodies' (8:23). He sees the whole cosmos caught up in a desire-filled movement that will eventually lead to 'the glory about to be revealed' (8:18), with the word 'glory' here essentially referring to God. Paul says:

> For creation waits with eager longing for the revealing of the children of God; for the creation was subjected to futility, not of its own will but by the will of the one who subjected it, in hope that the creation itself will be set free from its bondage to decay and will obtain the freedom of the glory of the children of God. We know that the whole creation has been groaning in labour pains until now; and not only the creation, but we ourselves, who have the first fruits of the Spirit, groan inwardly while we wait for adoption, the redemption of our bodies (8:20–23).

Certainly these verses negate the earth being wiped out in a cataclysmic apocalypse, as they describe a scene where the whole of nature is engaged in the process of giving birth to something better. Some commentators argue that here Paul is laying the foundations for a theology of nature, or at least providing the basis for a more positive interpretation of the world.

But the situation is more complex, and the passage has been described as 'a particularly muddy watering hole' and 'frustratingly allusive'.[36] Paul was not a modern environmentalist; his primary preoccupation and focus was Christ. The Christ he experienced so vividly on the road to Damascus is the image of the unseen God whose glory shines forth 'in the face of Christ' (II Corinthians 4:4, 6). The story of nature is part of the story of Christ, but that is not Paul's primary concern. However, that doesn't mean creation has no significance. For Paul, Christ, 'the children of God' and creation are all intimately intertwined. What the text seems to be saying is that God has subjected creation 'to futility' and it has to pass through a birth-like process to come to a liberation that ultimately lies beyond the present world: 'Paul's narrative is … infused with ancient cosmological and mythological presuppositions that are radically different [from] the contemporary science that informs our understanding of the world.'[37] Paul remains anthropocentric, in that the liberation of humankind is the centre of the story and creation plays a secondary role.

So where does this leave us? Is the text useless from an environmental perspective? No, because it unequivocally links the fate of humankind to the liberation of creation. The material world is not merely an inert stage or backdrop against which the human drama is played out – it has an intrinsic purpose and it 'groans inwardly' until it reaches its fulfilment. God cares about creation because God will intervene to liberate and fulfil it. For Paul, both creation and humanity are caught up in a process that will lead to 'the redemption of our bodies'. He could just as easily have said 'the redemption of matter', because the Greek word translated as 'body' could also have been translated as 'flesh' or 'matter'. Paul believed, like most early Christians, that the end of the world was imminent, in the sense that it would quickly follow the death and resurrection of Christ. So for Paul, the process of the liberation of matter would be occurring soon, even perhaps within his lifetime.

In fact the failure of the end times to come in apostolic or sub-apostolic times led to a crisis in the early church. Today we have no such illusions: we know we are involved in a much more difficult and long-term process, and that we have no idea when the end of the world will occur. But what the text does tell us clearly is that humanity's fate and that of the rest of creation are inextricably bound together as the whole of reality longs for a liberation that only God can bring. And that is a positive basis for the beginnings of an environmental theology.

Another passage which is often quoted in the eco-theological context is Paul's Letter to the Colossians:

> Christ is the image of the invisible God, the first-born of all creation;
> for in him all things in heaven and on earth were created, things
> visible and invisible, whether thrones or dominations or rulers or
> powers – all things have been created through him and for him.
> He himself is before all things, and in him all things hold together
> (1:15–17).

This passage, which might have been an early Christian hymn used during baptisms, says that Christ is the medium through which creation occurs. He is a product of the invisible God's creativity and, as such, is an icon of God. The passage actually sets up a striking trinity: God–Christ–Creation. In my view this is probably the most positive text for an environmental theology in the New Testament: not only is Christ the mediator in the process of creating the world, but the cosmos is created 'for him'. That is, the material universe exists to glorify him and he is the personality through which 'all things hold together'. This text makes the incarnation the most natural of processes: Christ, the creator of matter, so values it that he enters into it in the most intimate way by sharing our humanity.

Paul goes on to say that it is in and through Christ that 'all things whether on earth or in heaven' can be reconciled 'in his fleshly body' (1:20, 22). The emphasis on the sheer materiality of Christ's humanity is significant. In his letters Paul constantly emphasises that God in Christ has entered radically into the human condition, so much so that he takes on our 'flesh'. In the Second Letter to the Corinthians Paul says that God 'made him [Jesus] to be sin who knew no sin' (5:21). The word 'sin' here doesn't primarily refer to moral failure, but to the fact that God in Jesus knew our weakness, vulnerability, illness, tiredness, frustration, fear and despair, and our unavoidable knowledge that we would all eventually die. He did not resile from anything that being human involved. He was born in a body the same as ours, his body was crucified, he rose in his body and ascended bodily into heaven. Paul is saying that the body is at the core of Christian faith. All of this means that matter really matters – so much so that it is in and through the flesh of Christ that we gain redemption and liberation.

In the Letter to the Colossians Paul is also absolutely unequivocal about the intimate interconnection between Christ and creation: 'all things in heaven and on earth' were created 'through him and for him' (1:16). The present tense that the text uses seems to suggest that Christ's creativity is a continuing process: 'in him all things hold together' (1:17). That is, Christ is involved in an ongoing relationship with the world. It is only through Christ that reconciliation is ultimately achieved: 'Through him God was pleased to reconcile to himself all things, whether on earth or in heaven' (1:20). In using the word 'reconciliation', Paul is referring to an ideal future in which the whole of creation works together for good.

The ethical consequences of this are staggering. It suggests that there is such an intimate link between Christ and the cosmos, they are so inseparable, that to destroy any part of the natural world is to destroy the image of Christ, who is himself the image of God. If we were to take this seriously it would impose a very severe limit on the moral right to use and abuse our environment. I will return to this issue in the last chapter.

While this is by no means a complete treatment of all the passages in the Bible that could be used to support an environmental theology, I think we have seen enough to arrive at some tentative conclusions.

First, the Bible is a mixed blessing for those seeking to build such a theology. It was written over at least a thousand years, and the books that make it up naturally reflect their time and cultural conditions. Christian teaching doesn't say that every word is literally dictated by God, but it does say that it is essentially God's word in human speech. So each writer reflects the human conditions of his own period. Modern environmental considerations were not a priority in the past, and it is only *per accidens* that there are any explicit references to environmental issues. The books that make up the Scriptures can certainly be read from an environmental perspective, as *The Earth Bible* suggests. Here I return to the comment of Glacken – that commentaries and interpretations of Scripture have become much more important than the actual biblical texts themselves.[38] As a result, those of us who seek to develop eco-justice principles can read the Bible in a way that makes sense for us today.

Second, this excursus tells us that the Bible will never be a sufficient source upon which to build an environmental theology. The Scriptures can provide some help, but in the end we will have to rely on our own creativity as we work within the Catholic-Christian tradition.

It is to that tradition that I will turn in the last two chapters. But before we do that we should meet some of the most important 'geologians', Christian thinkers who have attempted to develop a theology of the environment.

6 'Geologians'

Thomas Berry describes himself as a 'geologian' rather than a theologian.[1] While he has been enormously influential both inside and outside Catholicism, he is certainly not the first geologian in the Christian tradition. While Lyn White might want to blame Christianity for the environmentally destructive attitudes of Western culture, there have been many Christians who laid the foundations of an environmental ethic and spirituality centuries before scientists took up the cudgels on behalf of the natural world. These great figures were not 'environmentalists' or 'greens' in our sense; such categories had not been invented. They were simply Christians whose love of the natural world and all its creatures was an instinctive part of their spirituality and theology.

The best known is St Francis of Assisi (1181–1226). At the heart of his spirituality was a radical commitment to poverty and humility which overflowed into a passionate devotion to God and a love of nature. Many in his own time – and subsequently – have seen him as the most Christ-like Christian ever. He was utterly committed to following the poverty of Christ, the man who had nowhere to lay his head: 'Foxes have holes, and the birds of the air have nests; but the Son of Man has nowhere to lay his head' (Matthew 8:20). Francis' spirituality was not theoretical but lived.

His closeness to animals is often mentioned by his contemporaries; he saw every creature as a revelation of the nature of God.

In *The Life of Saint Francis*, his biographer, St Bonaventure, says that when Francis 'considered the primordial source of all things he was filled with an even more abundant piety, calling creatures no matter how small by the name of brother or sister because he knew that they had come from the same source as himself'.[2] Particularly striking was the fact that he was able to dispel natural fear and calm wild animals: 'His holiness seems to have somehow restored the atmosphere of the earthly paradise, in which man lived in friendship with nature.'[3] While Francis is sometimes appropriated by followers of New Age beliefs, he remained a loyal and orthodox Catholic throughout his life. Francis' intimacy with animals is vividly illustrated by his relationship with a giant feral wolf that had terrified the town of Gubbio, 30 kilometres north of Assisi. In the 12th century wolves were common right across Europe, and were feared and hunted. Francis eventually tamed the Gubbio wolf, and it came to lie at his feet and put its paw in his hand.

Spiritual theologian Evelyn Underhill notes that the ability to calm animals is common among mystics. She says that genuinely spiritual people discover an intimate contact with both nature and God. 'In the remaking of [the spiritual person's] consciousness which follows upon the "mystical awakening", the deep and primal life which he shares with all creation has been roused from its sleep. Hence the barrier between human and non-human life, which makes man a stranger on earth … is done away.'[4] Another example is the Irish monk and missionary St Columbanus (c.543–615), whose biographer, Jonas of Bobbio, says that Columbanus could influence wolves with his serenity. On one occasion 12 wolves surrounded him in attacking mode: 'He stood still and said "O God come to my aid. O Lord, hasten to help me". They [the wolves] came nearer and seized his clothing. As he stood firm they left him unterrified and wandered off into the woods.'[5]

At Easter time Christians sing Francis' wonderful hymn '*Cantico di fratre sole*' ('The Canticle of Brother Sun' or, in the translation of William Henry Draper, 'All Creatures of Our God and King'). It is a hymn in which the sun, moon, winds, clouds, stars, water, fire and the earth itself sing in praise of God. Based on the Psalms, it was written in Francis' Umbrian dialect during a period of acute illness six months before he died of tuberculosis on 3 October 1226, aged 45:

> All creatures of our God and King,
> lift up your voice and with us sing
> Alleluia, alleluia!
>
> Thou burning sun with golden beam,
> thou silver moon with softer gleam,
> O praise Him, O praise Him …
>
> Dear mother earth, who day by day
> Unfoldest blessings on our way,
> O praise Him, alleluia!
>
> The flowers and fruits that in thee grow,
> Let them His glory also show;
> O praise Him, O praise Him
>
> Alleluia, alleluia, alleluia.

The danger with Francis' mystical sensibility is that we tend to sentimentalise and secularise it, making him a kind of mawkish animal lover wandering the Umbrian hills mouthing pious, New Age clichés. However, Francis' care for the natural world was rooted in his radical commitment to Christ and Catholicism, and evidenced in his poverty, simplicity and understanding that every element of creation reveals the transforming presence of God. His disciple, Bonaventure, picks up this emphasis and says that 'every creature by its nature is a kind of effigy and likeness of the eternal Wisdom' and that everything in the world is ordered harmoniously according to 'artistic numbers', by which he could be referring to what we might call 'ecological interdependence'.[6]

Francis' approach was essentially spiritual and affective, but there were others in the Catholic tradition who took a more theological stance. One of the most interesting was St Irenaeus, Bishop of Lyons (c.130–c.200). His theology is quite different from the fall–redemption tradition inherited by Western religiosity (largely through Augustine). As Australian theologian Denis Minns points out, Irenaeus had a far less dark view of humankind and sin, and offered 'to those more used to a Catholicism overshadowed by the figure of St Augustine a remarkably fresh and different outlook'.[7] Irenaeus' theology was opposed to speculations which we loosely call Gnostic, against which his book *Adversus Haereses* (*Against the Heresies*) was directed. In reaction to Gnostic denials of the value of the material world, Irenaeus strongly emphasised the involvement of God in the creation of the cosmos. His opposition to Gnosticism led him to exalt the value of flesh and matter, which he said would be brought to its ultimate consummation at the end of the world, when all creatures would revert to a peaceful and mutually fulfilling co-existence.

Irenaeus was not alone. A similar theme was picked up by the Roman presbyter, theologian and anti-pope, Novatian (c.200–58). In *De Trinitate* he gives a detailed description of the natural world, emphasising the concordance between the air, earth and water. He sees God as the one who gives unity to creation:

> God, holding all things together, leaves nothing empty of himself … He is always present in his work, penetrating all things, moving all things, connecting in order to achieve concord between the

> discordant matter of all the elements, so that from the different elements, one world, both single and firm, should be forged by the harmony of the elements brought together.[8]

If it is God who creates the unity of all matter, then that matter must contain something of God and be somehow symbolic of an important aspect of God. While Novatian never loses his sense of God's transcendence, it is significant that in this early period of theological development God and the natural world are so intimately connected.

Irenaeus and Novatian's positive assessments of the world and the flesh were exceptional, and were pushed into the background in later Western Christian theology. The complete collapse of the Roman Empire in the West in the early 5th century and the chaos which followed the collapse of the Carolingian Empire in the 9th century led to a very negative view of both the natural world and humanity.

However, Celtic spirituality provides a striking exception. Here nature is central. However, while the Irish loved the world, they never romanticised it. Celtic spirituality accepts its beauty, mystery and productivity, as well as its capacity to terrify and destroy. The Irish saints lived in close contact with nature, experiencing 'the world of wildlife, trees, plants and forces of weather, the sea and the vast starry sky as manifestations of God's creative nature, a sacrament of divine presence' rather than as distractions from prayer and asceticism.[9] Many of the Irish hermits, monks and nuns were poets, who saw the world with the heightened, hypersensitive eye of the visionary.

Speaking about the hermits' poetry, Irish literary scholar Robin Flower comments that they brought into their natural environment:

> an eye washed miraculously clear by a continual spiritual exercise that they, first in Europe, had that strange vision of natural things in an almost unnatural purity ... Many of the most beautiful poems of the age were clearly born of these anchoritish conditions.[10]

Like St Francis, the Irish saints seem to have had a special love for animals, especially those that were hunted or endangered, like wolves and bears. We have already seen that St Columbanus could calm the wolves, and it was reported that he often wandered about in the wilderness calling the wild beasts and birds. They responded immediately and he stroked them with his hand. He often called squirrels down from the tree-tops and put them on his neck.

The Irish ascetics particularly loved isolated places that were difficult to access – mountain tops, islands – because they felt that they were places of clarity and vision. Climbing a mountain was itself a ritually purifying experience. One example is Skellig Michael, the hermitage built on the ledges of a rock rising 218 metres out of the Atlantic Ocean, 14 kilometres off the coast of Kerry. Founded in the early 9th century and abandoned in the late 12th century because of falling temperatures and increasing storms as the Little Ice Age took hold, the rock never supported more than a dozen hermits, and they lived a strict ascetic life. They faced fierce winds, rain, sun and ocean – the natural world in all its starkness, terror, beauty and transforming power. Living on their small, uneven terrace about 190 metres above sea level, the hermits co-existed with thousands of puffins and petrels flying to and from their nests. They saw the Atlantic in all its moods and colours below them, and experienced the hardness of the rock out of which their houses were built, as well as the flowers and soft moss on the sloping areas on which their tiny, vulnerable settlement was built.

Another pivotal element in Irish spirituality was *peregrinatio* – exile or pilgrimage. The motivation was to seek God. The Irish monks were very attached to home and clan, but many also had a kind of restless energy and a spirit of penance that motivated them to leave Ireland to seek God through the difficult life of a recluse, or the lonely life of a stranger in a foreign land. The idea was to go to a place where you were vulnerable and powerless and therefore totally dependent upon God. So Irish monks became great travellers. They went north on dangerous journeys across the North Atlantic to the Faroe Islands and Iceland – they were there several hundred years before the Vikings arrived. St Brendan of Clonfert 'the Navigator' (484–577) also apparently sailed north, probably visiting the Orkney and Hebrides Islands. Some monks may have even crossed the Atlantic to reach North America. There is a wonderful medieval story about Brendan and his party when they were at sea: Easter Sunday came and they were looking for somewhere to celebrate Mass. Suddenly a tiny island came into view. They landed and Brendan celebrated Mass:

> The brethren then took out some uncooked meat and fish … and put a cauldron on a fire to cook them. After … the cauldron began to boil, the island moved about like a wave; whereupon they all rushed toward the boat, and implored the protection of their father. 'Fear not, children,' said the saint, 'for God last night revealed to me the mystery of all this; it was not an island … but a fish, the largest of all that swim in the ocean.'[11]

They had been on the back of a whale, and for the next 7 years it appeared every Easter so they could celebrate Mass on its back. The Irish monks also went to the Continent, where they shared their learning with the pagans and half-converted Christians in what today are central and northern England, northeastern France, western Germany, Switzerland and northern Italy.

The extraordinary vitality of this Irish religious movement had a deep impact on continental Catholicism. But the brutal conditions of 9th and early 10th century life meant that many of the complex riches of patristic theology and Irish spirituality were lost as a kind of unworldliness crept into faith and spirituality; holiness became identified with withdrawal from a corrupt world. This attitude remained influential into the Middle Ages. However, there were thinkers who broke out of this pessimistic mindset, as Austrian historian Friedrich Heer comments:

> Everywhere in Europe during the twelfth century ... hearts and minds were waking to a new appreciation of the world, its color, its vastness, its perils and its beauty. There was curiosity about the world in all its aspects ... the world of the cosmos and the world of nature.[12]

Heer also mentions the scientific speculations of several scholars (most of whom became bishops) of the school attached to the newly built cathedral of Chartres, southwest of Paris. The scholars of Chartres had confidence in the power of logic and a fascination with numbers. They argued that there was *intellectibilitas*, something of the divine which could be perceived in everything: humankind, nature, the cosmos. Nature was seen as a cosmic power, the mother of all reality. Unfortunately, this strain of theological thought didn't last.

In the 13th and 14th centuries, natural science had, at best, an ambiguous position in intellectual life. Despite the fact that the German Dominican St Albert the Great (c.1200–80) was interested in both astronomy and Greco-Roman classical ideas of science and the environment, and that Oxford philosopher Roger Bacon (c.1214–92) engaged in the empirical investigation of nature, science continued to be closely linked with speculative areas such as alchemy, astrology, magic and sorcery. As Heer notes, 'Theology frowned on any attempt at reaching into the secrets of nature, an unlawful invasion of the sacred womb of the Great Mother.'[13]

In contrast to this negative attitude towards science, another more positive stream continued the tradition of earlier thinkers. Another of my 'geologians', Matthew Fox, has shown that the greatest of medieval theologians, Thomas Aquinas, understood the cosmos to be a form of revelation of God parallel to biblical revelation: 'Sacred writings are bound in two volumes – that of creation and that of the Holy Scriptures ... Visible creatures are like a book in which we read the knowledge of God.'[14] Aquinas, who lived a couple of generations after St Francis, takes up these questions in his theology of creation, in which he says that 'every creature ... *demonstrat personam Patris*' – 'shows forth the personality of [God] the Father'. He sees creation as God the Son's creativity, giving form and shape to creatures, and the ordered nature of reality as embodying the love of the Holy Spirit for the world.[15] Aquinas regularly returns to the notion of God as the *artifex* (artist or craftsperson) of the entire world: 'God acts just like an artist in creating things working from an idea conceived in the mind and from a love which bends the will to that work.'[16]

Aquinas also uses this image in Book I of the *Summa Contra Gentiles*: 'All artists love what they give birth to – parents love their children; poets love their poems; craftspeople love their handiwork. How then could God hate a single thing since God is the cause of everything?'[17] He is arguing, in reverse, that every aspect of creation conjures up and makes present something of the creative power of God. He makes this clear when he says *in creaturis omnibus invenitur representationem Trinitatis per modum vestigii*, which Timothy McDermott succinctly translates as 'all creatures bear traces of the Trinity'.[18] Aquinas is arguing that the whole of the natural world is an icon or sacrament of the presence of God: 'Since God is the universal cause of the whole of being … it must be that wherever being is found, the divine presence is also there.'[19]

Thus Catholicism has an articulated theological understanding that the cosmos and the natural world sacramentally and iconographically represent and make present the creativity of God. In other words, nature is such a powerful symbol or icon that the perceptive, spiritual person can intuit a deeper resonance that points beyond nature to a kind of transcendent but real presence that many call 'God'.

Something of this tradition is also found among medieval mystics. One example is the abbess St Hildegarde of Bingen (1098–1179). She typifies the tradition in that she has an instinctive feel for the natural world that is nevertheless informed by a solid spiritual and theological education. A more contemporary example is the English Jesuit poet Gerard Manley Hopkins (1844–89). In 'God's Grandeur' Hopkins expresses his profound conviction that God is revealed through the world, but that humankind has lost contact with nature because 'all is seared with trade'.

Hopkins had a deep affinity with nature and a profound respect for the natural world. For him every single thing was necessarily unique; no one being, even of the same species or genus, is exactly the same as another. Every individual reality in nature 'radiates back a meaning' that is unique to the intuitive and sympathetic observer.[20] This radiation is what Hopkins calls 'inscape': 'Inscape … is the expression of the inner core of individuality, perceived in moments of insight by an onlooker who is in full harmony with the being he is observing.'[21] The notion of inscape is original to Hopkins, but he had a real affinity with the thought of medieval Franciscan John Duns Scotus (c.1265–1308). Scotus has a unique doctrine of individuation: for him individuality was the ultimate inner core of each separate being, what he called the *haecceitas*, the 'thisness' of each particular being. It is that which makes a being this specific one and no other. Just as all humans are different, so all individuals of whatever species are different from each other. Hopkins found support in Scotus' theory for his own notion of inscape. Other elements in Scotus' thought attracted Hopkins, especially the notion that the incarnation was necessary because God had to be made available to the human senses. This in turn postulated that the material world was a symbol of God, not divorced from Him, a view to which Hopkins wholeheartedly subscribed emotionally, even if he needed the authority of Scotus to feel easy with it.[22]

Hopkins' notion of inscape is two-sided: it involves our sympathetic and committed gaze at a being, or place in nature, or living, sentient reality and, in response, our receiving the communication of the unique individuality of the being that we are contemplating. Implicit in that perception of individuality is the possibility of discerning the transcendent. By this I mean that in the very process of recognising the unique individuality of each being, the spiritually perceptive person intuits a kind of transcendent presence that stands behind it. Literary critic George Steiner says that behind every genuine personal experience of beauty in nature and art, and every meaningful and loving encounter with others, there lurks what he calls a 'real presence' – a personal and sacred presence, a non-empirical dimension – that gives meaning to and provides foundations for these experiences. This view draws on the Catholic doctrine of the presence of Christ in the Eucharist.[23] To be able to make this connection, the creative imagination of the observer must be active.

In this sense imagination is really the faculty of intuition. It is what Hopkins' contemporary, the English theologian and cardinal John Henry Newman (1801–90), called the 'illative sense', the ability to make the oblique connections which help to make sense of apparently unconnected realities.[24] So when someone 'inscapes' a reality, a more profound meaning is revealed. When we inscape a reality, or activate our illative sense, we perceive or intuit in each individual being that we encounter the sense of a presence that transcends that individual being. We need to develop this side of ourselves if we are to discover the transcendent in the natural world.

My next 'geologian' was also a Jesuit: the French priest and palaeontologist Pierre Teilhard de Chardin (1881–1955). Nowadays he has slipped into an undeserved anonymity. In the years around the Second Vatican Council (1962–65) his ideas were highly influential. He is certainly one of the most important Catholic thinkers of the 20th century.[25]

Teilhard was influenced by French philosopher Henri Bergson (1859–1941). Bergson was dissatisfied with the materialism of 19th century science, but he didn't want to lose the insights that came from empiricism, especially those that came from the theory of evolution. His aim was to place science within a broader context than the material, and his genius lay in his ability to apply the findings of evolutionary science to his metaphysical, almost theological, search for an understanding of the inner core of reality. Essentially, Bergson's philosophy attempted to articulate the meta-dynamic that underlies and sustains everything. This meta-dynamic expresses itself through what Bergson calls an *élan vital*, a vital impulse, a profound life drive which motivates the struggle of each individual being for survival and wellbeing. This impulse is the undifferentiated life-force which impels evolution onwards. It 'is a continuous process in which the original drive divides itself into a growing variety of forms, but retains a basic direction'.[26] What Bergson did was give a form of intentionality and direction to the evolutionary process.

Influenced by Bergson and the Catholic philosopher Maurice Blondel, Teilhard's thought moved towards the poetic and theological, rather than towards the strictly philosophical. Nevertheless he was also a traditional scientist, deeply interested in the origins of the world around him. It was his broad scientific knowledge of geology, palaeontology and evolution that led him to theorise an all-encompassing dynamic which embraced the whole of world history. In this process he reintegrated those realities that he saw as most separate in our dualistic world view: matter and spirit. His major contribution to environmental theology is his notion that matter itself is impregnated with a purposive energy that constantly evolves towards ever-greater complexity. For Teilhard, matter is not merely a static, inert mass; it is a living reality in constant evolution. As such, it is the indispensable precondition for spirit.

Teilhard held that there are several critical stages matter must pass through on its journey towards complexity. The first is when inorganic matter begins its evolutionary development towards the emergence of life. The second is the actual beginning of life, which, in turn, has evolved into the many species which have inhabited the universe. The third is the emergence of mind, the critical shift from the dominance of instinct to the dominance of consciousness in humankind. As Emile Rideau, in his guide to Teilhard's thought, says:

> Man is not a fortuitous or accidental phenomenon, but one obviously prepared and, in a sense, willed – evolution's growing success. Far from being an anomalous aberration, he is the key, the head, the growing point of the universe ... 'evolution become reflexively conscious of itself' ... the noosphere is grafted once and for all on the biosphere.[27]

Teilhard refers to consciousness as 'noosphere': 'Man is only the beginning, within the limits of our experience, who not only knows, but knows that he knows.'[28] It is in humankind that evolution becomes truly personal.

Teilhard says that we are still in the process of evolution towards higher consciousness. The ultimate development of this is the achievement of the spiritual convergence of individuality, personal freedom and inter-communion on a cosmic scale: what he calls Omega Point. Omega Point is the place at which everything is brought into union with God. Teilhard writes: 'But instead of a vague centre of convergence envisaged as the ultimate end of this process of evolution [we have] the personal and defined reality of the Word Incarnate.'[29]

A key point for Teilhard is that all matter contains within itself the potential for spirituality. Thus he moves from physics through metaphysics to mysticism. In 'The Spiritual Power of Matter' he suggests that in order to perceive the spirituality of matter, one must undergo a real conversion:

> Never say, then, as some say: 'The kingdom of matter is worn out, matter is dead': till the end of time matter will always remain young, exuberant, sparkling, new-born for those who are willing. Never say 'Matter is accursed, matter is evil' … Son of man, bathe yourself in the ocean of matter; plunge into it where it is deepest and most violent; struggle with its currents and drink of its waters. For it cradled you long ago in your pre-conscious existence; and it is the ocean that will raise you up to God.[30]

This is the absolute antithesis of a dualistic understanding of reality. It is more integrated than traditional theology and more open to the scientific view of the world which so dominates our contemporary consciousness.

The work that best represents his spiritual vision is *The Divine Milieu*, published in French in 1957.[31] By seeing the world as a 'divine *milieu*' (in this context *milieu* is best translated as environment), Teilhard refocuses theology on the temporal processes of this world. He shifts our attention from eternity to time, from heaven to earth. He makes it possible for us to think about reality in a different way. This is not to pretend that there are no difficulties in Teilhard's vision. For me the greatest difficulty lies in the integration of his ideas about the theology of Christ. For Teilhard, all of reality is ultimately summed up in the 'cosmic Christ'. But just how the cosmic Christ is related to the evolution of matter is not clear. There is a sense in which his views reflect, as Berry says, the piety of the bourgeois French Catholicism of his time. This is not to take away from Teilhard's achievement: his influence on contemporary Catholicism and modern theology is widespread and profound.

In a way Thomas Berry is Teilhard's successor. He was a cultural historian and anthropologist of vast erudition, a genuine polymath. He has only gradually become known outside a small coterie of readers and thinkers in the United States. After a series of university appointments and running his own Riverdale Center for Religious Research, Berry decided to live his last years in the place of his birth: near Greensboro, North Carolina. He died there on 1 June 2009, aged 95.

He began publishing his ideas in the 1970s in the periodical *Cross Currents*, and in the Riverdale Papers. His first books (*Religions of India* and *Buddhism* and *Five Oriental Philosophies*) were published in the late 1960s.[32] His first work on the environment was *The Dream of the Earth* (1988). In 1992 he published, with Brian Swimme, *The Universe Story*, and in 1999 he published his most comprehensive book, *The Great Work*.[33] Every culture, he says, produces a 'great work', an overarching vision 'that gives shape and meaning to life by relating the human venture to the larger destinies of the universe'.[34]

Berry was born into a Catholic family in 1914 in the southern Appalachians. The determining element in his early life was his experience of the natural world; from his early childhood he was antagonistic to mechanistic views of existence. He joined the semi-enclosed Passionist order at the age of 20. As a student there he began to read the Chinese, Hindu and Buddhist classics. Much later he learned to read classical

Chinese and Sanskrit. He was ordained a priest in 1942. He completed a doctorate on the Italian philosopher Giovanni Battista Vico's philosophy at Washington's Catholic University of America in the late 1940s. Vico (1668–1744) sees history as a series of major periods, all very different from each other, that are connected by periods of transition that are characterised by gradual disintegration, then complete collapse.

Berry takes this formula and distinguishes four major cultural periods. The first is the tribal–shamanic period, which lasted until the second millennium BC. This was followed by traditional, classical civilisations that lasted in Europe and elsewhere – China and India, for instance – until the late 18th century. They were followed by the scientific–technological era of the 19th and 20th centuries, first in Europe and then in Asia. Berry says we are now moving through a difficult transition phase and into what he calls the Ecozoic period. He argues that we need to develop a new underpinning story, one that emphasises our intimate and interdependent relationship with the natural world.

It was Teilhard who showed Berry that a Christian need not be alienated from the natural world. Berry says that the 1962 publication of Rachel Carson's *Silent Spring* 'touched something deep in my thinking'.[35] He also maintained an interest in anthropology, especially in the Plains Indians of North America, and more broadly in North American Indigenous religion.

He describes himself:

> as a student of cultural history. I am primarily an historian. What I have to say are the probings of an historian into human affairs in a somewhat comprehensive context. During my university studies I sought to understand the unity and differentiation of human cultures and the dynamism that shaped their sense of reality and value ... The more I gave to the study of the human venture, the more clearly I saw the need to go back to the dynamics of life itself. I was progressively

> led back to … the study of the earth community, including its geological and biological as well as its human components. I call myself a geologian.[36]

This is reflected in *The Universe Story*, which is really a brief history of the cosmos. During the 1960s and 1970s Berry became increasingly concerned about the natural world. He told me that the fuel crisis and the escalating devastation of the world increased his awareness 'that the earth was troubled deeply in its very structure'. Over the last four decades of his life the natural world became the primary focus of his thought.

Fame came to Berry late in life. Had he not been a prophet and thinker he may have been called 'elderly', and, like most others of his age, relegated to irrelevance. He claims that one thing the modern world needs to recover is the tradition of respecting our 'elders', those wise and experienced men and women who interpret the world and give guidance to younger people based on their long experience of life – the ability to critique reality, he says, is especially important in our time, when so much change has occurred.

He says the key role of religion is to provide us with an interpretive pattern, a way of making sense of ourselves, the world and the cosmos. He believes that contemporary religion has failed us. He says that there are three central elements that make up contemporary history: (1) the devastation of the earth; (2) the incompetence of religion and cultural traditions to deal with this devastation; and (3) the rise of a new ecological vision of the universe. He says: 'The greatest failure of Christianity in the total course of its history is its inability to deal with the devastation of the planet.' He points out that Christians are sensitive to suicide, homicide and genocide, 'but we commit biocide (the killing of the life systems of the planet) and geocide (the killing of the planet itself) and we have no morality to deal with it'. Significantly, he notes that English lacks words to describe environmental destruction, and thus needs to invent neologisms – such as biocide and geocide – to describe it. Berry cites the number of papal statements on social and moral questions, but points to the lack of serious engagement with ecological questions; Benedict XVI seems to be beginning to remedy this. Berry says that 'religion is absorbed with the pathos of the human' and that this anthropocentrism is the dark side of biblical religion: 'there is an inherent tendency in biblical religion toward alienation from the natural world'. He claims that even the creed itself is unbalanced: it mentions the Creator–God right at the beginning but then goes on to focus almost exclusively on Christ, redemption and the church.

Christianity is a profoundly historical religion. Biblical history has a beginning (creation) and an end (the day of judgment). This gives the Western cultural tradition a linear notion of history rather than the cyclical one which is characteristic of most other great religions. And Christian thinking suffers from historical amnesia. It is fixated on what the Germans call *Heiligeschichte* – Holy History, or the history of salvation as recorded in the Bible and the history of the church – and lacks a sense of the broader history of the world.

Berry argues that the result of this historical amnesia is that those of us who live in the Western 'biblical–classical tradition' find it very difficult to adopt a non-domineering relationship with the planet. We act as though the whole world and all its processes were created, and evolved, exclusively for us. This has had very destructive consequences:

> Throughout the entire course of (Christian) tradition, the autism has deepened with our mechanism, our political nationalism, our economic industrialism ... [We need] a new interpretation of the Western historical process ... The only suitable interpretation of Western history seems to be the ironic interpretation. This irony is best expressed, perhaps, by the observation that our supposed

> progress toward an ever-improving human situation is bringing us to wasteworld rather than wonderworld.[37]

Berry says that the danger is that our theological view of God is incomplete if we do not take seriously the fact that it was God who created the world, and that therefore God is profoundly related to it: 'if we lose the splendour of the natural world, we lose our true sense of the divine'. The only solution, he says, is to shift Christian faith out of its sin–redemption fixation into a new environmentalist context.

He says that secularism and modern science have also failed to help us interpret the significance and meaning of the natural world:

> The supreme irony is that just at this moment, when such expansive horizons of past, present and future have opened up, mankind is suddenly precipitated into an inner anxiety and even into a foreboding about ourselves and the meaning of it all. Unable to bear such awesome meaning, men reject themselves as part of the world around them ... While primitive people ... had a sense of the magnitude of human existence ... we are beset by a sense of confusion and alienation ... Contemporary men have no spiritual vision adequate for these new magnitudes of existence ... To create such a skill, to teach such a discipline, are the primary tasks of contemporary spirituality.[38]

His interpretation of spirituality begins with the world itself, and he says that everything must be judged in the light of our relationship with it. He shifts the focus of modern spirituality outwards, away from its anthropocentric preoccupation with the human and psychological. He says: 'All human institutions, professions, programs and activities must now be judged primarily by the extent to which they inhibit, ignore or foster a mutually enhancing human–earth relationship.' Again he stresses that if we lose our sense of rapport with the world, we lose our sense of the divine, because it is the cosmos that stimulates and nourishes our imagination, and any diminishing of our sense of the natural world stifles our imaginative faculty.

The close connection between imagination and spirituality is further emphasised by Berry's definition of religion:

> Religion is poetry, or it is nothing! How can a person be religious without being poetic? Certainly, God is a poet – it is God who made rainbows and butterflies and flowers. It is the most absurd thing in the world to think of dealing with religion in any other way than poetry and music ... Take John of the Cross – all the great mystics have been poets. You cannot do it any other way.

I shall never forget the passion with which Berry uttered these words to me; they are an expression of the core of his religious conviction.

Berry says that genuine religion requires what he calls the 'Christ presence'. Ancient peoples always recognised the need for a person who could go 'beyond' the mundane into the spiritual world. In indigenous cultures, the person who did this was the shaman. Among Native Americans, for instance, the shaman goes into the spirit world and brings back guidance, healing and energy for the tribe. Berry points out the shamanic aspects of the Christ presence: Christ is a guiding, healing and empowering presence who comes to us from the transcendent world in human form. He argues that all peoples have the concept of saviour personalities who bear a divine presence. In the New Testament this presence is borne by Jesus. Berry emphasises that the historical realism of the incarnation is very important in the Christian and Western tradition: it is important that the man Jesus, the one who became the Christ presence, was a real, living, historical person.

According to Berry, we also need to develop a new cosmology to interact with theology. He says that four elements are necessary: first, Christian theology must take the world seriously; second, theology needs a larger concept of time; third, religion must recognise that life is an interactive biological continuum; and fourth, we need a new creation myth.

Taking the world seriously means that human beings have to see themselves in perspective: human history is minuscule in comparison with geological and biological history. The processes of the cosmos are 15 billion years old, and earth has been developing for about 4 billion years, but *Homo sapiens* has been on earth for just over 100,000 years. For Berry the starting point of theology must be the cosmos: 'We now experience ourselves as the latest arrivals, after some 15 billion years of universe history and after some 4.5 billion years of earth history. Here we are, born yesterday.'[39]

Next, Berry moves away from the traditional biblical and Western concept of time, in which God begins the process of directly creating the world on the first day and ends it on the last day. In this interpretation, historical time has a beginning and an end, and that makes it manageable for our minds. Biblical history says that God intervenes at specific times and in specific ways to guide the process of salvation, and that the peak moment of this was the life of Christ. In contrast, earth-time is, as noted above, about 4 billion years and cosmic-time is about 15 billion years. It is hard for us to conceive of a God who stands statically outside this enormous temporal range. Also, today the cosmos is understood as a dynamic, ongoing energy event, rather than something that was suddenly created at a specific point in time. The challenge for theology is to move towards discovering God within this process rather than positing the divine outside it.

Third, Berry's new cosmology demands that theology take biology, geology and theoretical physics seriously. In this he follows Teilhard. Berry sees life as an interactive continuum from the most primitive forms to the most highly evolved and complex – us! Human beings are not separate creatures whose lives and value somehow stand outside the rest of creation. We are a constituent part of it:

> Our bonding with the larger dimensions of the universe comes about primarily through our genetic coding. It is the determining factor. It provides constant guidance in the organic functioning that takes place in all our sense functions; in our capacity for transforming food into energy; in our thought, imagination and emotional life. Our genetic coding enables us to experience joy and sorrow ... It provides the ability to think, speak and create. It establishes the context of our relationship with the divine.[40]

Berry emphasises that all life is profoundly related genetically. It is the genes that pass on the ever-increasing complexity of life. He insists that we must rediscover our genetic coding, which will lead us back to our foundations in the processes of organic life. The realisation of our genetic relatedness with everything else will mean that, unless we are prepared to destroy something of ourselves, we must work to preserve our common life.

Fourth, the new cosmology demands a new myth – or as Berry calls it, a new 'story'. He says that creation myths are a fundamental substratum for all cultures and guide their historical evolution. These stories tell us where we came from and where we are going and define the nature of our relationship to the transcendent. The Genesis account of creation has provided Judeo-Christian culture with a monotheistic God; it defines the nature of humankind and our relationship to God and to nature. Genesis also explains the origin of sin and evil and the ambivalent attitude of human beings to their earthly lot: basically, we 'want to be like God, knowing good and evil' (Genesis 3:5), and we do this by breaking our ties to the earth. Creation myths define cultures and, in the process, divide cultures from each other. As long as religious traditions insist on their own myths, they will emphasise their differences from each other.

Berry says that a new situation has arisen in the world: for the first time we face the possibility of a shared origin myth because the scientific myth of creation has taken over from the biblical myth. He argues that science gives contemporary culture a common story of origin, a creation myth that is universal. A story that begins with the Big Bang and the primal atoms and moves through the whole evolution of life is a story that can unite us. We especially need this scientific myth as we face environmental problems that are worldwide. This doesn't mean that science will replace religion and faith, but it does mean that we have a kind of broad ecumenical ground upon which we can talk to each other. Perhaps on the basis of this we can go further to discover what the great religious traditions have in common in order to build structures of justice and peace.

In *The Universe Story*, Berry and Swimme, a mathematical cosmologist, attempt the ambitious task of sketching out the contemporary story of creation. Berry argues that we are now at the end of the Cenozoic period, the last 65 million years of geological time. Berry calls this the 'lyric period of the evolutionary process, the period of the flowers, the birds and the mammals'.[41] We are now at the terminal phase of the Cenozoic as our industrial economy closes down more and more of the world's living systems. 'An overlay of mechanistic patterns has been imposed on the biological functioning of the living world', although most people are only dimly aware of the terrible things that are happening to the planet.[42] Berry uses the word 'autistic' to describe modern humankind; he asserts that we are so self-obsessed, so myopically focused on economic, financial and technological developments that our interaction with the world around us is severely affected. We have withdrawn from reality and so closed ourselves to the natural world that we only see it as an object for our use.

We are now entering what Berry and Swimme call the Ecozoic period, a time when human beings realise their profound unity and connection with the whole of creation, when we jettison our abusive attitudes and realise that the individual subjectivity of all living things must be protected: 'That the universe is a communion of subjects rather than a collection of objects is the central commitment of the Ecozoic.'[43] Berry and Swimme argue that in order to achieve this we need to develop an integrated vision that will draw the whole of reality together. Unfortunately, the diversity and specialisation of scientific knowledge results in a very fragmented vision of reality. In order to draw the story together an imaginative vision that has shamanic overtones is needed. They say, 'The next phase of scientific development will require above all the insight of shamanic powers, for only with these powers can the story of the universe be told in the true depth of its meaning.'[44] Here the shaman is the wise one who can not only see the whole picture, but is also capable of expressing the underlying meaning, the spirit at the core of the vision:

> Both a competence and a willingness to engage in the immense effort needed to tell the story is what is now needed, especially if this story is to become what it should be: the comprehensive context of our human understanding of ourselves. This is a task that requires imaginative power as well as intellectual understanding. It also requires that we return to the mythic origins of the scientific venture.[45]

Berry and Swimme intend *The Universe Story* to be an attempt to construct something of this shamanic vision by telling the all-embracing mythic story of the universe. Berry clearly distinguishes the shamanic personality from 'the role of the philosopher, priest, prophet, or professor'.[46] The former draws wisdom from the world and interprets it in a comprehensive way, whereas people in the other roles tend towards purely rational explanations.

Berry's vision is not only theoretical; it is also practical. He points out that the earth economy pays an enormous price to support today's human economy. The absurdity is that the gross domestic product increases while the gross earth product decreases. Education, he says, also has to move further away from a dichotomised focus on specific issues and subjects and towards an integrated understanding of the story of the cosmos. We must understand that all things have subjective, individual value; they are not objects to support human consumption. The destructive myth of development must be replaced by the overarching myth of the story of the world. Both law and morality must recognise biocide and geocide as sins, social evils and crimes, just like homicide and genocide. Those who break the law and commit the sin of destroying the earth and its living forms must be held both morally and legally responsible. Moral theology must come to recognise that it is a sin, in the literal sense, to destroy the earth, no matter what the purpose.

We also need to develop an 'earth-centred' language. Just as feminists realised that patriarchal language is a means of oppression, so Berry says that we need to become sensitive 'to the non-human languages of the surrounding world'. It is already clear that animals communicate in complex ways. Berry takes this further:

> We are learning the mountain language, river language, tree language, the languages of the birds and all the animals and insects, as well as the language of the stars in the heavens. This capacity for understanding and communicating through these languages, until now enjoyed only by our poets and mystics, is of immense significance since so much of life is lived in association with the other beings of the universe.[47]

Berry says that this will involve the need to shift from the use of scientific, literal, objective language 'to a multivalent language much richer in its symbolic and poetic qualities'.[48]

Finally, Berry emphasises that the creativity of the earth only exists because of a delicate balance of forces:

> The universe is shaped in its larger dimensions from its earliest instance of emergence. The expansive original energy keeps the universe from collapsing, while the gravitational attraction holds the component parts together and enables the universe to blossom. Thus the curvature of the universe is sufficiently closed to maintain a coherence of its various components and sufficiently open to allow for a continued creativity.[49]

It is as a result of these forces that life has been able to emerge. The industrial age has profoundly upset and endangered this balance. The Ecozoic era will have to be the time when human activities are brought back into alignment with the earth's needs.

While Berry does not explicitly reflect upon the consequences if we fail to do this, it is quite clear that he thinks that if things do not change radically it will be the end of humankind as we know it today. Without the revelation of the image of God in the world of nature, it will be almost impossible for us to discover genuine religion and spirituality. Without the beauty of the world, the search for God will become meaningless. For when the glory and order of the world are distorted or destroyed, our chances of discovering the fundamental revelation of God are swept away. If we can find no image of God in the cosmos, we will never be able to discover it in ourselves – or anywhere else. The question is: is it already too late to stop the damage that the industrialisation of the world has brought about? Certainly not, if Thomas Berry has any say in it.

My next two 'geologians', Matthew Fox and Sean McDonagh, have both been deeply influenced by Berry, although their thought has moved in different directions that are complementary to his.

Fox was born in 1940 and grew up in Madison, Wisconsin, among 'the farmlands and lakes'. He joined the Dominicans at the age of 19 and studied theology in Chicago and the Institut Catholique in Paris. The most important of his books are *Original Blessing* (1981) and *The Coming of the Cosmic Christ* (1988).[50]

At the heart of Fox's theology is creation spirituality. He claims that this is the most ancient religious tradition to be found in the Bible, but that it also goes back beyond biblical times to the aboriginal religions of the world. Creation spirituality celebrates goodness and compassion. Fox says that the divine is inherent in the cosmos and especially in the human species, and it always seeks expression through art and mysticism. Because everyone is at heart an artist and mystic and can give expression to this, Fox maintains that creation spirituality is non-elitist, optimistic, and feminist. Central to Fox's thought is his notion of original blessing, which stands in contrast to traditional Christian theology's emphasis on original sin. Fox argues that the cosmos has been blessing humankind since its formation billions of years ago:

> It has made decisions on our behalf, decisions about the rate of expansion of the fireball and decisions about the temperature of the fireball, decisions about supernova explosions that gave birth to the elements of our body, decisions that allowed the sun, the earth, the rocks and the water to evolve. When we look back on it as scientists are doing today, we realize the universe has intended us and this is a blessing.[51]

For Fox, original blessing is ancient; original sin is recent, only going back to the theology of Augustine. Fox maintains that the notion of sin is very anthropocentric, and is only as old as the human race. The theology of original sin, which is not found in the Bible, feeds on human fears, and leads to the introspective conscience and to concern about personal salvation. The theology of original sin supports dualism, and the patriarchal church's control of personal morality. In contrast, he says, Jesus is a prophet of compassion. Fox quotes the beatitude 'Be compassionate as the Creator in heaven is compassionate' (Luke 6:36). He argues that in the gospels Jesus is not a theologian, but a cosmological storyteller and a prophet who spoke the truth and tried to liberate others from religious law and custom and ultimately death. He also notes that the New Testament and early Christians never thought of Christ in terms of personal salvation: 'They celebrate what they call theosis, the divinizing of the universe and they don't get stuck on the introspective conscience of the human.'

Fox is particularly scathing about contemporary fundamentalism, which he sees as a crude offshoot of Augustinian theology. He says that fundamentalism's 'Jesusolatry' is so extreme as to be heretical. An excessive focus on the man Jesus means that many people have lost the sense of God as Creator. This is why fundamentalists are so indifferent to the destruction of the environment, he claims. They have also lost a sense of the role of the Holy Spirit, 'which is the spirit of the Cosmic Christ'. In contrast to both fundamentalism and conventional church theology, Fox has attempted to articulate a broad cosmic spirituality that gives a context to contemporary environmentalism. While Fox's own spiritual foundations are in the medieval Christian mystical tradition, he stresses that deep ecumenism demands that all the mystical traditions of the world must be brought to bear on the salvation of the cosmos.

Sadly, in 1993 Matthew Fox was expelled from the Dominican order under orders from the Vatican.[52] This is deeply disturbing, and came at a time when the Catholic Church most needed creative thinkers in environmental theology. A passionate man, Fox had never adopted a cautious approach towards church authority and his theology upset fundamentalist Catholics. But it was his enormous popularity in the English-speaking world, both Catholic and non-Catholic, that probably tipped the scales against him. He didn't win many friends in high ecclesiastical places in August 1988 with his essay 'Is the Catholic Church Today a Dysfunctional Family?'[53] In it Fox describes the church as a maladjusted, addictive family led by an authoritarian, sadomasochistic and psychologically disturbed hierarchy. The Vatican, he argues, is a dysfunctional, fascist, self-deluded organisation that projects all its problems outwards, onto others with whom it never deals directly:

> The church's failure to share the great wisdom of our western mystical tradition constitutes a grave sin of omission which results in patriarchal cynicism and the loss of hope. It feeds a kind of collective hysteria that arouses the christofascists of our day, those who, in the name of Christ or Jesus, terrorize us.[54]

I believe there is much truth in what he says.

In May 1994 Fox was received into the priesthood of the US Episcopal Church. He has continued to develop his environmental theology in this more generous context. He has also continued publishing: his autobiography *Confessions: The Making of a Post-Denominational Priest* (1997) and *A New Reformation: Creation Spirituality and the Transformation of Christianity* (2006) are the most important of the books he has published since joining the Episcopal Church.[55] After the election of Joseph Ratzinger as Pope Benedict XVI in April 2005, Fox publicly nailed 95 theses for a new reformation of Christianity to the door of the Castle Church in Wittenberg, Germany, in imitation of Martin Luther's famous act in 1517, which began the Protestant Reformation.

He argues that today we are confronted with two versions of Christianity: the first is characterised by a punishing, vengeful, patriarchal God, a belief that we are immersed in original sin, a kind of ecclesiastical fundamentalism and rigid church structures, a fear of science, a hatred of nature, and an intolerance of alternative lifestyles. In contrast, Fox calls for a vision of Christianity which is centred on a God of love, compassion and justice, is focused on God's original blessing of the cosmos and the natural world, is ecumenical, embraces the feminine and is tolerant of different lifestyles, and that ultimately leads us to spiritual wisdom and to a religion that is part of the solution to the world's problems.

A different approach to the development of environmental theology is taken by Sean McDonagh, an Irish Columban missionary priest who spent 20 years in the Philippines working among the T'boli people in southern Mindanao. Here he saw the rainforest torn down and experienced the impact of this on the T'boli, a tribal people who had lived for centuries in forested hills and whose entire life and culture was centred on the forest. Born in 1935, he is the author of many influential books on eco-theology. His *To Care for the Earth: A Call for a New Theology* (1986) was a pioneering work. This was followed by *The Greening of the Church* (1990), which addressed the issue of why the church was so slow in confronting environmental issues. Among his later books are *Passion for the Earth* (1994), and *Patenting Life? Stop!* (2003), which focuses on the ethical questions surrounding genetically modified crops. His two most recent books are *The Death of Life* (2004) on the mega-extinctions which are occurring now across the world, and *Climate Change: Challenge to Us All* (2006).[56]

McDonagh describes what happened to the T'boli:

> I do not need weighty tomes to convince me of the seriousness of the problem facing the human community and the earth. I can see the trail of death opening out here before my eyes as I look at

> what was once an extraordinarily fruitful and colorful land. Until relatively recently, almost all of the Philippines was covered by dense, tropical rainforest. But over the past forty years the forests have almost disappeared. Lumber companies have attacked them with a vengeance in order to supply an insatiable appetite for tropical hardwoods in Japan, Europe, Australia and the United States. Landless farmers have followed the logger ... The scale of destruction is horrendous.[57]

The destruction of the forest has led to the erosion of the rich topsoils of the islands, which has blocked estuaries and caused flooding in coastal cities and towns. The sea and coral reefs around the Philippines are now polluted and being destroyed by the murky water from the erosion and run-off. Worst of all, the destruction of the forest produces 'the most despair-filled aspect of the ecological crisis', the irreversible destruction of species.[58] As a result of his Philippines experience, McDonagh's approach to environmental theology is practical. The question at the core of his thought is: 'Who has benefited most and who has borne the real costs.' While much of his ecological approach parallels that of Berry, his great contribution is to link social justice issues in a very practical way with ecology. For him the questions of culture, justice and ecology are intimately interconnected.[59]

He argues that the environment and the Third World poor bore the real costs of development in the 1980s, and that the rich have simply become richer. This is especially the result of the debt crisis which affects almost every third world country and which will become worse as a result of the global financial crisis of 2008–09. Both the environment and the poor are sacrificed by institutions such as the World Bank and the IMF to pay off debts that were run up decades ago in order to finance often failed or environmentally destructive 'development projects'.

McDonagh argues that there are good biblical precedents for wiping off these debts. Poor countries have had to accept structural adjustment programs that forced them to adopt the free market model. The result was that they had to reduce spending on education, healthcare and even food production for their own people. McDonagh points out that in contrast to the treatment of poor countries, in the market collapse of 2008, Western governments, despite their commitment to a discredited neo-liberal ideology, rushed in to bail out and socialise the debts of banks that were run up through grossly incompetent management. They also rescued US car-makers whose financial plight was the result of their own poor planning. McDonagh argues that if 'a similar situation arose in a poor country the IMF would oppose any government aid. But the IMF is silent about the request from the Detroit car manufacturing companies. The different responses indicate that there is one law for the rich and another for the poor.' He points out that a 'new economic institution ... will be needed to build the global economy on a just and sustainable foundation' and that the least appropriate people to do that 'are those who caused the problems in the first place'.[60]

He argues that a new theology needs to be developed to deal with these issues. The Catholic Church has been very slow to do this. There are two reasons for this: the church's deep-seated anthropocentrism, and the lack of a theological framework through which the sheer enormity of the ecological crisis can be grasped. McDonagh has also pointed out the weakness of the chapter on environment in the *Compendium of the Social Doctrine of the Church*.[61] Climate change and species extinction are dismissed in two paragraphs.

More recently McDonagh – and the Columban Fathers – have focused on the ethics of genetic engineering. This technology is dominated by utilitarianism: if something works, doesn't apparently hurt anyone and makes a profit, it's ethical. While there has been considerable ethical concern about the genetic engineering of human beings, little attention has been paid to the manipulation of animals, seeds and plants, he says.

Enormous amounts of money are involved in non-human genetic engineering, and yet there remain vital unanswered questions such as: Do human beings have the right to interfere in such an intrusive way by introducing exogenous DNA into the genome of another species? If we think that the world exists just for us, the answer would be 'yes'.

There is also the harvesting of animal organs, usually from pigs, to assist human beings. McDonagh believes that other species are the creations of God too, and thus have intrinsic rights. In that case, the onus is on us to demonstrate that there is a very good ethical reason to interfere so decisively in the life structure of another being. There is a sense in which this is technology gone mad. However, the profits made through genetic engineering are very real. For a start, we have no idea of the long-term effects of genetic manipulation. As McDonagh says:

> Given that these risks are potentially so destructive, research and production of genetically engineered organisms ought to be governed by the precautionary principle. This asserts that an action which is risky and could possibly cause widespread and irreversible damage should not be pursued, especially when there is a lack of full scientific certainty about the outcome of the action on the organism itself and the wider environment.[62]

That is exactly right.

So far, all my 'geologians' have been Catholics. However, Protestant theologians have been exploring this field for longer the Catholics. The earliest were the process theologians. Process theology emphasises God's intimate and vulnerable involvement with the entire life of the world, in contrast to theology that emphasises God's distance and omnipotence:

> God is not the external maker of the world but is, instead, the Spirit that breathes life into creatures and calls the higher organisms to a more abundant life of love. There is no compulsion or control here, only gift and persuasion. God is not before all creation but with all creation. Process theology is thus a thoroughgoing incarnational theology.[63]

The source of the tradition is mathematician, philosopher and polymath Alfred North Whitehead (1861–1947). The key figures in the movement are American theologians Charles Hartshorne (1897–2000) and John Cobb (1925–), and the Australian biologist Charles Birch (1918–2009), an Anglican with an evangelical background.

A key element of process theology is panentheism. This is different from pantheism, which essentially says that the world *is* God, or can be totally identified with God. Panentheism also seeks to indicate the intimate interconnection between the divine and the world, but it is more subtle. It says that God is present in all things and that the whole of creation mirrors something of the essence of God, but that God exists separately and absolutely. A sponge is often taken as an example of this relationship: water can saturate and impregnate a sponge, but the two are not identical. So the presence of God can be in all beings without being totally identified with them.

Where classical theology tends to separate God from the world, panentheism sees God as intimately involved with the world, as one who suffers with it. God is not a cold, distant, unfeeling divinity, but One who enters into the very of process of the cosmos and is intimately connected to all beings. Just as God creates the world, so in a sense we create God. What we do to other beings, we do to God. So we are called to care not only for each other, but for other beings as well, especially sentient animals. Process theology has a biocentric ethic: inflicting pain, suffering or cruelty on any living thing causes God to suffer. Birch says:

> God responds to the world with compassion. Compassion is to feel, as best one can, another's feelings. God as perfect love necessarily suffers with the world. God is not Aristotle's God of unilateral power: the 'Unmoved Mover'. The power of love, as of any relational power, is both the ability to effect and be affected. Love that is not responsive is not love but irresponsibility. [God is touched by the world,] feeling every feeling in the world ... Our own feelings are added to God's ocean of feeling.[64]

Birch has made a considerable contribution to the development of environmental theology, which was recognised when he received the international Templeton Prize for Progress in Religion in 1989. His work reflects his biological training, but he integrates his scientific knowledge with a profound and wide-ranging theological approach. His position is that all sentient creatures are, to a greater or lesser extent, able to choose:

> Richness of life depends upon the purposes we freely choose. That which animates human life animates alike the rest of the entities of creation. The evidence of science leads to a view of the universe as purposive in the sense that its entities exist by virtue of a degree of freedom which allows them a degree of self-determination ... the whole of the universe and its entities look more like life than like matter.[65]

Birch argues that there are different degrees of intrinsic value among living things. He says that a life-centred ethical approach will place upon us an obligation to work to maximise the wellbeing of all life-forms:

> Compassion is to be extended to all creatures who share the earth with us ... We should respect other creatures because of their intrinsic value and not simply because they are useful to us ... The

> gradation of intrinsic value implies a diversity of rights. The greater the richness of the experience of the subject the greater the rights … We need to develop a non-anthropocentric, biocentric ethic, which extends the concept of rights and justice to all living creatures.[66]

Birch's work is a fine example of the way in which theology and science can be integrated. His biocentric ethic finds its fullest expression in the word 'compassion': this is God's most fundamental characteristic, and it extends to all creatures, not just to humans. The challenge for the Christian, Birch says, is to mirror this deep and wide-ranging compassion.

The greatest Protestant theologian of the second half of the 20th century is without doubt Jürgen Moltmann (1926–). Moltmann is profoundly concerned about what is happening to the world. His Gifford Lectures for 1984–85, 'God in Creation: An Ecological Doctrine of Creation', are especially significant for the development of an environmental theology. He does not mince words:

> What we call the environmental crisis is not merely a crisis in the natural environment of human beings. It is nothing less than a crisis in human beings themselves. It is a crisis of life on this planet, a crisis so comprehensive and so irreversible that it can not unjustly be described as apocalyptic … it is the beginning of a life and death struggle for life on this earth.[67]

Moltmann had become deeply pessimistic as a POW in the United Kingdom during World War II, became a committed Christian there, and then came under the influence of Marxist Ernst Bloch's philosophy of hope. These experiences led him to produce his seminal book *The Theology of Hope*, which gave expression to the optimism of the late 1960s. But in 1973 he produced a very different book, *The Crucified God*.

Answering critics who argued that he had retreated to a negative theology, Moltmann replied:

> [*The Crucified God*] … cannot be regarded as a step back. *Theology of Hope* began with the resurrection of the crucified Christ, and now I am turning to look at the cross of the risen Christ … The theme then was that of *anticipations* of the future of God in the form of promises and hopes; here it is the understanding of the *incarnation* of that future, by way of the sufferings of Christ, in the world's suffering (emphasis in original).[68]

He had begun his journey towards an environmental theology.

In the late 1970s Moltmann began a systematic treatment of theology. *The Trinity and the Kingdom of God* took the identification of the suffering of Christ and the suffering of the world further, and revealed subtle hints of Moltmann's panentheism as he emphasised the immanence of God in both human history and nature. But it was *God in Creation* that affirmed his belief in the interpenetration, fellowship and mutual need between God and the world. This was taken further in his 1989 Christology, *The Way of Jesus Christ*, in which he argued that the process of God's incarnation, which began in Christ, will only be completed in the future deification of the cosmos.[69]

Moltmann says that since Renaissance Humanism, Western Christianity has taken humankind as the norm and focus of reality. This was not true of the Middle Ages, the New Testament or the Hebrew Scriptures, where the creation of humankind didn't indicate that we are the crown of creation, but rather that we are the most dependent of all creatures, reliant on all that had been created before us. Moltmann believes that the Sabbath, rather than humankind, was the crown of creation. In this context the Sabbath refers to the seventh day of creation, when God rested and reflected on all 'the work that He had done in creation'

(Genesis 2:3). Within this context all beings are icons of God and reflect the life of God.[70] Moltmann's theology has always been dominated by eschatology, the notion that God will come and will act in the future just as God has already acted in the past. This is the kind of hopeful expectancy that underlies all faith and acts as an alternative to the endemic hopelessness that characterises much contemporary culture.[71]

My last geologian is the German philosopher Martin Heidegger (1889–1976). He was concerned about ecological devastation and the effect of technology long before modern environmentalism arose.[72]

Heidegger's environmental thought is rooted in his profound ambivalence towards technology. He sees the ecological crisis as the direct result of technological culture. He defines technology in the broadest sense: it is human interference in the natural dynamics of the world to manipulate and use nature for some perceived good for individuals or the human community. Technology thus means everything from stem cell research to chainsaws, bulldozers, damming rivers for irrigation and hydro-electricity, to the massive dislocations of the landscape caused by extractive industries. Heidegger feels that we are unable to leave anything alone, including the very structure of our own bodies, and that we are dominated by a kind of an opportunistic, 'can-do' mentality; if something can be done, it should be done, and it needs no further ethical justification.

Heidegger believes that we behave, as Descartes says in the *Discourse on Method* (VI, paragraph 2), 'like masters and owners of nature … [who] enjoy without any pain the fruits of the earth'. He feels that this technocratic mindset is so built into our thinking and attitudes, has so possessed our intellectual horizons and penetrated into the very way we perceive reality that we are almost unable to think outside this context.

We apply a kind of measuring, calculating, management-style logic to everything.

The problem, Heidegger says, is our philosophy. He identifies philosophy with the Greco-Roman, Western tradition that has dominated our thought patterns for the last 2500 years. This emerges from two closely related sources: the metaphysical, intellectualising, idealising stream that finds its origins in Socrates, is developed by Plato, is carried into the late-Roman world by Plotinus and comes to dominate Western thinking through Christianity. The other, more analytical, empirical stream originates in Aristotle and flowed into Western thought in the medieval period. These two traditions came together in Descartes and the beginnings of the scientific revolution in the 17th century. According to Heidegger, this philosophical tradition comes to its end in modern technology. As George Steiner says:

> Heidegger will seek to prove that it is the continued authority of the metaphysical-scientific way of looking at the world, a way almost definitional of the West, that has brought on, has, in fact, made unavoidable the alienated, unhoused, recurrently barbaric estate of modern technological and mass consumption man.[73]

Berry agrees, saying that nowadays we live in a kind of technological trance.

Heidegger argues that technology so dominates the horizon of our being and so impregnates our attitudes that we cannot avoid being unconsciously immersed in it and dominated by it. It creates a cultural and intellectual *Ge-stell* (en-framing) that determines the way we think. And *how we think* is more important than what we think. Heidegger believes that the abstract, intellectualist tendency of Western philosophy cuts us off from actually ‘be-ing in the world’, from existence, from the miracle that we actually ‘are’, rather than ‘are not’. Here he is emphasising the participle 'be-ing' rather than the noun 'being'. For him 'is-ness', actual existence, occurred long before 'what-ness', the definition or the nature of a thing.

Here we begin to confront two of the great difficulties in understanding Heidegger. First, he is really pushing the boundaries of thought, challenging us to move beyond conventional ways of thinking. Second, there is the problem of language. He was intrigued by etymology, the history and origins of words, and he often gives meanings to words that are no longer common, or that strain a word to the edge of its definition. And that's when he's writing in German! This creates real problems for translation into English. To understand him, English speakers have to evolve awkward neologisms. However, the struggle is worth it.

Essentially, Heidegger wants to transcend philosophy by thinking completely outside the dominating Western dualist-intellectualist paradigm, getting back to the pre-Socratic Greeks such as Heraclitus (early 5th century BC), to a tradition of thinking that maintained humankind's organic connection with being and existence in the natural world. He wants to take his readers into 'an alternative order or space of meaning and being' so that they can experience and feel the strangeness of 'thinking outside the conventions of common logic and unexamined grammar'.[74] He attempts to shock us out of our predetermined and unconscious ways of thinking and open our imaginations to new ways of perceiving reality. Heidegger argues that we have lost any sense of the miracle of the fact of existence itself. To express this he uses the German word *Dasein* – from *da* (there) and *sein* (being): a 'there-being' is an existence-thrown-into-the-world, not an intellectual abstraction.

Heidegger argues that modern technology is simply the expression of the exploitative, calculating, mechanised, efficiency-oriented mentality that we apply to everything, but particularly to the natural world. This attitude is so built into our modern consciousness that we instinctively and without question assume that technology is a panacea for all our problems, both with the world and with ourselves. We implicitly and unconsciously define ourselves against the natural world, which, Heidegger says, we have reduced to a *Bestand* – a standing reserve – of resources and energy to be exploited for our own needs. In his 1954 essay 'The Question Concerning Technology', in an extraordinarily prophetic way, Heidegger pointed out that nowadays we even view ourselves as a kind of *Bestand*.[75] We have extended our manipulation of the natural world to the exploitation of ourselves as we harvest organs and manipulate our very DNA, which determines so much about us.

So what are we to do? What solution does Heidegger offer? First, he says, we have to realise that the issues surrounding technology and our divorce from the natural world are not problems that can be solved through acting ethically. It is very hard for Christians and people of goodwill to grasp this. These issues cannot be 'managed' by goodness; in fact 'managing' is part of the problem. The problem is essentially metaphysical; it is about a new paradigm, a new way of thinking and viewing reality. This is also what Moltmann is saying. The crisis we face can only be dealt with through the use of the imagination, through learning a whole new way of relating to the world.

In September 1966, a decade before he died, Heidegger gave an interview to *Der Spiegel* (*The Mirror* – a tabloid magazine). The interview was published in June 1976, after his death. Half of the interview was devoted to the question of technology. In the course of this discussion Heidegger said:

> Philosophy will not be able to effect an immediate transformation in the present condition of the world. This in not only true of philosophy, but of all merely human thought and endeavour. *Only a god can save us.* The sole possibility that is left for us is to prepare for a sort of readiness, through thinking and poetizing, for the appearance

> of the god in the time of foundering, for in the face of a god who is absent we founder (emphasis added).

So what is Heidegger saying? How do we make sense out of this odd statement?

First, he is saying we live in a time of *Untergang* – foundering, downfall or ruin. The word is significant. When a ship founders, it sinks, it's finished. Then he makes this extraordinary statement: 'Only a god can save us.' I think he is trying to convey that the reversal called for in our times is so profound that we will not be able to do it unaided. He told *Der Spiegel*: 'I know of no paths to the immediate transformation of the present situation of the world, assuming that such a thing is humanly possible at all.' As theologian Jan Van Der Veken says about the meaning of this sentence of Heidegger's:

> Whatever we do, Technology will go on to dominate nature. It is its very essence to do so. We cannot do anything about it. At the best we can try to alleviate the burden ... but, alas, the whole of humankind will want to harvest the fruits of Technology with little consideration for our common and unique heritage, Mother Earth.[76]

What we are dealing with here is what Marxist theorists call 'the impersonal force of history'. In other words this is something beyond our personal or communal will to change. Heidegger is trying to remind us that our freedom is very limited, that we need to learn a greater humility. We are not like those New York investment bankers in Tom Wolfe's *The Bonfire of the Vanities* (1987) who think that they are 'the masters of the universe'. We are, as human beings, extraordinarily vulnerable and profoundly dependent on nature for our survival. But we seem unable to stop ourselves tearing it apart.

Second, Heidegger argues that we need an acute awareness of the way technology creates a very specific *Gestell* – a thought-frame, a way of viewing the world. If we realise this we can then begin to perceive our predicament. We also need an attitude of *Bereitschaft*, meaning readiness, or being on stand-by. This word reminds me of the parable of the wise and foolish virgins in Matthew's gospel (25:1–12). The five wise virgins come prepared with oil for their lamps and are ready for the bridegroom when he comes, but the five foolish ones do not. 'Keep awake therefore,' Jesus says, 'for you do not know the day or the hour' (Matthew 25:13). The preaching of the early church focused on a kind of readiness for the end of the world and second coming of Christ which the earliest Christian generations expected to be just around the corner. There is a kind of similar apocalyptic in Heidegger's 'readiness'. It is precisely this which is lacking in our contemporary culture. We might act more quickly to deal with global warming if we had the sense that the world as we know it was on the edge of destruction.

Third, we can prepare ourselves for the coming of this god by what Heidegger calls 'thinking' and 'poetizing'. By thinking we will come to understand our metaphysical predicament, and by poetising we will develop our imaginations so that we will be able to perceive the actual presence of God, the saving being. And here I think it is reasonable to indicate some form of identification between Heidegger's 'god' and the Christian God with a capital 'G' – although he might have questioned this.

In fact the mature Heidegger moved very much in the direction of mysticism. There is much in his thought that is close to the medieval German Dominican mystic Master Eckhart (c.1260–1327), whom he often quotes. As theologian John Macquarrie has pointed out, Heidegger always had strong mystical elements in his thought.[77] For Heidegger, Be-ing is an image of God, not the conventional God, but more like the hidden God of the mystics, the Existent, the Presence that stands over and against us. Heidegger is trying to convey a sense that the absent God will come, that the passionate force of Be-ing will conquer the non-existence of technology and environmental destruction. Heidegger is arguing that if we understand the power that technology has over us, we will come to understand that the task that faces us is metaphysical: the evolution of a new *Gestell* through the prism of which we will begin to encounter nature and reality from a different, non-technological perspective. This frame will be, in a broad sense, essentially theological.

In developing this new theological perspective, the ability to poetise will be just as important as the ability to think. Poetising is what the poet does. In his 'Letter on Humanism' (1946) Heidegger says that we are 'not the lord of beings, but the shepherd of Being'. Essentially the poet names things, and by that process makes them present, real and lasting. The poet gives the divine Be-ing itself a *Heimkehr*, a homecoming. Real authentic poetry, like true art, is extremely rare. As Steiner says, the best art and poetry light up and illumine insights 'into the meaning of life which are, literally and demonstrably, *inexhaustible*' (emphasis added).[78] Like Steiner, I find this truer of music, especially a composer such as Beethoven. However, the notion of *Heimkehr* is extraordinarily theologically suggestive. This is what *anemnesis* ('Do this in remembrance of me') actually means: the real presence, the living reality and the grace-filled nearness of the risen Christ transcending history and touching our lives in and through the Eucharist.

Finally, Heidegger forces us to confront this question: if, as the great religions have consistently argued, the cosmos is somehow the product of God's creative action, will God stand by and allow the natural world to be destroyed? Or will God intervene? In what way? Is there a limit to technology's manipulation and destruction of the world – and have we reached that limit? If not now, when will we reach it? What is the nature of God's relationship to a world which has produced such rich diversity, when one species – humankind – seems intent on destroying so many species, as well as the very basis of life on earth itself?

All of this adds up to a fundamental question of absolute and central importance not just for the future of the human species, but for the future of the earth itself. I think that Heidegger has correctly posed the question. I am not certain that he has answered it, but his thinking is profoundly suggestive and takes us far beyond the politically correct clichés that so dominate contemporary public discourse in all the democracies of the Western world. Essentially this question is theological, and it is to theology and faith that we will turn now.

PART IV

THE CHRISTIAN RESPONSE

7 God's earth

At the core of the present environmental crisis is the manipulative attitude of human beings. We can't leave things alone. The natural world is not inherently self-destructive but constantly strives for balance and harmony. We're the problem. So what do we have to do? The answer: we are going to have to change quickly and profoundly. What is called for is the equivalent of deep spiritual change, and that is always a difficult and painful process. We are going to have to experience a 'conversion'. This will have to happen quickly or there will be little of earth left to save. Global warming has brought this to a head.

What does conversion involve? The best way I know to explain the process is through a profound personal experience of a place that is now destroyed.

In early 1971 I joined a group walking into Lake Pedder, a then pristine glacial lake in the wilderness of southwest Tasmania. It was about 10 months before this magnificent lake was drowned beneath a huge dam, which was built for an un-needed hydro-electric scheme. Despite a massive campaign to save the unique lake a myopic state Labor government ordered its destruction. The government, in turn, was dominated by a Hydro-Electricity Commission that was itself driven by an unquestioned technologism. It was a sinful action, a triumph of mindless vandals, an example of the stupidity, wilfulness and small-mindedness that can lead whole groups of people into profoundly evil actions.

Pedder was a magnificent place, a cathedral of nature. During my time there I experienced something that put me in touch with a presence far beyond myself, something I had never encountered before. At Pedder my awareness was heightened and I felt that my vision of the world around me was clarified. When I was on my own, away from the group, I began to feel that I had entered a kind of time beyond time. This made me feel vulnerable and frightened:

> yet there was nothing threatening me except the profound otherness of the place. Paradoxically, at the same time, I felt deeply at home with myself and this acute juxtaposition of alienation and belonging was held together in a strange, tense resolution.[1]

As the experience of Lake Pedder's sheer otherness began to seep into me, 'I began to perceive a kind of lurking "Presence" that was both personal and remote at the same time.' This is an oddly ambivalent experience. While the 'Presence' touches 'something profound inside you, at the same time it takes you out of yourself'.[2] As a Catholic, I would use the word 'God' to describe this presence; perhaps other people would not. However, what I remember vividly from that day was facing out towards a transcendent and mysterious presence that touched me deeply and influenced the rest of my life.

For me it was the beginning of a sense that the natural world was a sacrament or icon of the divine presence, but that despite this, it was very vulnerable. It was also the start of deep outrage at what was happening to the world. While my revulsion was real, for a number of years I left Lake Pedder in the background and got on with practical life. But the experience came back to me in the mid 1980s, and I began to make a more serious commitment to environmentalism.

Lots of people have experiences like these and most environmental activists understand what a conversion to the environment means. These experiences take you into a much deeper sense of time. While you don't leave the present behind, you do enter into a kind of timelessness that connects you in a mysterious but real way with both the past and the future.

My conversion to the environment brought me to a point at which I started to see what was happening to the world from a totally new perspective. It begins when you first see the colour of the landscape and you begin to pay attention to the animals and plants that inhabit it. Most committed environmentalists have come through a similar process, although they would not necessarily see it within a Christian or religious context. But the process is explicitly spiritual, and it is only when we pass through it that we realise that spirituality and the environment are not mutually exclusive; indeed they belong together. This applies to genuinely secular people as much as to believers. The result will be a strong sense of biological and existential identification with other living things and ultimately with the land and the earth itself. The processes may vary from individual to individual, but there are common elements.

The Bible knows about the psychological dynamics of repentance and conversion. The New Testament is very practical about the process. Conversion normally occurs at a time of personal or communal crisis, at a point when basic and far-reaching decisions can no longer be avoided. In the Hebrew Scriptures it is usually the prophets who challenge people to turn from their hard-heartedness and blockheadedness to God. In the gospels Jesus introduces a note of crisis, a time of decision, when a commitment for or against God's reign has to be made. Today we face the monumental crisis of global warming, a time of choice for or against the life of the earth itself. In classical Greek this is a *kairos*, a moment of crisis, a time when decisions have to be made.

The second element in the conversion process is repentance, or the ability to see oneself in perspective. It is only when we can break out of the narrow confines of our self-made world that we realise we have been caught up doing what the prophet Jeremiah describes as 'stubbornly following our own hearts' (9:14). The net result has been an obstinate and deliberate failure to see ourselves as 'the affliction of the world, its demonic presence', as Thomas Berry says. When we realise that we are not the ultimate fulfilment of cosmic process, but instead a destructive force, a plague on the earth, it is an appalling and frightening moment. This is the significant moment in the conversion process. It generates vulnerability and creates the possibility of a profound new vision, a fresh approach to life. This is a painful process: there is nothing more searing than finally seeing our own destructiveness.

It is also the moment when we see ourselves in our real place within the context of the natural world. We discover the humiliating truth: the entire world does not revolve around humankind, and never has. We realise that for almost all of geological history humans were absent and therefore totally irrelevant. In religious and Christian terms, this recognition of our real place in the scheme of things provides a chance for what the New Testament calls *metanoia*, a dramatic moment of humble realisation, repentance and conversion. Central to the conversion process is that we recognise that, as human beings, we are genetically and biologically rooted in the earth and totally dependent upon it. As the priest said as he put the ashes on the recipient's forehead in the old Ash Wednesday Catholic ritual: *Memento, homo, quia pulvis es, et in pulverem reverteris* – Remember that you are dust, and unto dust you will return. This prayer clearly says that we have come from the earth, that we live in dependence upon it, and that ultimately we will be re-absorbed by it. Yet our anthropocentric myths continue to deceive us and shield us from these truths. This moment of perspective, of seeing ourselves as the rest of the cosmos sees us, is a real spiritual, psychological and philosophical breakthrough, a painful moment of vision that leads to freedom and a whole new attitude.

Environmental conversion also involves a commitment to a completely new way of seeing reality. We are only at the edge of what this might mean in practice. A theology intersected by environmentalism and an environmentalism shaped by theology will demand not only a whole new ethical attitude to the world; it will revolutionise our approaches to ultimate questions of meaning and purpose. Bringing to consciousness our sense of oneness with the earth manifests itself first in a deep feeling of sympathy and unity with specific places as profoundly and personally connected with oneself. We feel in our own bodies the suffering, joy and beauty of this particular piece of the world, this landscape, this place. It is only on the basis of this experience of the local that a broader, more inclusive and universal sympathy for the suffering world can take hold within us.

Just as it is difficult for a normal sensitive person to read about or see the injuries and sufferings of our fellow human beings, especially when these are deliberately inflicted, so we need to develop a parallel sensitivity regarding other living things. Just as it is painful to read the Annual Report of Amnesty International about the torture of prisoners of conscience, so for the person who is environmentally sensitive it is searing to read about or see the destruction of old-growth forests by wood-chippers, or to view the slaughter of small animals on our roads, or to hear about or see on television the destruction of sea life by fishing and whaling. Alongside this experience must be the determination to do something active about this kind of human destructiveness towards the environment.

Environmental conversion involves sacrificing the extreme elements of our modern sense of individuality as we begin to recognise our commonality with and interdependence upon all other species. This sense of our rootedness in the whole of reality works unconsciously, at a level parallel to religious belief, and like belief, it needs to be articulated and brought regularly to consciousness. It is an expression of what Berry calls 'biological connectedness' with the whole of reality. Also just as with religious belief, environmental conversion requires a reflexive, intellectual understanding. St Anselm said in 1097 that *fides quaerens intellectum* – faith seeks understanding. Genuine belief always seeks to understand itself within its cultural and intellectual context. We need to understand how the environment actually works, how interactions affect each other, and what our human relationship is to it all. Environmental commitment must be underpinned by knowledge and science.

One of the most important elements in this process is staying connected to the natural world. This becomes real through a sense of relationship with a specific place, a particular landscape. This is well illustrated by the indigenous people of the eastern North American woodlands. These people use specific words for this personal interaction with the animals and plants of their landscape, words which take us to the heart of North American religion and its intersection with nature. Among these indigenous people there is no dichotomy between nature and spirituality. There is no real concept of nature as an abstract, neutral reality at all, as there is in Western scientific thought. Instead, there is a sense of the power of personal and spiritual presence in various aspects of the natural world. Also there is a belief that there are other-than-human *persons*. These other-than-human persons interact with human beings as causative agents in the world. Anthropologist A. Irving Hallowell says:

> All other 'persons' – human or other than human – are structured the same as I am. There is a vital part which is enduring and an outward appearance that may be transformed under certain conditions.
> All other 'persons' too have such attributes as self-awareness and understanding. I can talk with them … they have personal identity, autonomy, and volition.[3]

When things are seen this way the natural world takes on a whole wealth of personal meanings and presences that city-bound people may not experience. Berry says:

> These experiences are extraordinarily deep manifestations of spiritual presence throughout the universe. They convey the notion of the mystique of the land and vegetation, what might be called a mystique of the cosmological order.[4]

It is only when we concretise environmental awareness through a deep existential and spiritual connection with this or that being, presence or place that we begin to make a genuine and lasting environmental commitment.

In the United States some moral philosophers have taken the idea of the personhood of the non-human world and applied it in a legal context. This is based on the premise that nature doesn't exist merely to fulfil human needs or satisfy utilitarian demands. Since it is not merely a resource to be exploited at will, these philosophers have developed a system of legal rights for nature. Christopher D. Stone, of the University of Southern California, has discussed the ethical and legal issues raised by the protection of what he calls the 'nonperson' in his essay 'Should Trees Have Standing?', and in the book *Earth and Other Ethics*.[5]

Essentially, what Stone is doing is personifying nature and thereby endowing animals, plants and natural systems with rights that have legal standing in court. This claim has not been accepted in US legal circles, or in the legal systems of the United Kingdom, Canada or Australia. However, it has had an influence on environmental thinking in North America. The questions become particularly acute when tough choices have to be made between the needs of human beings and those of vulnerable and endangered species. I have sympathy with the extension of a notion of personhood to the natural world. However, I think the rights approach is too legalistic, and too dependent on judicial interpretation. Setting limits on our interferences in nature should be based on moral norms.

If environmental conversion is the first step in the process, what happens next? How do we develop an environmental theology and spirituality?

I want to begin this discussion by saying something about what is usually called 'natural theology'. Specifically, I want to focus on the fifth of the five traditional arguments used by theologians for God's existence: the argument from design. This may seem a diversion, but it is actually a way into some of the connections between the environment, theology and spirituality.

The origins of the argument from design are found in Greek thinkers such as Xenophon and the Stoics.[6] The idea was then adopted by early Christian apologists and has been used ever since as a way of underpinning the faith of believers. In the 13th century it was one of Thomas Aquinas' five *viae*, ways to God. Early in the *Summa Theologiae* Aquinas assemblies five arguments for the existence of God, although 'persuasions' is probably a better word to use than arguments – medieval theologians saw these so-called proofs as ways through which a person *who was already a believer* could underpin and strengthen their faith.[7] Also, they were arguing philosophically, not scientifically. This is an important distinction: science aims to arrive at a demonstrable fact, philosophy at a conclusion or consequence.

This distinction between science and philosophy has been completely lost in the unseemly brawl between Darwinian evolutionists and fundamentalists who espouse creationism. Here the philosophical argument about the design of the world has been treated by creationists as if it were a scientific 'proof'; they, in turn, have been accused by writers such as Richard Dawkins of merely trying to introduce their anti-evolutionary views into school science curricula. Simply stated, the argument from design claims that the apparent arrangement of the world – seen in its beauty, order, intelligibility and the interconnectedness of its parts – tells us something about an intelligent Creator who thought it out and designed it. The creationists began this brawl by trying to disprove evolution. They have wrenched the traditional argument out of its philosophical context and applied it literally and scientifically. As the Creation Design web page puts it:

> Rather than a history of haphazard mutations, all of life presents an intelligent design that extends from the logic of the body as a whole (like the design of a bird to fly) down to an intentional structure and organization of the very molecules and atoms that compose it … We find a perfection and complexity of organization that is so deep and so profound that simple common sense rebels at the proposition that it occurred as the result of millions upon millions of unobserved and undocumented accidental mutations.[8]

This kind of 'reasoning' leads to equally fatuous arguments by Dawkins:

> The claim that something – say the bacterial *flagellum* – is too complex to have evolved by natural selection is alleged, by a lamentably common but false syllogism, to support the 'rival' intelligent design theory by default. This kind of default reasoning leaves completely open the possibility that, if the bacterial *flagellum* is too complex to have evolved, it might also to have been too complex to have been created.[9]

Dawkins then argues against God's existence from statistical improbability. But what creationists and Dawkins fail to understand is that there are forms of knowledge other than scientific, and they don't seem to be able to comprehend that this is not a scientific but a philosophical discussion. The original and proper focus of the design argument is natural theology, not science. The argument posits the notion that the beauty, order, purpose and the benign environment of the world for living beings points towards, but doesn't prove, a Creator who is wise, powerful and good.

There are obvious philosophical problems with this argument: the natural world is not always a benign place. Nature is often destructive. Darwinian thinkers have argued that the evolution of even the most complex aspects of biological life is not actually driven by any sense of divine purpose, or by design at all, but simply by instinctual need. Dawkins argues along these lines in *The Blind Watchmaker*, which rejects the whole notion of evolution following a planned scenario.[10] His book is subtitled 'Why the evidence of evolution reveals a universe without design'. And there are others, such as French biologist Jacques Monod, who argue that the cosmos results from pure evolutionary chance.[11]

An interesting restatement of the argument from design has emerged recently from physicists and astronomers. They seem to have more sympathy with philosophical and theological approaches. Biologists, in contrast, are generally much more critical of religious belief. As physicist John Polkinghorne has said:

> Biology at the end of the twentieth century is more or less similar to what physics succeeded in doing in the eighteenth century, with the Newtonian theory of the solar system ... Two hundred years later physics has become wiser, and found that the world is somewhat more interesting than that.[12]

As a consequence, physicists and astronomers tend to be inclined toward more comprehensive views of the cosmos.

Physicists with a Christian commitment, such as Owen Gingerich of Harvard and Polkinghorne of Cambridge (he is an Anglican priest), have argued that the extraordinary facts of cosmic evolution cannot be sufficiently explained by instinct, random evolutionary events, or pure chance. Both these men contend that the intimate details of the development of the big bang, the nuclear resonance of carbon and oxygen, the process of stellar evolution, and the survival of biological life are all too finely and perfectly balanced to suggest anything other than, as astronomer Fred Hoyle says, the guidance of a super-intelligent mind. Physicist Paul Davies speaks of *The Mind of God*.[13] But it must be said that none of this is a 'demonstration', much less a 'proof' of the existence of God. Natural theology is more about hints and observable coherences; it is about persuasive arguments and intimations rather than proofs. It finds intimations of mind and purpose in the cosmos which point to bigger questions, questions which are essentially religious and theological.

Natural theology has developed a specific epistemological explanation of the relationship between God and the natural world. It is best expressed in what the great medieval thinkers Aquinas and Bonaventure called 'analogy'. Aquinas says that our comprehension of God is derived from our experience of the perfections that we can see in our fellow humans and in the creatures and the world around us. For instance, we know that God is beautiful because we can see beauty in the natural world; we know that God is good because we can see goodness in the people and creatures around us; we know that God is wise because we experience human and natural wisdom. However, our experience of beauty, goodness, and wisdom is not the same as beauty, goodness, and wisdom in God; God's reality and our knowledge are not univocal, but neither is it true that divine reality and human knowledge are equivocal, that is there is no deception or ambiguity between our perception and the reality of God. While our knowledge is not a knowledge of God as God truly is, it still gives us passing glimpses, fleeting perceptions, a sense of an intangible but real personal presence. Analogy is, as the Jewish scholar Eliphas Lévi says: 'the last word of science and the first word of faith'.[14]

Bonaventure approaches analogy more poetically than Aquinas. Bonaventure, as a Franciscan, took on the outlook of Francis of Assisi. He says that every creature is a *vestigium Dei*; *vestigium* here literally means a footstep, a track, a footmark. So each creature contains a trace of the divine and a trajectory towards God. In the case of human persons, Bonaventure takes this further, saying that we are the *imago Dei*, the image of God, for humankind alone possesses the spiritual powers which allow us to be more conformed to God. Philosophy, however, is merely the starting point for contemplation and the beginning of *The Journey of the Mind Into God*, as Bonaventure called his major spiritual work.

There are both strengths and weaknesses in the analogical approach to God. Its strengths are that it sees the whole world as a sign or symbol of God and grounds this recognition in a coherent philosophical argument. If analogy is used in a broadly symbolic way, the world and all that is in it is seen as pointing beyond itself. Thus, in a broad sense, it has transcendent value and is not a mere object; it has sacramental connotations. At least it posits the foundation for a theology that accepts the world as symbolic of the transcendent, and moves beyond dualism. In a way Bonaventure points in a direction that helps us begin to answer Heidegger's question: what type of God will save us?

Spiritual maturity soon teaches us that we know little or nothing of the *mysterium tremendum* that we call 'God', and that all even the most spiritually mature person can say is that they can perceive traces of the infinite in their experience. These traces of transcendent mystery are often actuated by an encounter with nature. They can also arise through deep contact with another person; through intellectual, scientific, or intuitive insights; through art, literature and – especially – music; or through other transforming things that occasionally happen to us. I am speaking here of profound and metaphysical realisations that Steiner calls 'real presences'. In a striking phrase, he says we are 'monads haunted by communion'.[15]

We find the transcendent and the divine in the midst of the world. There is a vector towards the sacred right at the core of ordinary life. But to be able to perceive it one must leave psychological interpretations behind and shift one's perception towards the deeper plane of spirituality and mysticism: the task that confronts the spiritual person is to move beyond the symbol and its psychological interpretation to perceive the transcendent reality that stands behind it. But our age is immersed in the psycho-therapeutic interpretation of experience. We seem to have lost the ability to discover the deeper meaning of our most significant experiences. There is a sense in which modern psychology, especially in its more superficial 'pop' forms, is the tag end of the anthropocentrism of the last few centuries: all meaning in the world has been invested in human subjectivity and human experience. All significance arises through connection with us.

The strength of an environmental theology is that it shifts us away from humanity's being the focus of all conscious, ethical, and religious endeavours: it points outwards, towards the wider world of the cosmos and challenges us to broaden our perspective as we try to interpret the meaning of reality and sort out our relationship to it. The deep shift occurring now is that it is increasingly in the natural world rather than in human subjectivity that we are discovering genuine traces of the transcendent. The dominance of psychology as the interpreter of our experience is, thankfully, coming to an end. It is by looking outwards to the natural world that we will discover the context and meaning of our existence, and experience genuine mysticism.

Many people argue that nowadays God is the problem. Who and where is God and how does the divine impinge on us? Paradoxically, it was not only modern science that drove God out of the world. The older style of theology, both Protestant and Catholic, also drove God out of the cosmos. That theology maintained the ultimate inexpressibility of the divine, but in the process of protecting this it drove God out of the reach of our experience and defined transcendence in a most unworldly way. We have seen something of the origin of this in the Platonised theology that entered the Christian tradition in the early church. But the active expulsion of God from the cosmos really occurred from the 17th century to the present. Nature was mechanised by Newtonian physics and came to be viewed solely as a repository of resources to be exploited by humankind. Christian theology simply accepted this cosmology; no coherent critique was offered. Theology allowed God to be driven out of nature – not intentionally, but as a byproduct of the mechanistic view of the world. The secularisation of nature drained it of all its sacramental and iconographic significance. An increasingly unworldly God was created. The so-called God of the gaps was merely an intermediary stage in the progressive mechanisation of the world, a stage when the divine was called in to plug the holes in scientific understanding. God was finally driven out of nature in the mid 20th century. The 'death of God' theories and the secularised theology of the 1960s and early 1970s was a signal of God's final banishment from the cosmos.

The environmental movement has created a unique opportunity for the recovery of the temporarily departed God. With the development of a less mechanised and more integrated notion of nature, it is now possible to rediscover the iconographic value of the cosmos. The task that faces theology today is to try to retain a sense of God's mystery and otherness while maintaining a perception of God's presence in and through the cosmos and earth's life-forms. In order to be able to rediscover God in the world, we need to develop the ability to perceive God in new ways.

Paradoxically, these draw on some very traditional Christian notions.

I have said that God is the *mysterium tremendum*. What does this word 'mystery' mean? Peoples of pre-technocratic culture, such as the Australian Aborigines or the Native Americans, understood mystery extremely well because they lived their religious lives in a natural world that they saw as full of symbols. Their beliefs emphasised the sacramental, symbolic nature of reality rather than its rational explanations. Specific places, times and ceremonies drew them beyond the obvious, banal, everyday world into a more transcendent realm of inner experience and meaning. Their interior lives were lived in relationship to quite specific places in the landscape and to a cycle of religious ceremonies which gave a sense of purpose and direction to their lives. Their sense of time was cyclic and repetitive rather than linear.

It is difficult, if not impossible, for those of us who live in Western technocratic society to recover the religious world of indigenous people. Our sense of time and history are too strongly felt as a consistent movement forward, and our sense of attachment to place is weakened. We have a desperate need to rediscover, through a more sacramental and iconographic approach to reality, the sense of the presence of the transcendent in the natural world. This is actually quite possible for those who are spiritually and environmentally attuned and it does not require us to abandon our sense of time and history.

As long as there is wilderness we have the chance to enter into what theologian Rudolf Otto has called the experience of the 'holy' or the 'numinous'.[16] We can still experience the sheer sanctity of specific parts of a landscape and to apprehend the holy, transcendent presence that stands both within and yet beyond the place. But to do this we have to be able to find such places. As more and more wildernesses and places of natural beauty give way to exploitation, commercialism and space for an ever-growing human population, our ability to experience the holy in nature is reduced.

But it is not just the disappearance of wilderness and the natural world that is the problem. We are so pragmatic in our approach to virtually everything, and our minds are so highly developed analytically, that it has become very difficult for us to apprehend the presence of the transcendent in the world around us. Our perceptions are simply not tuned to this channel. That is why we can destroy nature so casually. We have examined every aspect of the natural world, analysed its component parts and estimated its economic value. In the process we have lost the ability to see nature as an interlocking whole. We are entirely focused on the use-value of the environment. We have lost any sense of iconographic mystery in the natural world.

Wood-chippers, for instance, along with the governments, industries and trade unions that support them, have no perception at all of the mysterious beauty of an old-growth forest, nor of its value as an ecological micro-environment. Their crude pragmatism focuses entirely on however many tons of export products they can gain. Destroying old-growth forests – for whatever purpose – is evil and sinful, in my view, and it happens because people so narrow their focus that all they see is economic exploitation, profit and maintaining jobs. This is a prime example of the 'autism' that characterises our society and that has led straight to the global financial crisis. And we think the solution to the crisis is to be found in a further application of capitalist economic 'rationalism'!

The fact that we can analyse how the natural world works doesn't mean we have exhausted the question of its meaning. Nor does it show that we actually understand the significance of what we analyse. I am not suggesting that modern analysis is bad, or that we should surrender to the pseudo-intellectualism and puffed-up self-importance of New Age spiritual movements. I am saying that we live at the tail end of rationalism's usefulness as the dominant mode of thought. Antonio Salieri, in Peter Shaffer's play *Amadeus*, talks about a northern Italian image of God with what he calls 'trader's eyes'. At the crudest level Western culture still tends to see everything with trader's eyes; we break everything down into a cost-benefit analysis whereby reality is judged by its economic value. A forest or landscape is assessed almost exclusively in monetary terms. Can we sell the timber? Will it be economically viable if we develop it? Will it support cattle or sheep? Can we bring in tourists? We cannot let anything simply 'be'.

There is another modern way of seeing reality which derives from our analytical attitude, but it can work either for or against environmentalism. It is seeing with 'scientist's eyes'. This is the tendency to analyse everything in order to understand how it works. It is not as crude a view as that of the traders but it too is on the analytical spectrum. Nowadays some aspects of science are beginning to change: the study of ecology leads to the discovery of the inter-relationships between things, and is moving the analytic approach in a more integrated direction. Again, this is not to argue that analysis is bad. I have never supported the irrationalists who want to do away with all the advances of European Humanism and the Enlightenment. The Enlightenment has brought us too many benefits. I am saying that analytical thought needs to be integrated into a more comprehensive approach to reality.

Behind analysis stands the mystery of things. 'Mystery' is a poverty-stricken word in English – it can simply mean putting the pieces of a puzzle together to solve a problem, as Agatha Christie's Hercule Poirot or Conan Doyle's Sherlock Holmes do. In this sense, a mystery is solvable. It is a matter of using the clues to find the solution. But the Greek word *musterion* means much more than this. The origins of the word lie in the Greek mystery religions, but the word has been Christianised and transformed in meaning. It is often used by St Paul. For him the ultimate mystery is God's plan to bring salvation, unity and fullness to the whole created cosmos. He is a universalist who sees the *pleroma* – the fullness of God – permeating all reality. We have already seen Paul's colourful image of the whole world 'groaning in one great act of giving birth' until everything is set free from the bondage of sin and limitation. So for Paul, the core of the mystery is the process of bringing everything into unity and producing the fullness of life's potential. For him, this is a gift that only God can give.

Theologian Karl Rahner has described God as the 'holy mystery'. He uses this term as a way of escaping the circumscribed concept that the word 'God' can often conjure up; he contrasts holy mystery with the subjective, limited, and often legalistic and destructive notion that many people have of God.[17] Berry says that he too has abandoned the use of the word 'God' because of its connotations. Rahner's use of 'holy mystery' taps into the Christian mystical tradition of the intense longing for the transcendent, for bringing the human person face to face with the sheer, incomprehensible mystery of God. Unfortunately, however, it still lacks the sheer single-syllable brevity of the Anglo-Saxon word 'God'.

It is the mystery and indescribability of God that lures many of the most perceptive human beings to undertake the search for the transcendent. Genuine Christianity is a dynamic, restless religion, because it encourages a desire to search for God. The 4th century theologian Gregory of Nyssa, in his *Life of Moses*, expresses this restlessness in terms of a constantly deeper exploration:

> This truly is the vision of God: never to be satisfied in the desire to see him. But one must always, by looking at what he can see, rekindle his desire to see more. Thus no limit would interrupt growth in the ascent toward God, since no limit to the Good can be found, nor is the increasing of the desire for the Good brought to an end because it is satisfied.[18]

In Christian mysticism this search is often expressed in terms of negation. God is not to be found in expected places nor through predictable means. The early Christian theologians often refer to this as the *theologia negativa*. Gregory of Nyssa defines this as 'the seeing that consists in not seeing, because that which is sought transcends all knowledge, being separated on all sides by incomprehensibility as by a kind of darkness'.[19]

Gregory's mystical theology was taken up and developed by an anonymous 5th century writer, probably a Syrian monk or bishop, whom we know as Pseudo-Dionysius. He was a spiritual writer of great and continuing influence, especially after his works were translated into Latin in the Middle Ages.[20] At the core of his theology is the notion that no word can describe the reality of the transcendent. God dwells in a super-essential darkness, far beyond the realm of light. We ascend to our primitive glimmerings of the transcendent by following the *via negativa*. The *via negativa* is explained in *The Mystical Theology*, where Pseudo-Dionysius refers simply to the transcendent as 'it' as a way of avoiding all the connotations that are loaded onto the word 'God':

> Again, as we climb higher we say this. It is not soul or mind, nor does it possess imagination, conviction, speech, or understanding ... It cannot be spoken of ... It is not number or order, greatness or smallness, equality or inequality, similarity or dissimilarity. It is not immovable, moving or at rest. It has no power, it is not power, nor is it light. It does not live nor is it life ... It cannot be grasped by the understanding since it is neither knowledge nor truth.[21]

Here is the *via negativa* in its most arresting form. The point of this type of theology is to stress the absolute mystery of God, the fact that analogous knowledge is never more than a glimmer and that we don't even remotely begin to understand the transcendent mystery that confronts us. Thomas Aquinas stresses that after every effort has been made to discover God through natural reason and revelation, we have to admit that 'the ultimate in human knowledge [is] to know that we do not know God'.[22]

This notion of the incomprehensibility of God has long been emphasised in the Eastern Orthodox Church tradition. But the same human experience of darkness is also explored by many of the Western mystics, including the Spanish saint and poet John of the Cross (1542–91). He describes the driving passion that propels the mystic out into the darkness of incomprehension towards the extraordinary yet fleeting presence that alone will satisfy. Roy Campbell's translation of St John's poem '*En una noche oscura*' conveys something of the continuing compulsion to enter into a presence that is ultimately transforming:

> Upon that lucky night
> In secrecy, inscrutable to sight,
> I went without discerning
> And with no other light
> Except for that which in my heart was burning.[23]

In the poem he refers twice to 'presence' without further specification. It is this same experience of transforming personal presence that we can discover in the natural world. John had a great love for the natural world and was filled with a desire to be alone in it and experience it. However, Australian theologian Ross Collings points out that there seems to be a great gulf between St John's clear love for nature and his insistence on the terrible naked nothingness of the mystical ascent.[24] For John this is resolved through the paradox of experiencing everything by sacrificing everything.

The dynamics of mysticism stand in stark contrast to fundamentalism. The problem with fundamentalism is that it takes religion far too literally. It sees that which is essentially poetic, metaphorical and expressed in symbolic language as a simple kind of literalism and legalism. It fails to see religion as a vehicle that conjures up and points towards a reality which, by definition, transcends everything in our knowledge and experience. Religion brings us into the realm of symbols.

Symbolic thought has certainly become more difficult in our sanitised, technocratic culture. We are dominated by the superficially rational and our imaginations have become stultified. This explains the growth of fundamentalism in all religious traditions: it is an expression of the atrophy of the imagination, of our alienation from the natural world which is the original source of the religious quest. Fundamentalism is the application to spiritual experience of a superficial rationalism that results in the literal and limited use of religious language and that excludes the symbolic and sacramental. It is a symptom of deep spiritual sickness that can only be cured by the rediscovery of the natural source of human religiosity.

How then can this desire for the mysterious presence of the transcendent be understood? And how can it be applied to the natural world?

The natural world is the original source of religion and spirituality. As I said earlier, indigenous people have traditionally seen specific places in their landscape as numinous, where deeper levels of consciousness and spirituality are released. Such places take indigenous people away from banal, everyday concerns and insert them into a space that points beyond itself towards the transcendent. It is significant that the Hebrew people, after their escape from the quasi-urban environment of ancient Egypt, experienced their God in the isolated and stark landscape of the desert and mountains. This is not, for one moment, to say that God cannot be experienced in the products of human culture, in sacred art, music and worship. Nor am I saying that God cannot be experienced in everyday reality. I am simply saying that the natural world is where human beings experienced the transcendent for many centuries before the advent of Christianity, and that we need to recover some form of that primal experience. Most people in the contemporary world cannot undertake the rigours of religious mysticism, so we must find another way to experience the transcendent.

There are still areas in many countries, including Australia and the United States, where one can be alone in places of great natural beauty and mystery. To be in a place like this is to experience a silence that opens one up to solitude and to an experience of physical and spiritual vulnerability. At the same time, there is a deep sense of the oneness of the self with itself and with the place. I have also emphasised that mystical experience is characterised by a similar intense sense of the transcendence of space and time, usually accompanied by an intangible but real sense of personal presence. Sometimes this is quite specific (when the presence of God is invoked), but mostly it is unspecific – there is just a powerful sense of something transforming which cradles the individual who experiences it.

Up to this point I have talked as though cosmic consciousness or nature mysticism was compatible with the kind of mystical experience that is common to the great religious traditions. However, historian of religion R.C. Zaehner questions this:

> In strictly religious mysticism, be it Hindu, Christian or Muslim, the whole purpose of the exercise is to concentrate on an ultimate reality to the complete exclusion of all else; and by 'all else' is meant the phenomenal world or, as the theists put it, all that is not God. This means a total and absolute detachment from Nature, an isolation of the soul within itself either to realize itself as God, or to enter into communion with God. The exclusion of all that we normally call Nature is the *sine qua non* of this type of mystical experience.[25]

Zaehner argues that cosmic consciousness, on the other hand, is a real, spontaneous, mystical experience characterised by a sense of the transcendence of space and time. It is not confined to a particular type of person; 'nor does it appear to be the result of a particular desire to transcend oneself'.[26] He emphasises that there is no necessary reference to

God or transcendence in nature mysticism, and that it can be experienced by anyone. On the other hand, religious mysticism, in his view, refers explicitly to belief in God and requires of the participant deep commitment, profound detachment and asceticism over a long period. It is not called the *theologia negativa* for nothing!

For me, Zaehner drives too sharp a wedge between religious mysticism and cosmic consciousness. In contrast, Jesuit philosopher Joseph Marechal is more inclusive. He says that the fundamental characteristic of all mysticism is a 'feeling of the immediate presence of a Transcendent Being'. He argues that this intuition can be experienced in all religions, and 'even apart from all religious belief'. Marechal says that mysticism is experienced through an intuition which he defines as:

> the empirical feeling of presence, the perception of a spacialized reality … [the] direct assimilation of a knowing faculty with its object … mystical contemplation is neither a sense-perception nor an imaginative projection nor a discursive knowledge, but … one of those intuitions whose exact type we do not in our ordinary experience possess.[27]

In Marechal's view, mystical experience ranges across a spectrum that includes cosmic consciousness, mysticism inspired by nature, art or beauty, and the transforming and radical events that characterise religious mysticism at its deepest and most extraordinary, such as is seen in the lives of Sts Teresa of Avila and John of the Cross.

This is why, if we are to be religious beings who are turned outwards towards the transforming presence that pervades the whole cosmos, we desperately need the natural world, isolated wilderness, places of beauty and silence. We need to look out beyond the borders of the self to place ourselves where the intuition of cosmic consciousness can pervade our being. Since the vast majority of us will not undertake the hard road to the highest forms of religious mysticism, we need the natural world. It is through our experience of nature that most of us will find the meaning of our own lives and make some sense out of life on earth; nature will also provide us with experience of transcendence, or, if you prefer, God.

Rahner, in *Nature and Grace*, argues that human beings have, as part of their very essence, 'a natural desire for the beatific vision' – we all long for an ecstatic vision of goodness and beauty that will transcend and complete us.[28] Rahner's view is that God's grace pervades the entire created cosmos and that all of us, in our inner core, are oriented towards the transcendent. Thus the world becomes, in the literal sense, a sacrament of the presence of God, a 'mysterious infinity', where the transcendent is to be discovered:

> Man can try to evade the mysterious infinity which opens up before him ... Out of fear of the mysterious he can take flight to the familiar and the everyday. But the infinity which he experiences himself exposed to also permeates his everyday activities ... Man experiences himself as an infinite possibility.[29]

Genuine mysticism not only brings a sense of haunting presence. It is also about transcending time. To experience a time that stands outside ordinary time, we have to attain what theologian John S. Dunne calls 'time out of mind': we have to be able to escape from the present, from the prison of the now, and see ourselves in the context of the totality of our lives and of all life. Basing his work on Augustine's *Confessions*, Dunne argues that we only become ourselves and discover God through a process of recollection and memory that puts us in touch with the time that transcends the present. He says that to encounter God we have to appropriate personally all of our experiences and the totality of our whole life story.[30] T.S. Eliot seems to be saying something similar in his poem 'Burnt Norton'.

This is what I experienced that day at Lake Pedder. I was full of a sense of timelessness, a real awareness of the continuity of the whole of life. It was not a feeling that I had somehow gone back via some type of time machine to the past. It was much more a sense of actually standing outside time. What is also interesting is the intimacy between the words 'presence' and 'present'. Both are derived from the Latin *praesens*, which means now, at hand. The experience of transcendent presence means escaping the dominance of the chronological present and achieving a rare sense of unity with all that is and has been.

This is what the church has tried to do through its liturgy and the celebration of the Eucharist and sacraments. But worship seems no longer able to touch people's lives. So they seek other forms of religious expression. The beauty of nature and the wilderness has become vitally important for the spirituality of many people. It is increasingly in the cathedral of the environment that our contemporaries are rediscovering a way into the realm of the transcendent and encountering the sacred presence that stands within the natural world.

I am not talking about pantheism or some form of nature worship. There is a sense in which the biblical suspicion of the dangers of polytheism and Canaanite fertility belief has developed into a near paranoia in the Judeo-Christian tradition about the worship of nature. Any attempt to find God in nature is branded by literalist Christians as pantheism or New Age. Environmental theology is not about nature worship. It is simply an expression of the modern search for that which transcends individual and societal existence and which contextualises both the self and society; it is an expression of our innate religiosity and spirituality. It is part of the genuine mystical tradition.

Essentially I am saying that all of us have a facility for spirituality. But what is it and how does it work?

Rahner calls this facility the 'supernatural existential' – a mouthful if ever there was one. What he is referring to is the deep desire in everyone for some way of transcending subjectivity and the self. Rahner says it is the ability to look outwards to the world to discover that it is beautiful and good, in theological terms, a grace-filled place that reveals God. Clearly there is also evil, hatred and destruction, but in the end these will not prevail. Another approach is through what John Henry Newman calls the 'illative sense'. As we've seen, Newman, who believed strongly in the sacramentality of the material world, says that the illative sense is the ability to discern the kind of coherence that emerges from an accumulation of probabilities. It is the ability to make inferences and perceive connections between seemingly unrelated realities. He says that it is the act of connecting the inferences that brings us to religious certitude. It is about trusting probabilities, not about waiting for empirical evidence.

There is a real spontaneity about the process of almost unconsciously drawing all the implicit evidence together. In a way, this is much more about the imagination making connections than it is about logical thought. Perhaps we should call it the 'illative imagination'. Imagination is 'the facility to perceive affinities and correlations between apparently disparate and unconnected realities'.[31]

Fundamentalists lack, or have foregone, an illative imagination. They believe that their interpretations of the biblical text are literally true, not historically and culturally conditioned. The illative imagination 'is precisely what the great scientific theories are about: they are almost poetic visions that give form and create order among disparate and apparently unconnected material'.[32] The theory of evolution is an example of this: it was Charles Darwin's brilliant intuition about the connections running through all the material that had come down to us from cosmic, geological and natural history. Evolution provided us with a way of making sense out of it all. Above all, it was an exercise of the imagination.

At the deepest spiritual level the illative imagination is the intuition of the transcendent in our experiences of the beautiful, the good and the true. It is based on, and indeed requires, the conviction that the divine and the holy lurk everywhere in the world. We need only the imaginative ability to be able to perceive them. In other words, faith – and the experience of the transcendent – is not a kind of separate wisdom or understanding restricted to people who have some type of special religious gift; it is a way of imagining the world and all our interior and external experience as including, being part of, something transcendent and divine. In simple terms, it is the ability to make a connection between an experience of the natural world and the presence of a reality that stands both within and beyond it.

It is precisely this kind of imaginative intuition that we need to develop if we are ever going to discover the presence of the transcendent in the natural world.

8 Christ ... and some tentative conclusions

Until now I have said very little about Jesus Christ and the role that he might play in environmental theology. The reason: once you change your view of the age and size of the world, you also have to refocus all of the key elements of your theology, including the role that Christ plays.

Until the development of critical historical studies and the expansion of our knowledge of the long history of humankind in the 19th and 20th centuries, it was easy to see why the life of Jesus was the centrepiece of history for our ancestors. His pivotal role was obvious within the circumscribed ambit of biblical history, especially if you believed that the world was created in 4004BC, an idea that was popularised in the late 17th century by the French Bishop Jacques Bénigne Bossuet in his *Discourse on Universal History*. Bossuet had calculated the age of the world from the biblical text itself.[1] This theological cosmology placed Jesus at the centre of history and allowed God to stand outside the world's historical process in an eternity from which He could supervise the business of human history, intervening when and where necessary. It is precisely this cosmology that lost its grip on our imaginations as we moved toward a scientific understanding which sees the world as beginning with a big bang 15 billion years ago, and the human race as the offspring of an insignificant subsection of mammalian evolution, the hominids, that emerged a couple of million years ago.

In this context Jesus seems insignificant. But as a Catholic-Christian I must take on the challenge of trying to comprehend his importance within this broadest of all cosmological contexts. How can Jesus be the focus of the whole cosmos and the definitive mediator between God and humankind, as Christianity argues, when he is such a late arrival on the world stage? The 2000 year history of the church is a mere blink in the human story, let alone in the story of the universe. Biblical scholars and theologians make a distinction between the significance of the historical man Jesus who lived 2000 years ago and the resurrected, glorified Christ of faith, the 'anointed one' of God. They argue that the historical Jesus of Nazareth was the man who lived in the Roman imperial province of Judea in the time of the Emperors Augustus (27BC–14AD) and Tiberius (14–37AD) who, in the words of the Apostles' Creed, 'was conceived by the power of the Holy Spirit, born of the Virgin Mary, was crucified, died and was buried'. On the 'third day' he was raised up by the power of God and the early Christian community experienced him as alive and as saviour. They then gradually came to believe that not only had he risen from the dead, but that he pre-existed, that he was the creative Being who had brought the whole cosmos into existence.

This understanding of Christ as the pre-existing Creator of the world is summed up in the Letter to the Colossians, where Paul focuses on Christ's role in the process of cosmic-coming-to-be: 'He is the image of the invisible God, the firstborn of all creation; for in him all things ... were created ... all things have been created through him and for him. He himself is before all things, and in him all things hold together' (1:15–17). A similar theology of a descending God in Jesus and an ascending and exalted Christ can be found in the New Testament writings attributed to St John. These images are powerful and striking, and

Pierre Teilhard de Chardin was especially influenced by them.

At first sight this theology seems to fit in nicely with environmental concerns. As the ultimate source of creativity in the world, the glorified Christ could surely be expected to be a dedicated environmentalist. Thomas Berry, Matthew Fox and other theologians have shown some sympathy for the notion of what they call the cosmic Christ. Fox's influential book *The Coming of the Cosmic Christ* distinguishes between the post-Enlightenment's preoccupation with the historical Jesus and what he claims is the more ancient figure of the cosmic Christ. He correctly points out that the cosmic Christ cannot be divorced from the historical Jesus: 'A theology of the Cosmic Christ must be grounded in the historical Jesus, in his words, in his liberating deeds, in his life and orthopraxis. The Cosmic Christ is not a doctrine that is to be believed in and lived out *at the expense of the historical Jesus*' (emphasis in original).[2] Fox maintains that a kind of dialectic (he uses the word 'dance') is needed between time (which he identifies with the historical Jesus) and space (which he attributes to the cosmic Christ).

Berry developed the idea of the cosmic Christ along different lines. He attempted to integrate the figure of Christ with spiritual and cosmological ideas from various religious sources. Berry's thought is rooted in the theology of the Trinity and in the image of Christ as Creator, as presented in Paul's Letter to the Colossians, in which Christ is the hovering 'breath of God' that holds all things together. So Christ and the Spirit are intimately interrelated. Berry implies that there is a purposive aspect to creation by saying that everything is ordered to an ultimate human presence, which he identifies with Jesus. This is in tune with Teilhard's views; it is also rather anthropocentric. Berry also introduces some interesting concepts from Hindu, Buddhist and Chinese thought. He shows that in most of the great religious traditions there are similar forms of saviour-personalities. He claims that the Hindu notion of *Purusha* suggests something of this. *Purusha* is a complex term that refers to the uncaused spirit that permeates all reality, perhaps resembling Bergson's *élan vital.* It is the pure consciousness to which all things aspire and the transcendent spiritual principle which is to be found everywhere.[3]

The notion of a saviour-personality emerges more clearly in Buddhism. Berry makes reference to the continuing influence of the personality of the Buddha himself: 'Looked upon as a savior-personality, he became progressively identified with the transcendent experience of which he spoke so often.'[4] Something of the notion of Buddha as a saviour-personality is expressed through the term *Tathagata.* Of this Berry says:

> Few terms in the entire range of Buddhist terminology are so difficult to comprehend as this one. It must have existed prior to the time of Buddha to designate a prophetic personality with a salvation mission to all mankind ... Such a person could not be considered as just another one of many great personalities known and praised extensively in one of the traditional societies of mankind. Seen by his followers as a unique savior-type personality, he was a bringer of salvation, the supreme good sought by man. He was the healer of anguish, the bringer of blessedness, and a guide to that final blissful state so much desired by a suffering world.[5]

This notion also includes the sense that the 'Buddha personality' permeates every person and the whole of reality. Berry also finds elements of the notion of the saviour-personality in the thought of the neo-Confucian scholar Wang Yang-ming (1472–1529). He says that Wang 'tells us that a truly developed person is someone who realizes that we form one body with heaven, earth and all living things'.[6]

Despite the provocative and interesting insights of these thinkers, I think they drive too sharp a wedge between the cosmic Christ and the Jesus of history, almost implying that they are distinct realities. By emphasising the cosmic Christ, the awkward problem of Jesus' limited historical and cultural context is neatly, if unconsciously, sidestepped. This is too easy a solution; the historical Jesus is not so easily dismissed. So how do we make sense of him?

The historical Jesus, the man who actually existed 2000 years ago in Judea and Galilee, is not only a model for Christians. He also attracts many unbelievers. Sceptics – and even atheists – say that they admire both his life and his teaching. Jesus' well-established historical reality makes him attractive today because for many people God is no longer needed to explain the creation or existence or development of the world. Many believe that science does that for us. And as we have seen, for many the natural world is no longer viewed as a theophany – it is merely a source of materials and energy that can be used to attain human self-sufficiency.

Traditional Christianity has always viewed Jesus as the pivotal point in human history and the central focus of God's revelation. Without him Christianity would lose its *raison d'être*. So we are back to the problem with which I started this chapter: how can a man who lived in an obscure part of the Roman Empire 2000 years ago really be the central figure of cosmic history? How can someone whose whole life was culturally and historically conditioned, no matter how revolutionary his teachings may have been, become a major influence on the formation of a new environmental vision of life and spirituality in the 21st century? This problem is reinforced if you take seriously the conclusion of scholars such as John Dominic Crossan, who says that in his own time Jesus would have been seen as a 'peasant nobody' who was really only known in the unimportant and troublesome Roman province of Judea.[7] What does such a person have to offer to our time? What does the historical Jesus have to do with a whole new environmental vision of life, and in what sense is Jesus normative for faith and belief?

Contemporary Christian theology is only beginning to take these questions seriously. As a result I am not really sure if I can answer my own questions. However, I believe, with Fox, that the awkward link between the historical Jesus and the cosmic Christ must be somehow maintained. While I agree that the emphasis in an environmental theology might need to shift to the cosmic Christ, the intimate connection between all of this and the man Jesus cannot be lost. We cannot retreat from the importance of the historical and the factual. Christianity can never afford to lose its rootedness in and contact with what really happened. Yet at the same time, I agree with Fox that the present overemphasis on Jesus, the kind of idolatry of Jesus that you tend to find among fundamentalists – 'Jesusolatry', as he calls it – is actually the last gasp of the 19th century's almost manic search for the historical Jesus.

Perhaps a clue to the solution of the problem is provided by Australian theologian Denis Edwards. Drawing on the thought of Karl Rahner, Edwards sees Jesus as the most important person in history, someone who, in his own flesh, expresses the essence of God's self-revelation and who, at the same time, expresses in his crucified body the essence of the cosmic longing for the transcendent: 'He is the self-transcendence of the world of matter reaching out to God ... This self-transcendence of the cosmos, in its highest and final stage, is identical with the absolute self-communication of God.'[8] It seems to me that Edwards points in the right direction: the real, historical, material existence of Jesus and the fact of his death is the beginning of the final stage of world history, the beginning of what the New Testament calls the kingdom or reign of God. This term refers to the transforming presence of God already at work in the world bringing about reconciliation and the transformation of the world which will come to its fulfilment in the second coming of Christ at the end of history.

Having written that sentence I immediately ask myself: what does this mean, especially within the context of the way in which the natural world is presently being raped and destroyed? To try to answer it I think we need to explore a little more deeply the closely connected Christian teaching about the incarnation of Jesus.

Paradoxically and curiously, the doctrine of the incarnation was largely lost in the search for the historical Jesus. Theologians and biblical scholars became so focused on the historical facts of Jesus' biography that they seemed to lose, or forget, the significance of his human existence. The unique characteristic of Christianity as a religion is the importance it places on the material, on the flesh, on that which most roots us in the history and processes of the earth. For Christianity, matter really matters. This is unequivocally the attitude of the New Testament. The First Letter of John, for instance, makes belief in the identity between the physical, human Jesus and the divine Son of God normative for Christian belief: 'By this you know the Spirit of God: every spirit that confesses that Jesus Christ has come in the flesh is from God' (4:2). John's Gospel also refuses to back away from the reality of Jesus' physicality and the fact of his human existence and history. John will not compromise with those who want to turn Jesus into an abstraction, a mere appearance of the Divine in an adopted and disposable body. It is in the actual human body of Jesus that we discover God, and this is reinforced when consuming Jesus' flesh is made the touchstone of continuing in his company. In John's Gospel Jesus lays down an ultimatum to his disciples: 'Unless you eat the flesh of the Son of Man and drink his blood, you have no life in you. Those who eat my flesh and drink my blood have eternal life' (6:53–54). Writing late in New Testament times, probably in the 90s of the 1st century, the author of John's Gospel was clearly aware of the church's regular celebration of the Eucharist. In this chapter Jesus had already referred to himself as the 'true bread from heaven' (6:34–35), another clear reference to the Eucharist. In Eucharistic formulas nowadays Christians normally used the word 'body' rather than 'flesh': 'This is my body.' Somehow it is less confronting. But many scholars think that Jesus actually used the word 'flesh' because his aim was to confront. This was too much for many of his followers and they turned away: 'When many of his disciples heard this [the teaching about eating his flesh and drinking his blood], they said, "This teaching is difficult; who can accept it?" ... Because of this many of his disciples turned back and no longer went about with him' (John 6:60–6).

Like those who turned away then, there are many Christians today who are also Gnostics at heart. In other words, they don't believe in the full humanity of Jesus, or that God in the flesh of Jesus embraced the fullness of the human condition. They spiritualise the incarnation through an exaggerated emphasis on Christ's divinity at the expense of his humanity. In reality, what John's Gospel is saying is that the reception of the Eucharist establishes a most intimate connection between the life of Christ and the life of the Christian. In a literal sense the two become 'one flesh'.

The word 'flesh' here is the important clue; it is an essential key to understanding biblical anthropology and the nature of the human person. God alone is 'Spirit'. All else is 'flesh': *sarx* in Greek, *basar* in Hebrew. But the biblical word does not only refer to the 'meat' of the person, the material and animal side in contradistinction to the spiritual. As we have already seen, it has no relationship to the Greek idea of a body of flesh animated by a spiritual soul. For the Bible, a person does not *have* a body; he or she *is* a body. Each of us is *soma*, an animated body, a psycho-spiritual unity that is summed up in the word 'flesh'. It is our bodily existence that roots us in the human community. It is also what directs us towards transcendence and the divine through communion with Christ in the Eucharist.

But 'flesh' also refers to the physical – the vulnerable and mortal body, destined for sickness and death. We have seen that both Platonic and neo-Platonic philosophy have had a profound influence on the development of Christian theology, especially in terms of spiritualising faith and almost denying the significance of the body and the flesh. For Platonists, immortality was achieved by jettisoning the body and returning to the pure, supposedly limpid life of the soul. But our actual human experience is different, for it is only when we admit and embrace bodily existence that we can face the fact of death. Genuine Christian theology has always understood this and has never embraced immortality in the Platonic sense. It has never denied the reality of death. Christ, after all, 'was born of the Virgin Mary, suffered under Pontius Pilate, was crucified, died, and was buried', as the Apostles' Creed says.

For the Christian, as for Christ, death is seen as an opening out to a transforming process of union with God through bodily resurrection and a profound sense of continuity with this life, rather than as some type of disembodied, 'spiritual' existence separate from the here and now. The belief in the bodily resurrection of Christ is unequivocal. The Christian teaching is that after his death on the cross Christ rose in his body. Jesus makes this clear to his followers and apostles when he appears to them after the resurrection. They think he is a spirit or ghost, but he says: '"Why are you frightened, and why do doubts arise in your hearts? Look at my hands and feet; see that it is I myself. Touch me and see, for a ghost does not have flesh and bones as you see that I have"' (Luke 24:38–39). He then asks for something to eat. Clearly he is emphasising that he has risen in his body, just as he died in his body.

The Apostles' Creed also says 'I believe in … the resurrection of the body.' Christian teaching is that we will also ultimately rise in our bodies. Until the century just before Jesus, the Hebrew notion of an afterlife was very vague, and any notion of immortality which didn't involve the body would have been thought nonsense. As already mentioned, the idea of the immortality of the soul was a very late development in Hebrew thought, and in fact originated in Greek philosophy. The notion of resurrection is clearly part of New Testament teaching, but with the exception of Christ's resurrection, it tends to be vague about the notion of our bodily resurrection. As we will see below, the doctrine of the resurrection of the body is really only clarified in the post-apostolic period, and was certainly clear by the time the creeds began to be used in the late 2nd century.

Underlying Christian notions of resurrection is the doctrine of the incarnation, which is that God literally assumed human flesh in Christ and entered intimately into the stuff of the world, into matter. Despite Christianity's poor record on sexuality, it actually supports the centrality of matter and the body. Jesus entered into the human condition totally. St Paul says, in the Second Letter to the Corinthians, that God 'made him [Jesus] to be sin who knew no sin' (5:21). The word 'sin' here refers to the fact that God in Jesus knew our weakness, failures, mistakes, vulnerability, illness, tiredness, frustration, fear, despair and our frightening knowledge that we will all eventually die. He did not resile from anything human. Jesus was born of a woman in a body the same as ours. His body grew and developed and he experienced health and weakness. As an adult he stood against the prevailing religious and political systems and as a result was tortured, crucified and died. He rose again 'on the third day' in his body, and he ascended bodily into heaven. In the vivid phrase of Paul we 'see the glory of God shining in the [bodily] face of Christ' (II Corinthians 4:6).

Throughout the New Testament it is crystal clear that the flesh of Jesus is basic to the definition of who Christ is.[9] Christians believe that in baptism they become incorporated into the very living body of Christ, that in the Eucharist they receive his flesh and blood, and that they will share in his resurrection through the resurrection of their own bodies. In the Letter to the Colossians Paul sums it up by saying that in Christ 'the whole fullness of the Godhead dwells bodily' (2:9). In other words, the material body is at the absolute core of Catholic-Christian faith. That is why I keep saying, 'Matter really matters.'

But despite the theology of the incarnation, neo-Platonist ideology – the notion of the person as a kind of combined body and soul made up of material and spiritual-intellectual aspects – has continued to dominate the Christian tradition. As a result, most people in our culture tend to think of the spiritual as immortal and the body as destined for death and decay. The Christian doctrine of the resurrection of the body confronts the denial of the body and materiality head on and refutes it. This is why the doctrine of the resurrection of the body created so much difficulty for Platonised theologians. Augustine, for example, struggled for many years with this teaching. Many people today are still confused about life after death. They tend to identify continuing existence with the Platonic notion of the immortality of the soul, when Christianity is really talking about a continuing life in the glorified flesh of the body (by 'glorified', theology means the fulfilment of all human potential). Many Christians are still unable to distinguish clearly the Christian teaching about the resurrection of the body from the Platonic philosophical notion of the immortality of the soul. Platonism should be the first ideology abandoned when a genuinely environmental spirituality and theology begin to permeate Christian life. Environmental theology has to place the incarnation at the centre of its focus because it literally means that God takes the flesh, matter, and the world seriously – so seriously, in fact, that in Jesus the divine and the transcendent enter into the very processes of material existence.

The corollaries of this are obvious. If God takes matter so seriously that God becomes identified with matter in the flesh of Jesus, then surely we too must take the material world seriously. In environmental theology the incarnation of God assumes a central symbolic and real role: 'God so loved the world (the Greek word used here is *kosmos*) that he gave his only Son' (John 3:16). It is only through a thorough-going emphasis on the historical, enfleshed Jesus as the living image of God that theology will be able to rid Christianity of its dualism and its contempt for the world and matter. The incarnation means that it is incumbent on the church to take the cosmos and the earth seriously. For it is in and through matter that God is revealed. As a consequence, I see Christ not so much as the central point of history, but as the ultimate symbol that God takes God's material, natural world utterly seriously. It is matter that is sacramental, the symbol of the presence of the ultimate. The incarnation is all about the environment.

So to answer the question I posed some pages back about how we make real the kingdom of God on earth today: we do it by standing up for the natural world, by defending other creatures and other species, by making a stand against human rapaciousness and anthropocentrism, by placing the defence of the earth at the centre of Christian morality, by moving beyond immature distinctions between body and soul, by seeing global warming and human over-population as the greatest moral challenges of our time and actually doing something about them. By tackling these issues we cooperate in the building of God's reign.

I want to look a little more closely now at the often misunderstood Christian doctrine of the resurrection of the body. This doctrine says that just as Jesus rose 'in his body', so we too will rise 'bodily'. It will not be a reunion of a separated soul with inert body, but an animated body rising towards the embrace of God. Also as theologian Richard McBrien points out, resurrection is not purely individualistic; it is the foundation of belief in what the church calls the communion of saints. As McBrien says, 'life after death is also communal life'.[10] Here it is important to recall that all doctrines are symbols: they are metaphoric and poetic, and ought be taken more as pointers to a reality beyond our understanding than literally. The resurrection of the body is about the continuation of human bodily life beyond death and indicates that this continuation will not be a purely individualistic act: just as human life now involves us in community, so will our life with God. In its oddly anthropocentric way, Christianity is saying that the body and the flesh are so important that it is in and through the body that each will come to what St Paul calls the *pleroma* – the fullness of wisdom, peace, justice, joy, love, and all possible experience in God. Paul, as we saw, also applies this notion of fullness to the world itself, which, he says, has been 'groaning in labour pains' until the world and each of us achieves 'the redemption of our bodies' (Romans 8:22–23). All this language is metaphorical, but this positive vision of the material world and everything within it immediately bestows intrinsic value on matter.

This is a different picture from that presented by those elements of mainstream Christianity (and Christian fundamentalists) who see the destruction of the world as a kind of cleansing process in which 'the sheep and the goats' are separated, with the goats going off to hell, and those who are saved marching off to heaven to be with God. Paul's image of the completion and fulfilment of the world's potential is intimately linked to human salvation and fullness of life: for Paul, there is no human fulfilment without the cosmos itself coming to completion. According to this view, if we destroy the world, or large parts of it, we will destroy ourselves and our chance of salvation. It is these neglected elements of Christology which need to be re-emphasised as we move towards the development of an environmental theology.

Yet I have to admit that I still find myself dissatisfied with the traditional presentation of Christ. I am far more preoccupied with the search for God in the world than I am with the quest for Jesus. Perhaps that is because I have been formed in a community that is committed to the gospels and the person of Christ and I have integrated that. I completely accept that Christian faith without Christ is a meaningless and empty system, that, as Martin Luther said, *crux probat omnia* – the cross of Jesus is the test of everything. Nevertheless, the sense of transcendent presence that I find in the natural world of wilderness and sea, among the wild animals, and in the beauty of the stars and the vast history of the cosmos, is now far more influential on me than the traditional forms of theological and spiritual discourse. While in past cultures the focus on Christ and God worked, with the dominance of science today I think we need to commence our search for the transcendent with our experience of the mysterious presence of God in the world rather than with the Bible and Christian revelation. That comes later, when one comes to explicit faith and commitment.

So in my view, we need to reinvent the way we present Christianity. We need to discover a new starting point. Christians must look outwards from their historical preoccupations with Christ, the Bible, salvation and the church and instead focus on the history and reality of the cosmos. It is here that the elusive presence of the transcendent God is to be found. It is in the world and cosmos that the ultimate meaning of existence is to be discovered. It is the natural world which is the primal revelation of God and the place where the transcendent is most sacramentally present.

However, as recent thinkers such as Thomas Berry, Brian Swimme, Matthew Fox, Diamuid O'Murchu and Michael Morwood have pointed out, once you take the cosmos seriously, in terms of its history and its extent, you have to expand your theology enormously, and the nature of belief changes.[11] We have to take contemporary cosmology seriously, not because it is 'modern', but because it is the only way in which we can speak coherently to our world. Science today sees the world as having reached the present by means of a long and complex evolutionary process. In other words, the sheer proportions and time span of our world have been expanded enormously.

This demands an expansion of our understanding of God's interaction with the world. In a way, environmental theology turns the traditional theological process on its head. In the past it worked from Jesus to God to the world. Now it works from the world to God to Jesus. In other words, we intuit the divine presence out there in nature and the cosmos. It is only once we articulate that that we have a chance of encountering Christ as the ultimate enfleshed expression of God's love and understanding.

Hans Küng is a contemporary theologian who understands the nature of modern culture well and, as the success of his many books indicates, has a great facility in speaking to it. He believes deeply in the need for genuine and open dialogue among beliefs and communities. At the core of his theology is one key word: ecumenism. His entire theological output constantly comes back to the practice of openness among people of differing views. From his original work on Karl Barth, through his books on inter-Christian dialogue, to his current concern with Christian dialogue with the other great world religions, and with the need to develop a global ethic that will underpin all our activities and relationships, he always comes back to the importance of a truly ecumenical attitude.

In his book *Theology for the Third Millennium* Küng uses the word 'ecumenical' in its broadest sense, to describe the emerging cultural epoch. He says that he prefers this term to the modern cultural buzzwords 'postmodern', 'post-history' and 'post-enlightenment':

> I would prefer to call this emerging epoch of ours 'ecumenical', in the sense of a new global understanding of the various denominations, religions and regions ... We have reached a crisis which some today would understand apocalyptically as an 'end time', which others, unwilling to abandon all hope, would see as a time of transition.[12]

Küng, of course, belongs to the latter group. Comparing his life to that of Joseph Ratzinger, Pope Benedict XVI, Küng says that given his background and training, he could have committed himself 'to the hierarchical Roman system' (which would have probably resulted in his becoming a bishop or even a cardinal), but that instead 'Without ever giving up my roots in the Christian faith, I embarked on a life of expanding concentric circles: the unity of the churches, peace among the religions, the community of nations.'[13] For me, this was a far more important commitment than becoming a churchman – or even, like Ratzinger, a pope.

Küng stresses that this new ecumenical culture is only just starting to emerge and that it will lead us to a new understanding of ourselves and our relationship to the world. We need to construct an *oikoumene* (the Greek word from which 'ecumenism' is derived) which is characterised by a world view which is able to reach across the particularities of religion, culture and nation to give us a sense of being citizens of the whole earth. He suggests that while the epoch of modernity was secular in outlook, characterised by the 'God is dead' debate and the denial of the significance of faith and spirituality by writers such as Christopher Hitchens and Richard Dawkins, the ecumenical world view has rediscovered that religion and commitment to a deeper life are an essential part of being human. God is alive today and is being found anew.

Despite the ravages of rabid fundamentalism in all the great religious traditions, as well as among neo-Darwinians and other scientists, it is important for the sake of peace and the survival of the world that genuinely religious people tackle the task of which Küng speaks.[14] This task is to focus on what binds the world together rather than on what separates us. Küng actually takes this further, asking whether or not there is 'one true religion', or one true church. This is a frightening question for some Christians, given their traditional emphasis on the exclusivity of Christ – Christ as the one and only manifestation of God – and their rejection of all other possibilities of God revealing God's self to us.

Actually, the task confronting us sits squarely between fanaticism and indifference and is of profound importance:

> Blind zeal for truth has brought on unrestrained injury, burnings at the stake, destruction, and murder at all times and in all churches

> and religions. Conversely, fatigued forgetfulness of truth has as its consequence disorientation and anomie, so that many people no longer believe in anything at all.[15]

The Catholic Church has come a long way in dealing with these questions. It recognised at the Second Vatican Council that the other great world religions are genuine vehicles of grace and salvation: 'The Catholic religion rejects nothing of all which is true and holy in these religions' the *Declaration on Non-Christian Religions* says.[16] Catholic theology has moved right away from the notion that one has to be, in that odd phrase of Karl Rahner, an 'anonymous Christian' to attain salvation. The same cannot be said for some branches of evangelical Protestantism. Despite vigorous debate in the World Council of Churches at several general assemblies, the Protestant evangelical tradition generally does not yet accept that the majority of the humans come to grace, truth and genuine morality through their own faiths.

Not that there has not been some backtracking within Catholicism, as the September 2000 Declaration of the Congregation for the Doctrine of the Faith, *Dominus Jesus* (DJ), makes clear. This document was written under the aegis of the then-Cardinal Joseph Ratzinger. Parts of DJ are particularly inept. As I pointed out in my book on Benedict XVI, DJ was criticised by many, including bishops and cardinals, and 'it largely ignores all of the work that has been achieved in ecumenical dialogue with the other Christian churches and other religious traditions … since the end of Vatican II'.[17]

However, the kind of approach espoused by Küng is increasingly being recognised even by civil governments as a real contribution to breaking down the barriers that lead to the so-called clash of civilisations. A good example of this is the Australian and Indonesian governments' cooperation in promoting this kind of dialogue between Christians and Muslims.

Deep ecumenism also has much to offer to environmentalism. A truly ecumenical theology can underpin a trans-religious approach of caring for the natural world. That is why fundamentalists, capitalists and pro-development activists are suspicious of it. As we saw at the beginning of this book, more and more people from different religious traditions are committing themselves to caring for the world because they realise that nature and the material world are the deepest and most pervasive symbolic images of that which all genuine religions seek – the transcendent. At the heart of all true religion is the search for God, for the God that transcends all the revelations of the religious books – Bible, the Quran, the Bhagavad Gita – for the God who is more often found in music, in art, in the wilderness, and above all in the natural world than in the self-engrossed, sad faces of the followers of particular revelations and saviours. There is only one non-negotiable, and that is that we only have one world – this one – so it must be here that we will find God. If we destroy the world, we destroy not only ourselves, but also the most important symbol of God that we have.

So what hope is there that we will change our ways radically? To be honest, as a historian I think it unlikely. People in wealthy countries are unlikely to embrace a drop in their standard of living, even in the face of global warming. Also, as became clear at the Copenhagen Climate Change Conference:

> Western governments underestimated the strength of developing countries' entrenched grievances – that the imperialist West had industrialised and grown wealthy at their expense, even today through its continued dominance of global trade and financial systems.[18]

Countries such as China, India, South Africa and Brazil don't see why they should limit their development just because many people in the developed West are concerned about climate change, 'particularly when the science validates the idea of a massive Western debt to the South, in the form of dangerous quantities of carbon dioxide accumulated in the atmosphere during the West's 300 years of successful industrialisation'.[19] They ask, why should their emerging middle class bear the burden created by the West in the process of its development? And the problem of over-population threatens to overwhelm everything any of us try to do. And even if people in developed countries did choose simpler, sustainable lifestyles, some of the forces that work against this particular type of change (such as the extractive industries, particularly coal and oil) have extraordinary resources. Because it is so sensitive to powerful lobbies representing vested interests, there is a real sense in which our large, participative democracy is particularly ill-adapted to deal with these kinds of environmental challenges, particularly given the tight time-frames we face with global warming and environmental destruction.

It is wishful thinking to imagine that suddenly everyone will understand the problems and take action to deal with global warming. We are still not even able to control deforestation in developed countries, let alone the Third World, despite the fact that old-growth forests are the best carbon sinks we have. The disconnections and disjunctions in human 'reasoning' remain mind-boggling. Thus the scenario outlined by James Lovelock – of a remnant humankind living in the few inhabitable places left on earth in a new Dark Age, and dominated by those with tactical nuclear weapons – has increasing plausibility.

Sure, there are many people of goodwill who are seriously committed to changing attitudes and who are willing to make the sacrifices needed. I've lost count of the number of meetings and gatherings I've been to where people have preached the need for local action and personal change and conversion. But as Martin Heidegger pointed out, we don't face an ethical as much as a philosophical problem. His view is that, sad to say, we are not going to change things – or change things quickly enough – by acting ethically. It is even more absurd to think that we will achieve anything through carbon trading. After all, it was capitalism in its economic rationalist incarnation that created the problem in the first place, so to use the system which created the problem in the first place seems to be contradictory. As James Hanson said in relation to global warming, a straight tax on pollution would be a much more logical and simpler solution. Christians and others of goodwill will find it hard to grasp that ethics will not solve the problem. And it is indeed a great shame that this is not an issue that can be 'managed' by goodness. It can't even be achieved by the abandonment of free-market capitalism, even though that system has been and remains a crucial factor in the process of environmental destruction. Neither is socialism a panacea. It has been as destructive as capitalism.

Don't misunderstand me. This is not a call to 'eat, drink and be merry for tomorrow we die'. I still believe that we have to act ethically, and we have to do everything we possibly can to change our own and other's attitudes. I would not have written this book if I didn't think we have been called to act to stop environmental destruction. But we have to be realistic about the time constraints we face with global warming and species extinction, and the difficulty of getting democratic governments to face intractable, long-term issues which will have an impact immediately on their electorates, especially if that impact constrains consumption or challenges individualism. So this is not a call to take it easy, but it is a caution for those who act on climate change or the environment to be realistic about what can be achieved when the odds are stacked against change.

Nevertheless, the last thing I want to encourage is cynicism. We have to do as much as is humanly possible. We have to, as the Second Letter to Timothy says, 'fight the good fight', finish the race, keep the faith (4:7).

So people of goodwill confront a far-reaching challenge. Even though our religious and intellectual systems have failed us, we need to hang on to hope. We need to be convinced that hope is not just wishful thinking, a velleity (a mere wish without any accompanying effort), or an inclination to do the right thing. Rather it involves a determination not to sit back and accept things, not to 'cop it sweet' as the slang expression puts it. Hope is intimately linked to imagination, and imagination is the ability to discover other, new ways of viewing reality. It is about conceiving of the world differently. It is, as Heidegger says, the facility to 'poetise', the capacity to create new and different possibilities, to bring things together and make new, unexpected connections.

So in order to survive we are going to have to see and value the natural world differently. This will mean abandoning a purely utilitarian view of nature, a view that sees it merely as resources to be exploited. We need to perceive the world and the cosmos as a kind of poem that conveys a deeper meaning to us, that takes us beyond superficial consciousness and into the realm of the sacred. We must begin to see nature as a theophany, a manifestation of the transcendent.

But how is this going to happen? How will profound change like this come about? All the evidence seems to point to our inability to re-conceive or re-calibrate our vision of the natural world.

This is where we have to recall again Heidegger's words: 'only a [G]od can save us'. Another aspect of hope is trust. We need to trust that God will not abandon creation. How God saves the natural world is God's business. Perhaps the answer lies in serendipity, in the unexpected, in the kind of sudden and unforeseen change that comes out of left field. I said earlier that as a historian I was not very optimistic that enough of us would change quickly and radically enough for the natural world to be saved and environmental destruction reversed. But as a historian I also know that radical and far-reaching change often comes serendipitously – in the least-expected way and from utterly unpredicted sources. Even in 1988, who would have expected the complete collapse of the whole Soviet system in Russia and Eastern Europe and the fall of the Berlin Wall as ordinary people seized control of it while the once-dreaded East German secret police stood looking on helplessly? And when King Louis XVI was beheaded by the French revolutionaries in 1793, who would have expected that France would have an Emperor 12 years later in 1805: Napoleon I?

So things can change, suddenly and unexpectedly. Keeping that in mind, we also need to confront the metaphysical (and ethical) challenge before us. We need to exercise our imaginations to develop a new paradigm, a new way of thinking about and viewing reality. We face so great a crisis that it can only be solved by opening ourselves up to completely new ways of perceiving reality.

Despite the overwhelming odds that we face, we need to hang on tightly to hope. Hope is at the core of Christian faith, and as St Paul says, 'hope does not disappoint us' (Romans 5:5). My trust is in a Creator God who will not abandon the world, which is product of divine creativity. If God 'so loved the world that he gave his only Son ... in order that the world might be saved through him' (John 3:16–17), my hope is that we won't have to do it on our own. God will save the world, and the whole process is in the hands of the Creator.

Notes

1 CURSED

1 Paul Collins, *Burn: The Epic Story of Bushfire in Australia*, Melbourne: Scribe, 2009, pp. xxvii–xxviii.
2 Paul Collins, *God's Earth: Religion as if matter really mattered*, Melbourne: HarperCollins Religious, 1995, p. 1.
3 Rev Jerry Falwell in Alex Johnson, 'More evangelicals say God is green', www.MSNBC.com, 6 November 2007.
4 Steven Douglas, 'How to "green" your church', *Eureka Street*, 6 March 2009.
5 Mary Evelyn Tucker and Christopher Chapple (eds), *Hinduism and Ecology: The Intersection of Earth, Sky, and Water*, Cambridge MA: Harvard University Press, 2000.
6 All quotations from Marjorie Hope and James Young, 'Islam and Ecology', *Cross Currents*, www.crosscurrents.org/islamecology.html.
7 Thomas Berry, interview in TV documentary, *God's Earth*, ABC TV.
8 Thomas Berry, *The Dream of the Earth*, San Francisco: Sierra Club Books, 1988, p. 21.
9 Karol Wojtyla (trans. H.T. Willetts), *Love and Responsibility*, London: Collins, 1981, p. 121. See Paul Collins, *Mixed Blessings. John Paul II and the Church of the Eighties*, Melbourne: Penguin, 1986, pp. 169–72.
10 See *Summa Theologiae* (ST) I, Q 76, art 2 and the *Summa Contra Gentiles* (SCG) II, 76, 78, 79 and especially 82.
11 Berry, *God's Earth*.
12 St John of the Cross, '*En una noche oscura*' ('Upon a gloomy night') in Roy Campbell's translation of the *Poems of Saint John of the Cross* (London: Fount/Collins, 1979, p. 11).
13 From Berry interview, *Insight*, ABC Radio National, Sunday, 27 January 1991.
14 Berry, *Dream*, p. 17.

2 WARMING

1 See Collins, *Burn*, pp. xvii–xxviii.
2 Ibid., pp. 1–50, 108–35, 216–32.
3 Bureau of Meteorology, Special Climate Statement 17: 'The Exceptional January–February 2009 Heat Wave in South-Eastern Australia', 9 February 2009, pp. 3–4.
4 David Karoly, 'Bushfires and extreme heat in south-east Australia', guest commentary in *Real Climate*, 16 February 2009 at www.realclimate.org/index.php/archives/2009/bushfire-and-climate.
5 Ibid.
6 David Spratt, 'This is an emergency', paper based on David Spratt and Phillip Sutton, *Climate Code Red: The case for emergency action*, Melbourne: Scribe, 2008.
7 NASA climatologist Dr Jay Zwally, quoted in Spratt, 'This is an emergency'.
8 George Monbiot, 'The latest science suggests that preventing runaway climate change means total decarbonisation', *The Guardian*, 25 November 2008.
9 Andrew Glikson, 'The methane time-bomb', *Crikey.com*, 10 October 2008.
10 Ian Allison et al., *The Copenhagen Diagnosis, 2009*, Sydney: UNSW Climate Change Research Centre, 2009, p. 23.
11 Spratt, 'This is an emergency'.
12 Guy Pearse, *Coal, Climate Change and the End of the Resources Boom*, Quarterly Essay, 33, Melbourne: Black Inc., 2009, pp. 31–57, 62–74.
13 For 2009 levels see co2now.org. James E. Hanson et al., 'Target Atmospheric CO_2: Where should humanity aim?', *Open Atmospheric Science Journal*, 2, 2008, pp. 217–31. Copy at arvix.org/abs/0804.1126.
14 Clive Hamilton, 'The return of Dr Strangelove', Australian Policy Online, p. 2.
15 Andrew Glickson, '350ppm CO_2: The upper limit of human habitats', privately distributed paper, 22 October 2009.
16 Andrew Glikson, 'Warning from the past: Implications of abrupt atmospheric changes in the recent history of the earth for 21st century climate projections', paper given at Research School of Earth Science, ANU, 2 September 2008.
17 Andrew Glikson, *Crikey.com*, 5 September 2008.
18 See Will Steffen, Paul J. Crutzen and John R. McNeill, 'The Anthropocene: Are humans now overwhelming the great forces of nature?', *Ambio* (Royal Swedish Academy of Sciences), Vol. 36, No. 8, 2008, pp. 614–21.
19 Ibid., p. 615.
20 Ibid., p. 618.
21 James Hansen, 'Global warming twenty years later: Tipping points near', US Congress House Select Committee on Energy Independence and Global Warming, 23 June 2008. Text can be found at www.columbia.edu/~jeh1/.
22 *The Guardian*, 29 November 2009.
23 *The Guardian*, 20 December 2009.
24 James Lovelock, *The Revenge of Gaia*, London: Allen Lane, 2006.
25 W.S. Broecker, 'What if the conveyor were to shut down? Reflections on a possible outcome of the great global experiment', October 1998, available at williamcalvin.com/teaching/Broecker99.html.

26 Tim Flannery, *Now or Never: A sustainable future for Australia?*, Quarterly Essay, 31, Melbourne: Black Inc., 2008, p. 5.
27 Ibid., p. 25.
28 George Monbiot, in *The Guardian*, 25 November 2008.
29 Allison et al., *The Copenhagen Diagnosis, 2009*, pp. 39–40.
30 Quoted in Andrew Glikson, 'Why Penny Wong's Ferrari is hardly a lifeboat', in privately distributed paper, 11 March 2009.
31 Ross Garnaut, *The Garnaut Climate Change Review: Final Report*, Melbourne: Cambridge University Press, 2008, p. 595–96.
32 Berry, *Insight.*
33 Sean McDonagh, privately distributed paper, 'The Catholic Church and Climate Change', 1 December 2008, provided by Rev. Dr Charles Rue.
34 Australian Catholic Bishops Conference, *2002 Social Justice Statement: A New Earth - The Environmental Challenge*, Canberra: ACBC, 2002.
35 Charles Rue, *Let the Son Shine: An Australian Catholic Response to Climate Change*, Sydney, Columban JPIC Office, 2009, p. 27. See also his article 'The perverse skills of climate change deniers', *Eureka Street*, 30 November 2009.
36 Aquinas, ST, I, q 45, a 7. All translations are by the author unless otherwise noted.
37 Berry, quoted by McDonagh, *The Tablet*, 30 April 1994.
38 Berry, *Insight.*
39 Aristotle deals with prudence in several places in his writings. In the *Nicomachean Ethics* (VI, 5) he refers to it as 'practical wisdom'. He also deals with it in the *Eudemian Ethics* at 1250a, 30–39. See W.D. Ross (ed.), *The Works of Aristotle*, Oxford: Oxford University Press, 1915, vol. IX.
40 Aquinas, ST, II II, q 142, a 8.
41 Aquinas, ST, II II, q 77, aa 2–16.
42 Aquinas, ST, II II, q 48, a 1.
43 Aquinas, ST, II II, q 47, a 2, reply to second objection.
44 Aquinas, ST, II II, q 47, a 1.
45 Aristotle, *Eudemian Ethics*, 1250a, 35.
46 Aquinas, ST, II II, q 19, aa 1–8.
47 Karoly, quoted in Clive Hamilton, 'Climate emergency a crisis of democracy', *Crikey.com*, 4 February 2009.
48 Aquinas, ST, II II, q 123, a 3.
49 Aquinas, ST, II II, q 128, a 1.
50 Aquinas, ST, II II, q 123, aa 6, 10. The reference to attacking is at q 123, a 10, reply to third objection.
51 Bernard Häring (trans. Edwin Kaiser), *The Law of Christ*, Cork: The Mercier Press, 1967, Vol. III, p. 37.
52 Ibid., Vol. III, p. 22. See pp. 22–34.
53 Aquinas, ST, II II, q 58, a 1.
54 Häring, *Law*, Vol. III, p. 25.
55 Aquinas, ST, II II, q 58, a 12.
56 Häring, *Law*, Vol. III, p. 26.

3 POPULATION

1 Fred Spoor et al., *Nature*, Vol. 448 (August 2007), pp. 688–91.
2 Richard E. Leakey and Roger Lewin, *People of the Lake: Mankind and Its Beginnings*, New York: Anchor Press/Doubleday, 1978, p. 254.
3 A.J. McMichael, *Planetary Overload: Global Environmental Change and the Health of the Human Species*, Cambridge: Cambridge University Press, 1993, p. 34.
4 Ibid., pp. 105 and 82–83.
5 Steffen et al., 'The Anthropocene', p. 616.
6 Al Gore, *Earth in the Balance: Forging a New Common Purpose*, London: Earthscan, 1992, p. 307.
7 Boris Johnson, 'Global over-population is the real issue', *The Telegraph*, 25 October 2007.
8 Ibid.
9 Gore, *Earth*, p. 307.
10 Alvin Powell, 'Former VP Calls for Change in Thinking', *Harvard University Gazette*, 14 December 2006.
11 Columban Mission Society, *Unjust Genes – Life and Death for Sale*, DVD and booklet on genetically engineered food. See www.columban.org.au.
12 Gore, *Earth*, p. 307.
13 United Nations (UN), *World Population Prospects Report: The 2006 Revision*, Press Release (POP/952), 13 March 2007.
14 These statistics are based on the UN, *World Population Prospects Report: The 2006 Revision*. Slightly conflicting figures can be found the Central Intelligence Agency's *World Fact Book*, at www.cia.gov/library/publications/the-world-factbook/fields/. I have followed the UN figures. The Niger figure is for 2009.
15 Australian Bureau of Statistics, Media Release, 'Australian Demographic Statistics, June 2009'. Issued 3/12/09.
16 John Caldwell, 'Paths to lower fertility', *British Medical Journal*, 9 October 1999, pp. 985–87.
17 Paul Ehrlich and Anne Ehrlich, *Population Explosion*, New York: Simon & Schuster, 1990, p. 216.
18 Chakravarthi Ram-Prasad, 'India's middle class failure', *Prospect Magazine*, Issue 138, September 2007.
19 For the Black Death see David Herlihy, *The Black Death and the Transformation of the West*, Cambridge MA: Harvard University Press, 1997. For the 1918–19 outbreak see John F. Brundage and G. Dennis Shanks, 'Deaths from Bacterial Pneumonia during 1918–19 Influenza Pandemic', *Emerging Infectious Diseases Journal*, Vol. 14, No. 8, August 2008.
20 WHO, 'Pandemic preparedness', at www.who.int/csr/disease/pandemic/en.html.
21 Optimum Population Trust, 'Modest Footprint Carrying Capacity as calculated from Ecological Footprints of Nations Data; Calculations of Human Population Sustainability by countries', at www.optimumpopulation.org.
22 For Australia, see Paul Collins, *Believers: Does Australian Catholicism Have a Future?*, Sydney: UNSW Press, 2008, pp. 43–46. For Ireland, see William H.

MacNeill, *Population and Politics since 1750*, Charlottesville VA: University Press of Virginia, 1990, pp. 58–60.

23 Lambeth Conference 1958, 'The Encyclical Letter from the Bishops; together with resolutions and reports', London: SPCK, 1958, p. 147.

24 Basim F. Masallam in Warren T. Reich (ed.), *The Encyclopedia of Bioethics*, New York: Macmillan, 1978, Vol. 3, p. 1268.

25 Xavier Rynne, *The Third Session. The debates and decrees of Vatican Council II September 14 to November 21, 1964*, London: Faber & Faber, 1965, pp. 161, 162.

26 *The Tablet*, 19/26 December 1992.

27 *The Tablet*, 6 November 1982.

28 J. Brian Hehir, *Encyclopedia of Ethics*, Vol. 3, p. 1254.

29 Paul VI, *Populorum Progressio*, 26 March 1967, paragraph 37.

30 Ibid.

31 John Paul II, Apostolic Exhortation *Familiaris Consortio*, 22 November 1981, paragraph 30.

32 Ibid.

33 John Paul II, Encyclical *Solitudo Rei Socialis*, 30 December 1987, paragraph 25.

34 John Paul II, Angelus Address, 17 July 1997.

35 David Willey, *God's Politician: John Paul and the Vatican*, London: Faber & Faber, 1992, p. 164.

36 Ibid., p. 165.

37 *The Tablet*, 30 April 1994.

38 Benedict XVI, *Caritas in Veritate*, paragraph 44.

39 Hehir, *Encyclopedia of Ethics*, pp. 1255, 1256.

40 Asoka Bandarage, 'Control cash not people', *Ecologist*, 38/8, October 2008.

41 Ehrlich and Ehrlich, *The Population Explosion*, p. 216. Paul Harrison, *The Third Revolution: Environment, Population and a Sustainable World*, London: I.B. Tauris, 1992, pp. 288–91.

42 *ANU Reporter*, 27 April 1994, p. 12.

43 David G Schultenover, *A View from Rome: On the Eve of the Modernist Crisis*, New York: Fordham University Press, 1993, p. 171.

44 Matthew Connolly, *Fatal Misconception: The Struggle to Control World Population*, Cambridge MA: Harvard University Press, 2008.

45 Ralph B. Potter, in *Encyclopedia of Bioethics*, Vol. 3, pp. 1244–49.

4 ENVIRONMENTAL THUGS

1 Lynn White, 'The historical roots of the ecologic crisis', *Science*, 115, 1967, pp. 1203–07.

2 H. Paul Santmire, *The Travail of Nature: The Ambiguous Promise of Christian Theology*, Philadephia: Fortress, 1985, p. 7.

3 Simon Schama, *Landscape and Memory*, London: HarperCollins, 1995, p. 13.

4 Rupert Sheldrake, *The Rebirth of Nature: The Greening of Science and God*, London: Century, 1990, p. 26. See also pp. 25ff.

5 Thomas Berry, *Insight*, ABC Radio National, 30 June 1993.

6 Edward O. Wilson, *The Future of Life*, New York: Alfred A. Knopf, 2002, p. 92.
7 Ibid., pp. 90–2 and 94–6. Quotation from p. 102.
8 John Man, *Atlas of the Year 1000*, London: Penguin, 1999, p. 131.
9 John Mulvaney and Johan Kamminga, *Prehistory of Australia*, Sydney: Allen & Unwin, 1999, p. 124.
10 Josephine Flood, *Archaeology of the Dreamtime: The story of prehistoric Australia and its people*, Sydney: Angus & Robertson, 1992, p. 158. See pp. 157–70 for megafauna.
11 Tim Flannery, *The Future Eaters: An ecological history of the Australasian lands and people*, Sydney: Reed Books, 1994.
12 Mulvaney and Kamminga, *Prehistory*, p. 124.
13 J.N.D. Kelly, *Early Christian Doctrines*, London: A. & C. Black, 1968, p. 24. See also pp. 22–28.
14 Rosemary Radford Ruether, *Sexism and God-talk: Toward a feminist theology*, Boston: Beacon Books, 1983, pp. 79–80.
15 E.R. Dodds, *Pagan and Christian in an Age of Anxiety*, New York: W.W. Norton, 1965, pp. 9–10.
16 Arthur O. Lovejoy, *The Great Chain of Being: A study of the history of an idea*, Cambridge MA: Harvard University Press, 1936, pp. 24, 25. See also pp. 24–35.
17 Dodds, *Pagan and Christian*, p. 29.
18 Lovejoy, *Great Chain*, p. 35.
19 Margaret Miles, *Augustine on the Body*, Missoula MT: Scholars Press, 1979. See also *Fullness of Life: Historical foundations of a new asceticism*, Philadelphia: Westminster, 1981, and *Reading Historical Theology: Before, during and after Augustine*, Eugene OR: Cascade Books, 2008.
20 Peter Brown, *The Body and Society: Men, women and sexual renunciation in early Christianity*, London: Faber & Faber 2008 [1988].
21 Ibid., pp. 29–30.
22 Ibid., p. 438.
23 Ibid., p. 442.
24 Ibid.
25 Cicero, *De natura deorum*, 13:35 quoted in Clarence Glacken, *Traces on the Rhodian Shore: Nature and culture in Western thought from ancient times to the end of the eighteenth century*, Berkeley: University of California Press, 1967, p. 56.
26 Cicero, quoted in Glacken, *Traces*, p. 144.
27 Ibid., p. 175.
28 Sheldrake, *Rebirth*, pp. 12, 33.
29 Heinrich Wolfflin, *Renaissance and Baroque*, London: Collins/Fontana, 1964, p. 38.
30 René Descartes (trans. Donald A. Cress), *Meditations on First Philosophy*, Indianapolis: Hackett Publishing Company, 1993, First Meditation, paragraph 12.
31 René Descartes (trans. Donald A. Cress), *A Discourse on Method*, Indianapolis: Hackett Publishing Company, 1980, part 4.
32 Sheldrake, *Rebirth*, p. 37.
33 Theodore Roszak, *Where the Wasteland Ends: Politics and transcendence in a post industrial society*, New York: Doubleday, 1973, pp. 234–35.

34 Geoffrey Barraclough, *History in a Changing World*, Oxford: Basil Blackwell, 1957, p. 223.
35 Ibid., p. 224.
36 E.O. Wilson in *Salon.com*, 14 January 2002. See also E.O. Wilson, *The Future of Life*, New York: Alfred A. Knopf, 2002.
37 CSIRO, 'Water availability in the Murray–Darling Basin: Summary of a Report from CSIRO to the Australian Government', CSIRO, October 2008.
38 Ibid., p. 5.
39 Thomas Berry, 'The dream of the future: Our way into the future', *Cross Currents*, Summer/Fall, 1987, p. 210.

5 BIBLE

1 The five volumes of *The Earth Bible* were published between 2000 and 2002. The volumes are: Norman C. Habel (ed.), *The Earth Bible. Readings from the perspective of earth*, Sheffield: Sheffield Academic Press, Vol. 1, 2000; Norman C. Habel and Shirley Wurst (eds), *The Earth Bible. The earth story in Genesis*, Sheffield: Sheffield Academic Press, Vol. 2, 2000; Norman C. Habel and Shirley Wurst (eds), *The Earth Bible. The earth story in wisdom traditions*, Sheffield: Sheffield Academic Press, Vol. 3, 2001; Norman C. Habel (ed.), *The Earth Bible. The earth story in the psalms and the prophets*, Sheffield: Sheffield Academic Press, Vol. 4, 2001; Vicky Balabanski and Norman C. Habel, *The Earth Bible. The earth story in the New Testament*, Sheffield: Sheffield Academic Press, Vol. 5, 2002.
2 *The Green Bible* uses the NRSV (New York: Harper One, 2008). Throughout the writing of this chapter I have consulted the *Green Bible* and found it confusing. It is difficult to discern the principles used to choose the verses that have green connotations.
3 See Norman Habel in 'Geophany: The earth story in Genesis 1', in Habel & Wurst, *The earth story in Genesis*, pp. 34–48.
4 Habel, *The earth story in Genesis*, p. 36.
5 Ibid., p. 37.
6 Ibid., p. 42.
7 Ibid., p. 43.
8 Jürgen Moltmann (trans. M. Kohl), *God in Creation: An ecological doctrine of creation*, London: SCM, 1985, p. 277.
9 Habel, *The earth story in Genesis*, p. 47.
10 John L. McKenzie, *Dictionary of the Bible*, London: Geoffrey Chapman, 1966, p. 829 and John Bright, *The History of Israel*, London: SCM, 1972 (revised edn), pp. 216ff.
11 David Atkinson, *Renewing the Face of the Earth: A theological and pastoral response to climate change*, Norwich: Canterbury Press, 2008, p. 63.
12 John L. McKenzie, *The Two-Edged Sword: An interpretation of the Old Testament*, Milwaukee: Bruce Publishing Company, 1956, p. 75.

13 Eugene H. Maly, 'Commentary on Genesis', in Raymond E. Brown (ed.), *The Jerome Biblical Commentary*, Englewood Cliffs NJ: Prentice-Hall, 1968, Vol. I, p. 12.
14 Glacken, *Traces*, p. 151.
15 Mark David Futato, *Interpreting the Psalms*, Grand Rapids MI: Kregal Publications, 2007, p. 115.
16 Peter L. Trudinger, 'Friend or Foe? Earth, Sea and *Chaoskampf* in the Psalms', in Habel (ed.), *The earth story in the psalms and the prophets*, pp. 29–41.
17 Philip J. King, 'Commentary on Amos', in Brown (ed.), *Jerome Biblical Commentary*, Vol. I, p. 245.
18 Bright, *History*, p. 328.
19 Ibid., p. 333.
20 Keith Carley, 'Ezekiel's formula for desolation: Harsh justice for the land/earth', in Habel (ed.), *The earth story in the psalms and the prophets*, p. 145.
21 Kalinda Rose Stevenson, 'If earth could speak: The case of the mountains against YHWH in Ezekiel 6:35–36', in Habel (ed), *The earth story in the psalms and the prophets*, p. 158.
22 Norman C. Habel with the Earth Bible Team, 'Where is the voice of earth in wisdom literature?', in Habel & Wurst (eds), *The earth story in wisdom traditions*, p. 26.
23 See Laura Habgood-Oster, 'Wisdom literature and eco-feminism' and Shirley Wurst, 'Woman wisdom's way: Ecokinship', in Habel & Wurst (eds), *The earth story in wisdom traditions*, pp. 35–47 and 48–64.
24 Habel with the Earth Bible Team, 'Where is the voice of earth in wisdom literature?', p. 29.
25 McKenzie, *Dictionary of the Bible*, p. 440.
26 Ibid., p. 441.
27 Ibid., p. 514.
28 Habel, 'Earth first', in Habel & Wurst (eds), *The earth story in wisdom traditions*, p. 69.
29 Habel & Wurst (eds), *The earth story in wisdom traditions*, pp. 65–77, 78–91 and 116–25. See also Norman C. Habel's fine commentary, *The Book of Job*, Louisville KY: Westminster John Knox Press, 1985.
30 Jerusalem Bible (JB) translation. I will use the JB translation for Job chapters 38 to 42 because it has captured the confrontational irony of the original.
31 McKenzie, *Dictionary of the Bible*, p. 442.
32 Habel, 'Earth first', in Habel & Wurst (eds), *The earth story in wisdom traditions*, p. 74.
33 Moltmann, *God in Creation*, p. 65.
34 William Loader, 'Good news – for the Earth? Reflections on Mark 1:1–15', in Balabanski & Habel, *The earth story in the New Testament*, p. 41.
35 Dean Rich, *Evidence for God*, at www.godandscience.org/apologetics/life_universe_everything.html.
36 Cheryl Hunt et al., 'An environmental mantra? Ecological interest in Romans 8:19–23 and a modest proposal for its narrative interpretation', *Journal of*

Theological Studies, NS Vol. 59, Pt 2, 2008, pp. 546 and 556. See also Brendan Byrne, 'Creation groaning: An Earth Bible reading of Romans 8:18–22', in Habel (ed.), *Readings from the perspective of the earth*, pp. 193–203.
37 Hunt et al., 'An environmental mantra?', p. 573.
38 Glacken, *Traces*, p. 151.

6 'GEOLOGIANS'

1 Anne Lonergan and Caroline Richards (eds), *Thomas Berry and the New Cosmology*, Mystic CT: Twenty Third Publications, 1987, p. 3.
2 Bonaventure, *The Life of Saint Francis*, VIII. See Ewert Cousins' translation in *Bonaventure. The Soul's Journey into God; The Tree of Life; The Life of Saint Francis*, New York: Paulist Press, 1978, pp. 254–55.
3 Jean Leclercq, Francois Vandenbroucke and Louis Bouyer, *A History of Christian Spirituality: The Spirituality of the Middle Ages*, New York: The Seabury Press, 1968, Vol. II, p. 291.
4 Evelyn Underhill, *Mysticism: A Study of the Nature and Development of Man's Spiritual Consciousness*, New York: E.P. Dutton, 1961 [1911], p. 260.
5 Jonas of Bobbio (English translation), *Life of Saint Columbanus*, Philadelphia: Department of History of the University of Pennsylvania, 1895, para 15.
6 St Bonaventure, *The Soul's Journey into God*, Ch. I, 12 in Cousins, *Bonaventure*, p. 69.
7 Denis Minns, *Irenaeus*, London: Geoffrey Chapman, 1994, p. 135.
8 Novatian, *De Trinitate*, 2. Quoted in Jean Danileou, *The Origins of Latin Christianity: A History of Early Christian Doctrine before the Council of Nicaea*, London: Darton, Longman & Todd, 1977, Vol. III, p. 238. See pp. 233–44.
9 Richard J. Woods, *The Spirituality of the Celtic Saints*, Maryknoll NY: Orbis Books, 2000, pp. 182–83.
10 Robin Flower, *The Irish Tradition*, Oxford: Clarendon Press, 1947, pp. 42–43.
11 Quoted in Katherine Scherman, *The Flowering of Ireland: Saints, Scholars and Kings*, Boston: Little, Brown & Company, 1981, p. 139.
12 Friedrich Heer (trans. Janet Sondheimer), *The Medieval World: Europe from 1100 to 1350*, London: Weidenfeld & Nicolson, 1962, p. 96.
13 Ibid., p. 289.
14 Matthew Fox, *Sheer Joy: Conversations with Thomas Aquinas on Creation Spirituality*, San Francisco: Harper SanFrancisco, 1992, p. 59–60.
15 Aquinas, ST, I, Q 45, a 7.
16 Aquinas, ST, I, Q 45, a 6.
17 Aquinas, SCG, Book I, Ch. 95, a 6 (translation from Fox, *Sheer Joy*, p. 66).
18 Aquinas, ST, I, Q 45, a 7, p. 87 (trans. Timothy McDermott, in *Summa Theologiae: A Concise Translation*, London: Eyre and Spottiswoode, 1989).
19 Aquinas, SCG, Book III, Ch. 68, 4. Translation from Vernon J. Bourke, *On the Truth of the Catholic Faith: Summa Contra Gentiles*, New York: Image Books, 1956, p. 224.
20 Robert Bernard Martin, *Gerard Manley Hopkins: A Very Private Life*, London:

HarperCollins, 1992, p. 205.
21 Norman H. MacKenzie, quoted in Martin, *Hopkins*, p. 205.
22 Ibid., pp. 206ff.
23 George Steiner, *Real Presences: Is there anything in what we say?*, London: Faber & Faber, 1989.
24 J.H. Newman (ed. I.T. Ker), *An Essay in Aid of a Grammar of Assent*, Oxford: Oxford University Press, 1985, pp. 221ff.
25 See Claude Cuénot, *Teilhard de Chardin: A Biographical Study*, Baltimore: Helicon Press, 1965 and Emile Rideau, *Teilhard de Chardin: A Guide to His Thought*, London: Collins, 1967.
26 Leszek Kolakowski, *Bergson*, Oxford: Oxford University Press, 1985, p. 58.
27 Rideau, *Teilhard de Chardin*, p. 53.
28 Pierre Teilhard de Chardin (trans. René Hague), *Toward the Future*, London: Collins, 1975, p. 171.
29 Pierre Teilhard de Chardin (trans. Norman Denny), *The Future of Man*, London: Collins, 1964, p. 34.
30 Pierre Teilhard de Chardin (trans. Gerald Vann), *The Hymn of the Universe*, London: Collins, 1965, pp. 59–71.
31 Pierre Teilhard de Chardin (trans. Bernard Wall), *The Divine Milieu: An Essay on the Interior Life*, New York: Collins, 1960.
32 The first two were reprinted by Anima Publications (Chambersberg PA, 1989) and the third by Magi Books, Albany, 1968.
33 Brian Swimme and Thomas Berry, *The Universe Story: From the primordial flaming forth to the ecozoic era*, San Francisco: Harper SanFrancisco, 1992. Thomas Berry, *The Great Work: Our Way into the Future*, New York: Bell Tower, 1999.
34 Berry, *Great Work*, p. 1.
35 Biographical details and unacknowledged quotations from Berry come from author interviews and material broadcast on ABC Radio National, *Insight*, 27 January 1991.
36 Quoted in Lonergan and Richards, *Thomas Berry*, p. 3.
37 Berry, *Dream*, p. 17.
38 Thomas Berry, 'Contemporary spirituality: The journey of the human community', *Cross Currents*, Summer/Fall 1974, pp. 174–75.
39 Berry, *Dream*, p. 14.
40 Ibid, p. 196.
41 Berry in unpublished paper, 'The Ecozoic Period', p. 2.
42 Berry and Swimme, *Universe Story*, p. 241.
43 Ibid., p. 243.
44 Ibid., p. 238.
45 Ibid., p. 237.
46 Berry, *Dream*, p. 211.
47 Berry and Swimme, *Universe Story*, p. 258.
48 Ibid.
49 Ibid., p. 260.

50 Matthew Fox, *Original Blessing: A Primer in Creation Spirituality*, Santa Fe: Bear & Co., 1981; *The Coming of the Cosmic Christ*, Melbourne: Collins/Dove, 1989.
51 Quotation from author interview with Fox in 1989. Other unfootnoted quotations are from the same interview.
52 Disputes with the Vatican had come to a head when the Vatican imposed a year-long silence on Fox in December 1988. The Vatican then put pressure on the Dominican order to either deal with or silence Fox permanently.
53 *Creation*, November/December 1988.
54 Ibid.
55 Matthew Fox, *Confessions: The Making of a Post-Denominational Priest*, San Francisco: Harper SanFrancisco, 1997; *A New Reformation: Creation Spirituality and the Transformation of Christianity*, Rochester VT: Inner Traditions, 2006.
56 Sean McDonagh, *To Care for the Earth: A Call to a New Theology*, London: Geoffrey Chapman, 1986; *The Greening of the Church*, London: Geoffrey Chapman, 1990; *Passion for the Earth*, London: Geoffrey Chapman, 1994; *Patenting Life? Stop! Is Corporate Greed Forcing Us to Eat Genetically Engineered Food?*, Dublin: Dominican Publications, 2003; *The Death of Life: The Horror of Extinction*, Dublin: Columba Press, 2004; *Climate Change: The Challenge to Us All*, Dublin: Columba Press, 2007.
57 Sean McDonagh in Walter Schwarz (ed.), *Updating God*, Basingstoke: Marshall Pickering, 1988, p. 140.
58 Ibid., p. 141.
59 McDonagh, *Care*, pp. 3–11.
60 The quotations come from articles 'Challenging the "Washington Consensus"' and 'One Law for the Rich and One for the Poor' by Sean McDonagh from late 2008, made available by Rev. Dr Charles Rue.
61 Pontifical Council for Justice and Peace, *The Compendium of the Social Doctrine of the Church*, Washington DC: USCCB Publishing, 2005.
62 Quotations in this paragraph are from McDonagh, 'Engineering life: Ethics and genetic engineering', at www.sedos.org/english/McDonagh.html.
63 Charles Birch, *On Purpose*, Sydney: UNSW Press, 1990, p. xiv.
64 Charles Birch, *Science and Soul*, Sydney: UNSW Press, 2008, p. 170.
65 Birch, *On Purpose*, p. 174.
66 Charles Birch, *Regaining Compassion: For Humanity and Nature*, Sydney: UNSW Press, 1993, pp. 105–06.
67 Moltmann, *God in Creation*, p. xi.
68 Jürgen Moltmann (trans. James W. Leitch), *Theology of Hope: On the Ground and Implication of a Christian Eschatology*, London: SCM, 1967; *The Crucified God: The Cross of Christ as the Foundation and Criticism of Christian Theology* (trans. R.A. Wilson and J. Bowden), New York: Harper & Row, 1974. The quotation is from *Crucified God*, p. 5.
69 Jürgen Moltmann (trans. Margaret Kohl), *The Way of Jesus Christ*, London: SCM, 1989.
70 This material is drawn from an author interview with Moltmann for the TV documentary *God's Earth*.

71 Jürgen Moltmann, *The Coming of God: Christian Eschatology*, Minneapolis: Fortress, 1996.
72 See George Steiner's *Heidegger*, London: Fontana, 1992. For biography, see Rüdiger Safranski (trans. Ewald Osers), *Martin Heidegger: Between Good and Evil*, Cambridge MA: Harvard University Press, 1998. See also Hugo Ott (trans. Allan Blunden), *Martin Heidegger: A Political Life*, London: HarperCollins, 1993.
73 Steiner, *Heidegger*, p. 28.
74 Ibid., pp. 11–12.
75 Martin Heidegger (trans. William Lovitt), *The Question Concerning Technology and Other Essays*, New York: Harper Torchbooks, 1977.
76 Jan van der Veken, 'Only a god can save us', lecture at World Council of Churches, 7th General Assembly, Canberra, Australia, September 1991.
77 John Macquarrie, *Heidegger and Christianity: The Hensley Henson Lectures 1993–94*, London: SCM Press, 1994. For Heidegger's mysticism, see John D. Caputo, *The Mystical Element in Heidegger's Thought*, New York: Fordham University Press, 1986.
78 Steiner, *Heidegger*, p. 144.

7 GOD'S EARTH

1 Paul Collins, *Between the Rock and a Hard Place: Being Catholic Today*, Sydney: ABC Books, 2004, pp. 113–14.
2 Ibid.
3 Quoted in Elizabeth Tooker (ed.), *Native North American Spirituality of the Eastern Woodlands*, New York: Paulist Press, 1979, p. 27.
4 Author interview, 1993.
5 Christopher D. Stone, 'Should Trees Have Standing? Toward Legal Rights for Natural Objects', *Southern California Law Review*, 45, Spring 1972, pp. 450–501, later published as a book. See also Stone's *Earth and Other Ethics: The Case for Moral Pluralism*, New York: Harper & Row, 1987.
6 Glacken, *Traces*, pp. 42–44, 60–61.
7 Aquinas, ST, I, Q 2, art 3.
8 Introduction at w.w.w.creationdesign.org/
9 Richard Dawkins and Jerry Coyne, *The Guardian*, 1 September 2005.
10 Richard Dawkins, *The Blind Watchmaker: Why the evidence of evolution reveals a universe without design*, Harmondsworth: Penguin, 1990.
11 Jacques Monod, *Chance and Necessity: An Essay on the Natural Philosophy of Modern Biology*, New York: Vintage Books, 1972.
12 John Polkinghorne, *Religion and Current Science*, Sydney: New College, UNSW, 1993, p. 17.
13 See papers by Gingerich and Polkinghorne in Murray Rae, Hilary Regan and John Stenhouse (eds), *Science and Theology: Questions at the Interface*, Edinburgh: T. & T. Clark, 1994. Paul Davies, *The Mind of God: The Scientific Basis for a Rational World*, New York: Simon & Schuster, 1992.
14 Quoted in Underhill, *Mysticism*, p. 160.

15 Steiner, *Real Presences*, p. 140.
16 Rudolf Otto, *The Idea of the Holy*, Harmondsworth: Penguin, 1953.
17 Karl Rahner, The *Foundations of Christian Faith: An Introduction to the Idea of Christianity*, New York: Seabury, 1978, pp. 57–66.
18 Gregory of Nyssa (trans. Abraham J. Malherbe and Everett Ferguson), *The Life of Moses*, New York: Paulist Press, 1978, p. 116.
19 Ibid., p. 95.
20 For a translation of *The Celestial Hierarchy, The Ecclesiastical Hierarchy, The Divine Names* and *The Mystical Theology* see Colm Luibheid, *Pseudo-Dionysius: The Complete Works*, New York: Paulist Press, 1987.
21 *The Mystical Theology*, Ch. 5 (see Luibheid, *Psuedo-Dionysius*, p. 141).
22 Aquinas, *De potentia*, q 7, art 5, ad 14 (see Fox, *Sheer Joy*, p. 196).
23 *The Poems of Saint John of the Cross* (trans. Roy Campbell), Harmondsworth: Penguin, 1960, p. 11.
24 Ross Collings, *John of the Cross*, Collegeville MN: Michael Glazier/Liturgical, 1990, pp. 26–49.
25 R.C. Zaehner, *Mysticism Sacred and Profane: An Inquiry into Some Varieties of Praeternatural Experience*, Oxford: Oxford University Press, 1957, p. 33.
26 Ibid., p. 41.
27 Joseph Marechal (trans. Algar Thorold), *Studies in the Psychology of the Mystics*, London: Burns, Oates & Washbourne, 1927, pp. 103, 111, 98, 121.
28 Karl Rahner (trans. Dinah Wharton), *Nature and Grace and Other Essays*, London: Sheed & Ward, 1963, p. 10.
29 Rahner, *Foundations*, p. 32.
30 John S. Dunne, *A Search for God in Time and Memory*, London: Sheldon Press, 1975, pp. 1–31.
31 Collins, *Between the Rock*, p. 89.
32 Ibid.

8 CHRIST ... AND SOME TENTATIVE CONCLUSIONS

1 Paul Hazard, *The European Mind 1680–1715*, New York: Meridian, 1963, p. 40. See also pp. 198–216.
2 Fox, *Cosmic Christ*, pp. 75–79, especially p. 79.
3 Thomas Berry, *Religions of India*, New York: Columbia University Press, 1992, pp. 84–85, 213.
4 Thomas Berry, *Buddhism*, New York: Hawthorn Books, 1967, p. 31.
5 Ibid., pp. 32–33.
6 Berry, *Dream*, p. 15.
7 John Dominic Crossan, *The Historical Jesus: The Life of a Mediterranean Peasant*, Edinburgh: T. & T. Clark, 1991, p. xii.
8 Denis Edwards, *Jesus and the Cosmos*, New York: Paulist Press, 1991, p. 83.
9 There is a whole series of texts in the New Testament to support this contention: John 1:14–16; John 6:51–59; I John 4:2–3; II John 4:1; I Corinthians 15:35–49; II Corinthians 5:16; Philippians 2:6ff; I Timothy 3:16; Colossians 1:22.

10 Richard McBrien, *Catholicism*, North Blackburn: CollinsDove, 1994, p. 1174.
11 I have already referred to works by Berry, Fox and Swimme. Morwood and O'Murchu have written a number of books, but I recommend: Diamuid O'Murchu, *Evolutionary Faith: Rediscovering God in Our Great Story*, New York: Orbis, 2002 and *Quantum Theology*, New York: Crossroad, 2004; Michael Morwood, *From Sand to Solid Ground: Questions of Faith for Modern Catholics*, New York: Crossroad, 2007.
12 Hans Küng, *Theology for the Third Millennium: An Ecumenical View*, New York: Doubleday, 1991, pp. 3–4.
13 Hans Küng, *Disputed Truth: Memoirs*, London: Continuum, 2007, Vol. II, pp. 1–2.
14 Küng, *Third Millennium*, p. 227.
15 Ibid., p. 228.
16 Second Vatican Council, *Declaration on Non-Christian Religions*, paragaph 2.
17 Paul Collins, *God's New Man: The Election of Benedict XVI and the Legacy of John Paul II*, London: Continuum, 2005, p. 65. See pp. 65–67.
18 Tony Kevin, 'Reviving climate hope', *Eureka Street*, 9 June 2010.
19 Ibid.

Index

Born in Melbourne, Paul Collins is a historian, broadcaster and writer. A Catholic priest for 33 years, he resigned from active ministry due to a dispute with the Vatican over his book *Papal Power.* He is the author of 11 books on religion, the environment and history and has a Masters degree in theology from Harvard University and a Doctorate in history from the Australian National University. He lives in Canberra. UNSW Press published his book *Believers* in 2008.